The Talking

Jamie Michael Gregory

To Debbie,
Thank-you for supporting
& believing in my project.
I look forward to what we
can get from this upcoming
campaign.

Jamie :)

"Every act of creation is first an act of destruction."

-Pablo Picasso

About the Author

My name is Jamie Michael Gregory and The Talking Universe is the first book of three I plan to write. Not only have I survived my experiences, but I have gone on to excel in my life. My survival has afforded me the clarity to share with you my incredible journey, and what has made me the person I am today.

I have overcome the extreme lows of having to steal food out of shops to survive when I was homeless and sleeping on the streets, to the highs of having more money than I could spend when I went on to redevelop hotels for the second-largest hotel chain in the world. I hold nothing back and share with you everything I have learned, both good and bad, along with some very basic knowledge which will help you the reader, find what it is we are all so desperately in search of, purpose.

Website: www.jamiemichaelgregory.com

Foreword

From the subjects we are taught by the educational system to the medicine we are prescribed by the healthcare organisation, I have found that my best course of action came through searching and exploring myself. Through natural means, I was able to navigate a path which went against everything any doctor or teacher ever told me. When I learned the most important lesson in life that is not taught in school—the importance of truly loving myself—only then was I able to start creating a life I could have once only dreamed of.

Don't believe everything you are taught, everything you read, or what other people say. Go out and find your own answers because only then will you discover what resonates and works for you. Only when you start to take responsibility for your own life, will improvement start to happen. Relying on the social institutions which are in place will only result in one outcome, and that's back to square one each and every time. These systems have failed people for years as they are totally inverted. Instead of teaching a person how to think, they do the opposite and teach them what to think to create a manipulated, sick and lost society. The resulting factor is the chaos we see in the world today.

Table of Contents

Chapter 1 – Trauma

(A deeply distressing or disturbing experience)

My name is Jamie Gregory, and this is my story, but before I get to that, let me first explain the story of every human being on the planet.

In total, approximately 140 million babies were born globally in 2021, and each one came into this world via unique circumstances. The brain begins to record information when a baby starts to form in the womb, and this can be affected by various environmental conditions which each mother is exposed too. Within the first nine months of pregnancy, up to 20,000 new neurons are created each second, and if you consider that an adult will create 700 new neurons per day, we can see how significant this early period is for development. By the time birth takes place, a new-born will have accumulated in excess of 80 billion neurons, and these will continue to increase and connect to network systems inside of the body to start making sense of the world. With external senses becoming available, sensory organs enable a person to experience sight through the eyes, sound through the ears, smell through the nose, taste through the mouth and touch through the skin. Whenever any of these sensations are experienced, neurons will send signals to the brain to start identifying what is occurring.

Interoception is another system that allows a person to experience many bodily sensations; these include a rumbling stomach, a dry mouth or a racing heart, for instance. These sensory systems will continuously provide feedback information to be processed through the brain to keep a person balanced, healthy and safe. Whenever there is a disruption or dysfunction, the body begins to act to produce the necessary changes it requires to bring everything back to homeostasis.

The experiences we each encounter in the first years of life are the most prominent in organising how the brain will go on to operate. The brain quickly learns what is deemed safe or unsafe, familiar or unfamiliar, and real or false. As we begin to grow and develop, a person will start to make sense of the world by examining what is happening around them. What does that sound represent? What does that taste like? And what does that tone mean? Each person will then create their own unique understanding of the world, and this is moulded by what they have experienced. When in infancy, a child does not have the capacity to understand the complexities of many situations, so they will rely on their caregivers to help them interpret the world. Each caregiver will have their own unique version of life based on what they have experienced, and this is then transferred to each child, so they begin to experience life through their caregiver's filters.

So, now that we have a basic understanding of what each child experiences when growing up, I will begin to share my experience with you.

I was born into this world on the 4th of December 1985. My mother is English, and her name is Jane; my dad was Greek Cypriot, and he was called Anthony, although everyone called him Tony or The Greek.

From my understanding, my dad's childhood was very turbulent, and he was exposed to a lot of trauma that he should not have been. This trauma would cause my dad to develop unhealthy coping strategies, which would infiltrate his adult life until he was killed when I was 17 years of age.

A few years before my birth, my parents had their first child, my sister Christina. As she grew older, Christina did not develop at the same rate as other babies, and it emerged over time that she had been born with learning difficulties. This must have been a challenging time for both my parents, especially as it was their firstborn. Unfortunately, Christina's brain never developed beyond the age of four, meaning that my mum has the responsibility of looking after a child trapped inside an adult's body. My mum has dedicated her life to taking care of Christina's needs, and she became an author, telling her own story through her book, which is called: *Bringing up a challenging child at home: When love is not enough.*

After Christina, the thought of having another child must have been a terrifying scenario for both of my parents; however, a couple of years passed, and I was born, and a few years after me, my younger sister, Alexandra. In total, there were three of us children.

As I began to grow, my mum struggled with Christina's learning difficulties, and Alex being a new-born. This meant that they both warranted more attention than me, and I was stuck in the middle. With my dad working to bring money into the household, my mum was left to care for all of us children and look after the house.

From what I know from my mum, my dad was abusive towards her, both physically and mentally. When I turned four years of age, my parents separated, and my dad ended up in another relationship with a younger woman called Tracy. Yet again, this must have been a difficult time for my mum, as she was left to fend for herself as a single parent raising three children.

From a very early age, I had always been hypersensitive to any changes in my environment. I remember I was not allowed to drink Coca-Cola or eat sweets, for instance, because they would have an adverse effect on me as I would shake violently and become hyperactive. On some weekends, my dad used to collect me, and I would get to go and stay with him and Tracy. When my dad returned me back home, my mum would become frustrated because he would not set any boundaries, and I would return energetic, hyperactive, and wild. My dad would give me sweets and whatever else I wanted instead of showing me the consistent love that I required, and this was my dad's way of buying my affection throughout my life with him.

At the age of four, I started to gravitate towards my dad. Looking back, I remember feeling confused and not fully understanding the situation as to why my dad had left and separated from my mum. Going back and forth between two parents only made the situation confusing for me, and this was at an age when all children need stability, structure, and security in their life.

With the situation deteriorating at home with my mum, things were about to change. My dad used to constantly threaten her by saying that he would kidnap and take me back to Cyprus if she would not allow me to go and live with him permanently. Eventually, the threats wore her down, and she decided to give in to his demands. I was four years old when I went to live with my dad, so I was still very dependent on people taking care of me. I do know my mum had concerns regarding my dad's behaviour and ability to raise me, but she sought comfort in the fact that Tracy might be able to protect me if things were ever to escalate as they had done in the past.

Due to my dad's chaotic lifestyle and behaviour, he was too unstable to meet the demands of bringing up a child, and because of this, he was unable to offer me the protection, comfort, and attention I required. This interaction between a child and their caregivers goes an extremely long way in the development of healthy emotions, and without it, there can only be a disaster to follow, as you will go on to see.

After moving to London Colney to live with my dad, I remember it felt like my home immediately. I had my own bedroom, and it was nice to be with my dad as everything was incredibly joyful at the start. I do remember that I hated visiting my mum as it made me upset every time, I had to be apart from my dad. At my mums I became jealous of my sisters, so living with my dad meant that I did not have to compete for his affection.

The impact of the separation between my mother and father played a prominent role in the early development of my life. When parents separate, especially when a child is young, it can feel like pieces of them are being torn in different directions. With my mum no longer playing a prominent role in my life anymore, a new dynamic had been created with her replacement Tracy, and this then impacted the development of my brain as I formed trust issues, which in turn would affect my self-worth. Tracy was always kind and gentle towards me, but introducing a new caregiver to a child before they have created enough consistent repetitions in their childhood activates the stress response system. A child will view a new caregiver with doubt, and only when they receive confirmation through consistent nurturing will the new guardian be deemed safe and no longer a threat. As children grow and develop, they begin to organise their neurobiology (the biology of the nervous system). When a caregiver is removed from their life, the world begins to change causing an adaptation in the child, which ultimately causes confusion.

My new life had now begun, and it was time to start primary school. The early part of my schooling was enjoyable—I liked going to school and made friends easily. With primary school starting well, I eventually grew to see Tracy as my new mum, and I became very attached to her.

As time progressed, it became apparent that my dad suffered from extreme mood swings, and this caused his relationship with Tracy to eventually deteriorate. My dad would often explode into fits of rage, and this would consist of him screaming, destroying various objects in our house and behaving violently. This type of behaviour made me feel terrified, and I remember not feeling safe as a child. Tracy became afraid of him too, and she eventually decided to confide in my mum with nowhere else to turn. On several occasions in my childhood, I walked into arguments where I had physically seen my dad attack one of his girlfriends. On one occasion, in a fit of anger, my dad broke Tracy's jaw by punching her.

Inevitably, Tracy left, and my last memory of her is still extremely vivid. I was now five years old, and it was a school night when Tracy had decided to come into my room visibly upset; I remember she knelt by the side of my bed and kissed me goodnight on my forehead. Little did I know that this would be the last time I would see her. I had become attached to Tracy so when she disappeared out of my life, my brain had not created enough consistent repetitions with a single female to form a trusting bond.

The following day, I awoke, dressed, and went to school as usual. When I came home, I remember sitting down and putting the TV on like I usually did, but something felt different; I then noticed that various possessions from our house were missing, and this left me feeling confused, and I found myself in a situation that I did not fully understand yet again. As a child, when you do not understand certain situations, the mind will go on to create a warped version of reality in an attempt to make sense of the events. The damage this then causes any child as they grow older is very hard to overcome because a child's perception and view of the world are shaped and then developed by the environmental conditions to which they have been exposed. This is then what goes on to mould a child's core beliefs.

When my dad returned home from work that evening and realised that Tracy had left, he was distraught. He then proceeded to fall onto the floor, and he burst out crying, in my bedroom, with his head planted in his hands. It was very traumatic to see my dad cry as he was not someone who ever showed any sign of weakness. Seeing my dad so vulnerable left me feeling extremely upset, and after this occasion, I never saw him cry again.

A scary change then happened from this moment onwards, and my dad had said that Tracy had left because she no longer wanted to be with him because of me. I think my dad believed what came out of his own mouth; I certainly did, as any child would. If he could throw the blame elsewhere, I believe it made it easier for him to rationalise certain circumstances that he would cause himself.

My dad's behaviour had now started to influence the development of my brain as it scanned, processed then programmed what it was being subjected to. Much of this information becomes redundant over time, but when a strong emotional disturbance becomes embedded, such as childhood trauma, it becomes ingrained and recorded; this is what then causes the devastation in a person's future.

It broke my heart when Tracy disappeared from our lives. Tracy had told me she had loved me, but so had my mum, and she no longer wanted me in her life anymore in my distorted version of reality. Over the coming months, I became upset and cried to myself, thinking that Tracy had left because of me. All these thoughts were going through my immature and undeveloped brain, and at such a young age, my mind was formed with distrust—especially towards females. These experiences would go on to create some of my first perceptions of the world.

At the tender age of just five, my dad became abusive as he blamed me for all the failures in his own life. One thing I remember clearly is my basic thought processes back then. Some children were born good, and others, like me, were just born bad. *That is why Daddy hates me*, I used to say to myself, *because God has made me bad.* It was my way as a child of rationalising and trying to make sense of the world. Children's earliest

11

attachment patterns create inner diagrams on which to base relationships as they grow older. This is then centred upon how much pleasure and safety can be experienced as well as what to expect from other human beings. When you are a child, you are the centre of your own world, and if you receive constant abuse and are told you are to blame for everything in your surroundings, why would that judgement ever be questioned? Any child in my position would just assume that they must be exactly what they are told. As I grew older, I became imprisoned by my destructive thought processes which meant that there would be severe consequences in my future, and when I was treated badly, I would accept it as it felt familiar to what I had experienced as a child. A problem I had, which many others who experience childhood trauma also struggle with, is this: it is virtually impossible to break these beliefs without outside help because the abusive behaviour becomes ingrained and recognised from the most crucial moment in life when the brain is absorbing, developing, and forming.

As well as the varying forms of abuse I would go on to suffer with, I also began to get neglected. This meant genetic potential was missing from my experiences, so important capabilities never developed for me. When neglect is present in early childhood, the effects are catastrophic because they interfere with the rapid growth of a child's brain, which requires stimulation to get the correct development. The most common form of neglect is what I experienced, and that is fragmented caregiving. Some days I was fed and nurtured, and others, I was not. As a result, my world became a confusing place, which only dysregulated me further. Structure, reciprocation, and consistency are imperative for any child to receive a clear set of signals that will assist in developing a healthy brain.

When I was neglected or abused, it did not matter how much I screamed, pleaded, or cried because whatever I did would not register with my dad or stop what would transpire. Children who suffer from abuse or neglect could potentially go on to create a barrier when they are faced with challenges later on in life because they have been conditioned to feel helpless. Because I was unable to register, change or force a reaction from my dad, I would eventually give up, which created a destructive cycle with severe consequences to follow in my future.

As I began living my life through extreme emotions, I activated my stress response system, which over a sustained period of time, caused me to become sensitised and dysfunctional. Being hungry and not fed or scared and not comforted, will activate the flight or fight response. The term "flight or fight" represents the two choices our ancient ancestors used when faced with danger in their environment; they could either fight or flee, but if either fail to work, then the brain will record these responses as unsuccessful, and a person then has to adapt and find a new way to react. In my instance, this adaptation resulted in disengagement from the scary outside world, and I retreated further into myself. With this becoming my default response, I struggled to heal as I got older because I refused to trust the outside world; relationships are what help a person to heal, but relationship interaction became just too painful for me.

With my dad now blaming me for everything wrong in his world, he began to destroy all the innocence I had as a child, and after his indoctrination, he was the only person I had left to depend on. I believe this type of constant abuse turned me into an introvert from a young age. I remember, many times, I used to go upstairs to my bedroom and cry myself to sleep, seeking comfort in my teddy bears by talking to them; unfortunately, though, they never spoke back to me. My confiding in my teddy bears was something I held on to for an exceptionally long time—it's what brought me comfort, so I found it extremely hard and difficult when I

13

became an adult to sleep without the comfort and security that my teddies had brought me as a child.

My dad had an active social and work life that became entangled together. Due to this, I remember being passed around between several different childminders, and at times it would be as late as 9 pm when my dad would get me out of bed and say, "Jamie, get up and go to Jo's." Jo was one of my childminders who lived around the corner. Sometimes I just did not know if I was coming or going, and I became very unsettled because I needed routine and consistency in my life. While at Jo's, I would sometimes hear her partner, Andy, saying, "Why is he here again?" and "Well, just send him back!" He probably thought I never heard him, but I did—although I wished I had not. Every time I was unable to identify why no one wanted me, I reached the same conclusion: *God must have made me a bad child.*

A healthy relationship between a child and their parents is imperative to stimulate the right chemical balance for the brain to develop. As I grew, my brain did not secrete enough happy hormones, which in turn made me very unhappy inside. Luckily, the brain can be altered and changed over time as it is malleable, so eventually, growth was possible for me, likewise with other children who have experienced such damning childhoods. Through experience, I have found that many people make up for the lack of a parental relationship later on in life. This healing bond is essential for any individual to overcome the trauma they have been subjected to by receiving some form of safety, protection, and love. A loving relationship can come from a person towards an animal, a partner, or other members of the family or friends, but it must come from somewhere for that person to go on and eventually heal.

Due to the impact my dad's behaviour and words were having on me, I began to detest my mum, and my hatred towards her only grew as I got older. My dad told me that she was a slag who slept with many men, she was a whore who dumped me on his doorstep and under no circumstances could I ever trust her. The list that came out of my dad's mouth was endless. He would follow these statements up with, "You would have no one if it was not for me." The consequence of this abuse meant that when things got tough, I felt like I had no one to turn to, so I suppressed my emotions which then caused a severe disconnect. The damaging effects of feeding a child such disgusting things are inconceivable. I grew up to be solely dependent on a parent who constantly abused me, and I believed that no one else cared about my well-being, and this is what we call a trauma bond.

As time progressed, the abuse from my dad began to take a multitude of forms, ranging from severe physical beatings with weapons to mental torture. My preference was the physical beatings because the pain only lasted for the time it took him to kick the shit out of me. On some occasions, his attacks would leave me unconscious; on others, they left me with cuts, bruises, and several scars which I still have today. The reason I did not like the mental torture was because of how it made me feel internally. Being told I was not loved and that is why everyone had left me, apart from my dad damaged me so severely that it would alter how I interacted in my environment. The abuse I had to contend with produced prolonged feelings of fear, rejection, and abandonment. Unfortunately, I did not get the best start in life, and my world was one of danger, pain and suffering.

Trying to hide the abuse I was having to endure ended up becoming a task in itself, and the thought of going over to my mum's would only make me plead, scream and cry. Whenever I was naughty, my dad only had to say the words, "Carry on, and you will go to your mum's," and that was enough to send shivers shooting down my spine, and I would correct my behaviour immediately. At my dad's, I could do whatever I wanted from

15

an extremely young age, whereas at my mum's, I had to go to bed at a set time—which, to me, was ridiculously early, and she made me eat vegetables, and I fucking hated vegetables. With me being regularly covered in cuts and bruises, my mum would ask what had happened. My dad would always be nice to me on the drive to my mum's—he was very calculated in anticipation of me telling her anything. He would tell me in the car not to mention anything that happened at our house, and I remember he would bribe me by buying sweets or football hologram cards. To explain my injuries, I would say that I had fallen down the stairs or they had happened playing football at school. I did not trust my mum because of what I had been subjected to by my dad, so there was no way I was going to confide in her.

Growing up in constant fear meant that my brain had formed to always be on high alert, even in situations that were safe for me. The brain generates perceptions, emotions, and thoughts, which in turn guide our behaviour as human beings. Emotions, for instance, are primarily unconscious reactions which we experience as feelings, and the component of an emotion is formed in the brain, which then signals the body to react and take action. When I used to stay at my mum's I felt threatened but in actuality, I was safe. As I grew older and my brain continued to form, I constantly anticipated danger even when it was not present.

As well as going over to stay at my mum's, I used to be sent to my Greek grandparents. Their English wasn't the best, and I would find myself bored a lot of the time because they would stick me in front of the TV to watch Cartoon Network—if I was lucky, my grandad would take me to the allotment where he had a patch. He used to grow vegetables and fruit, and he also used to set traps to catch animals that he would then take home and eat. Out of boredom with nothing to do, I would misbehave to get attention, and as with my dad, I was subjected to physical beatings—this time from my

16

grandad and grandma with the broom and stick. They were not as strong as my dad, so I was not afraid, and at this point in my life, I was used to being beaten. When you are physically abused as a child, you become desensitised, and after the first few times, the pain is never as bad anymore because the mind creates a defence mechanism that enables a person to become immune to the pain by dissociating, which in itself is very disturbing. My grandparents were very old-school. Their view of moulding a child was the same as my dad's: violence solves everything.

The food my grandparents ate mainly consisted of what was either caught or grown in the allotment. One day my grandad decided to set a trap. He had put some raw meat on a wooden stick with superglue smeared onto it, and this attracted wild birds, which would fly down and get stuck while attempting to eat the meat. This trap was set in the morning, and once we returned late in the afternoon, there were several birds stuck to the stick. My grandad then proceeded to snap the necks of these birds and brought them home in a plastic bag. Once home, he cooked them in the kitchen, and they were then eaten for dinner. There was no chance I was eating any of this stuff—it really gave me a distaste towards food in general. The constant strange noises I heard in their kitchen would scare the life out of me, and this caused me to have nightmares about monsters who lived in their kitchen cupboards.

Not all the animals that arrived in the kitchen were dead, and some instead were killed in the kitchen. It was very unpleasant, but I now understand that this was my grandparents' culture from growing up in Cyprus. Due to my childhood experiences, kitchens and food have always horrified me, and this has contributed to me becoming the worst cook on the planet (many ex-girlfriends would testify). I knew what I liked, and I was either unwilling or too scared to try new foods. This, as well as other

17

circumstances, would eventually result in me becoming anorexic in the future when at the age of 17, I weighed just seven stone in weight.

My distrust which had now formed in humans coincided with my deep affection for animals which I still have to this day. After continuously asking my dad for a pet, he decided to finally get me a grey British short-haired cat which I named Gizmo. I was so excited when she arrived, and I loved her straight away. Gizmo was the best present I could ever have asked for, but my dad hated having a cat in the house from the moment she arrived. My dad wanted any excuse he could find to get rid of her, so after no longer than a week, the cat flap was miraculously locked, so Gizmo could not go toilet outside. Due to this, Gizmo decided to shit on my dad's bed, and his reaction to this could not have been any worse. After finding the cat shit, my dad stormed into my bedroom shouting and swearing. I had no idea what was going on at the time, but I accepted what was happening because I was a "bad child" in my mind. My dad proceeded to grab me by the neck as he dragged me to his bedroom; he then rubbed my face in the cat shit, saying that the cat shitting on the bed was my fault for wanting a cat in the first place. This made me feel extremely upset, and I proceeded to apologise while crying at the same time. That evening my cat was given to Jo, the childminder, and I was left heartbroken. After screaming, pleading and crying, I promised that I would never be a "bad child" again if I could just keep Gizmo, but my dad would not change his mind. Once again, I found myself in a situation where no matter how much I begged, I could not register a change in my dad's behaviour. I remember finding this incredibly difficult to get over, especially when I used to go over to Jo's and see my cat, but they had now given her a new name.

Having my face rubbed in cat shit was pretty gentle compared to some of the extreme beatings I took from my dad. On one occasion, he had chased me to my bedroom and had taken off his favourite black belt, which had silver metal spikes on it. He then began to lash me non-stop, screaming and calling me every disgusting name you could possibly think of. When this beating had finally finished, I fell asleep soon afterwards as I was exhausted by the amount of adrenaline my body had used to protect me. A lot of the time, his beatings left me feeling distant, docile and tired, so I would sleep for long periods. I remember I used to enjoy sleeping as a child because it was a way to disappear out of my reality.

After this particular beating, I remember waking up the following morning feeling stiff and struggling to move to put my clothes on. As the day progressed at school, blood began to seep through my white school shirt. On this occasion, one of my teachers noticed and decided to do something. I was then removed from my class, and the teacher raised her concerns with my mum on the telephone. I had decided to come up with my usual excuses, but after my shirt was taken off, I was asked why I had belt marks on my back and who had done them. Under pressure, I broke down crying, and I said, "It was my dad." Immediately, the police and social services were called, and my mum was now on her way to collect me from school. At the time, I had no idea what was happening, and all I wanted to do was to go back home. I felt like I had betrayed my dad by confiding in the school, and if I had known this was going to end up in me being placed into my mum's custody, I would have lied instead, like I always used to.

Finally, my dad was arrested, and I was placed on the child protection register. The guilt I felt for getting my dad into trouble made me continuously cry and beg for my mum to take me back home. I now hated my mum further and blamed her for getting my dad into trouble. All the nasty things my dad had said about my mum had just been reconfirmed to me by her actions which were taking me away from my dad and my

19

perception of what love was. I was too young to understand that my mum was trying to protect me, and instead, I just saw someone who was removing me from my dad to feed me shitty vegetables and put me to bed early. By speaking out, I felt that the consequences threatened my survival, so in the future, I focused all of my energy on not connecting with my emotions, so I did not have to feel the abuse I was enduring.

Being placed into my mum's custody felt like a fucking prison sentence! I could not stand her rules, and I could not stand her. Whenever I was at my mum's, it felt so different compared to what I had experienced with my dad, and every time she tried to set boundaries or show me affection, I would only reject it. I remember I used to swear violently towards her, showing no respect. I now spoke in the terminology I had learned from my dad, and I began repeating his words, "You dirty fucking slag" and "You fucking whore! I hate you, you fucking bitch. Return me nowwwww!" You name it, I said it. All I was doing was re-enacting what my environment had taught me, and I was now a vehicle to express and channel my dad's hatred towards my mother.

I now blamed myself for the situation I was in. In my distorted version of reality, I was taken away from my dad because I was a "bad child." Suffering abuse was a small price to pay if it meant I did not have to live at my mum's, so I decided to do something to accomplish exactly that. I made a promise to myself never to speak a word again about being beaten or what happened at home with my dad. I had become so accustomed to my environment that I was frightened of change. I had developed a strategy for survival, and there was no way I would relinquish that because I was terrified of the consequences of doing so. This behaviour which I went on to establish, worked successfully as I was never placed back into my mum's custody again, and every time I was beaten in the future, I would bottle it up internally rather than turning to anyone else for help.

After a month or so had passed, I was allowed to go back to my dad's but only on supervised visits as social services, had to be present. This was supposed to be an ongoing arrangement, but they only came once and then signed papers stating I was allowed back into my dad's custody. After this point, no matter what cuts or bruises I had, no one investigated further.

Once back at home, the beatings stopped for a short period of time, and I was grateful to be back at school. There was a certain degree of peace at the start, but inevitably it was not going to last long. Eventually, my dad's mask started to fall off, and the real Tony began to re-appear. The more abuse I was then subjected to, the more I became attached to my dad. This may sound strange at first, but children are programmed genetically to be loyal to the people who care for them. This is also why children can feel torn about the feelings they harbour towards an abuser.

With my dad's outbursts becoming more frequent as the days passed, his life started to decline, and it became one of chaos. He had now started to see a lot of females, and there were often sex parties happening in our house. These orgies used to be filmed and played back on the TV screen in our living room. On top of what I had already been exposed to, I was now being subjected to sexual abuse. Although this type of abuse was never performed on me physically, it is still classified as sexual abuse when a child is exposed to sexual activities at such a young age.

As the sex parties were going on in the living room, I used to sneak onto the stairs and look below to see what was happening, and sometimes there would be just one girl, but on other occasions, there would be as many as ten people having full-blown orgies. This sexual exposure at such a young age caused my perceptions to become skewed, and I grew up searching for what I thought was love in all the wrong places; the consequences of this will become apparent later on throughout my story when I tried to kill myself.

The older I got, the more my dad's behaviour became unpredictable, and I had no idea what mood he would be in when he arrived home from work. Sometimes he would have a present for me, like a big teddy bear or a new pair of football boots, and on other occasions, he would come back and start attacking me for reasons such as not washing up a plate. His weapons would range from tennis racquets, bats, and belts—it was literally whatever he could get hold of at the time he exploded.

On many occasions, I would see the lights of my dad's car shine through the downstairs window and upon his return, I would often wet myself in fear. I used to get told off for wetting myself, and my dad would say, "Big boys don't wet themselves." When he would ask me why I would do it, I would just shrug my shoulders and say, "I don't know". I did know, but I was not prepared to tell my dad that he frightened me so much that it caused me to wet myself in fear.

My life always felt in danger, and the threats became a reality on some days. One of these days was when I took a beating that resulted in scars. My dad had flipped and chased me up the stairs, but I had managed to get to the bathroom and lock the door before he caught me. I remember him going crazy and threatening to kill me. One of his sayings was: "I put you in this fucking world, and I will be the one to take you out this fucking world." Eventually, due to his constant smashing on the door, it fully snapped in half over my back while I was trying to block him from entering. I had nowhere to escape this time, and I was struggling to move, so I just cowered into a ball and accepted my fate. My dad then picked up a piece of loose wood that had broken from the door, and despite my pleading with him, he beat me violently with the wood. I most definitely lost a part of myself that day, and I remember having an out-of-body experience and not feeling the pain that a beating like this should warrant. Looking back, I can remember feeling as if I was inside the bathroom light, and I saw a person being attacked by my dad. That person was me. I cried at first, but as the beating continued, I just became numb, and I drifted off. There was no physical pain, and instead, all I remember is waking up in my bed, unsure how I got there. I was seven years old when this particular beating occurred. Today, I still have two scars on my leg, on the inside of my left thigh, from the deep gashes he caused me that day. Whenever I am naked and look at my leg, it is a constant reminder of the suffering I had to go through as a child.

As I was too small to fight back and many times I could not run away, I would end up being cornered like a scared animal. At this point, my body would prepare me for the onslaught I was about to receive by decreasing my heart rate and releasing opioids. Time would then begin to slow down, and I would become totally dissociated from the traumatic event, and this would reduce the impact that it would have on me in the present moment. Reading further about dissociation, I have found that amnesia can occur. Although I was able to separate myself from certain elements of my traumatic experiences, my subconscious mind would still record what had happened. The consequence of this would be the impact that it would have on my future. I would get flashbacks which were filled with intense emotions that created irrational behaviour patterns and heightened emotional responses to situations that would not merit such a reaction. The importance of the subconscious mind would eventually become the key to my transformation process in the future.

The majority of experiences a person has leave no permanent trace, but some are so prominent that they actually rewire the arrangement of the brain. The neural activity that generates the initial experience enables it to be recollected in the future, and when the impact is severe, it can become embedded and part of the brain's structure; this is because intense traumatic experiences increase attention. Therefore, they are more likely to be recognised and stored. The amygdala is the part of the brain that acts as a tunnel and participates in keeping an emotional experience alive by replaying it in a cycle, and this repetition will remain continuous until new neuron connections are formed. As we grow older, the brain begins to mature, but during the child maturation stage, if a window of opportunity for learning is missed, such as in my case due to the trauma I was exposed to, a person will find it virtually impossible to acquire the skills later on in life without some form of help.

The continuous abuse I had to face as a child left me with no foundation point to go on and excel in my future, and this would only create further disturbing experiences. When you are not loved correctly, you begin to ask yourself, *Am I not important?* And this message when a child is forming their world view is disturbing, to say the least. The capability of any person to express love depends on the loving interactions they receive early in their life. As I grew into an adult, I became a needy person who longed for somewhere to belong even when that place became destructive, and without the correct neurobiology, I did not have the capacity to even accept love when it tried to find me.

Despite my destructive upbringing, there were, however, times of positivity in my life, and I was not kept shackled to chains in some dungeon somewhere. I would hate for anyone who reads my book to feel sorry for me because, as you will go on to see, all the greatest gifts I have acquired in my life were attained through confronting and then working through my trauma in the correct way. Although my dad was very unstable, he was also

24

affectionate and caring towards me. From a young age, I was spoiled in terms of what I was given in a monetary sense, and I always had new football boots, designer clothes and the most up-to-date phones. My dad always had the latest gadgets, and I remember we used to sit and listen to artists such as Fleetwood Mac and Lionel Ritchie on his stereo. Going over to my Greek grandparents with my dad could be enjoyable at times, even if the food wasn't. There, I got to see my cousins the twins, Jamie, Nicholas and also their older sister Anthea. I was very fortunate to have friends when I was younger, and I remember I used to spend school evenings and weekends playing computer games or going down to the park to play football. I loved playing and watching football when I was younger, and it was something I became good at. So, in between the negative experiences in my life, there were also these times of positivity.

I had now turned eight years old, and I had joined a local football team. Football became my release, and I would practise for hours as it became a good form of dissociation, helping to regulate the stresses in my everyday life. Coaches and parents showed a keen interest in my abilities, and on several occasions, football scouts turned up at the house trying to persuade my dad to let me join various professional academies. The commitment involved meant that my dad would have to take me to practice regularly, but that did not fit in with his lifestyle. Whenever I tried to engage him in anything regarding school, football, or my life, he would usually be too busy and usher me away. This craving for attention would end up penetrating right through into my adult life, and on many occasions, I found myself in constant search of approval from others because I did not have the confidence to make my own decisions. Sometimes I just wanted an arm around my shoulder to tell me that what I was doing was right, but instead, I got no guidance.

In year five of primary school, I was diagnosed with dyslexia. I remember thinking that I was permanently stupid as no one had fully explained to me what this meant. A memory that sticks out was a malicious comment from my dad, which was, "Well, you're fucked now, aren't you? You probably got that from your mum's side of the family." He would often make comments like this, blaming my mum's genes for the reason Chrissy was disabled. I remember thinking that *if I'm dyslexic, then what is the point in trying in school?* "Catching dyslexia" from my mum just gave me more of a reason to hate her further.

My days at school became filled with a lot of frustration and communication difficulties. I was unable to express myself in various situations and this meant that I did not get the correct academic, emotional, or social learning that was required of someone my age. The educational system's unrealistic expectations left me feeling further alienated by punishment when I could not conform to their requirements.

I had now turned 11 years of age and while some of my friends were going to each other's houses to complete homework, play in the park, and eat ice cream, I was misbehaving and had started smoking cigarettes. I had now made a friend at school, and we used to get in so much trouble together! His name was Mark, and he became like the brother I never had. Mark and I would both sit behind the school, smoking our Lambert & Butler cigarettes as we watched the other kids carry on with their day; we were also kids at the time, but we did not classify ourselves as children. I saw myself as a full-grown adult by the age of 11.

I had now reached an age where no one told me when to go to bed, what to eat, who I could hang around with or what time I had to be home. I had zero boundaries, and this was far too much freedom for any 11-year-old. My dad would often leave home for a night, a weekend, or more—the longest being two weeks when he decided to go to Spain. On each occasion, I was left to fend for myself because my dad now deemed me old enough to not need a childminder anymore. Looking back, it does not take a rocket scientist to realise I should not have been put in a position to make fundamental decisions aged 11.

My dad's obsession with seeing countless females would continue, and although some of these were flings, a few did become serious. Every time he got a new girlfriend, I would think I had found a mum, but very soon afterwards, they would be gone one by one, and this happened too many times to even estimate a number. Eventually, after continuous disappointment, I just gave up and lost trust in any female because, as far as I could see, they all said the same thing and then disappeared.

At around the time I was about to start secondary school, my dad started to attract media attention as he began making various TV appearances—mainly due to his lifestyle. He was also in the *News of the World* middle-page spread, with the caption "Do not touch this man with a bargepole". He was now totally out of control.

Although my upbringing was anything but normal, it was only just the beginning. Things were soon going to reach a whole new level—and this would make everything that I have written so far seem like a fairy tale in comparison.

You do not have the capability to stop what was done to you as a child, but you do have strength when you become an adult in how you choose to overcome it.

—Jamie Gregory

Chapter 2 – React

(To behave or change in a particular way when something happens)

Life had become extremely difficult due to my dysfunctional upbringing. Mark and I had been accepted into the same secondary school, and in the second year, I'd had enough of the continuous abuse I was being subjected to at home, so I decided to run away with Mark. We then went to live with Mark's auntie in Bognor Regis, on the south coast of England. At the time, we were both 12 years old, and we got jobs working at a local fair on the sea front. The money we earnt was spent in the evenings at the local arcades, where we would gamble it away on the fruit machines.

The time I spent in Bognor Regis was a much-needed relief for me, as it was a very simple way of living. I no longer had to worry about what mood my dad would be in each day, and I no longer had to accept any further abuse from him. Despite Bognor Regis never being a long-term solution, it helped to calm my stress response system. Eventually, after missing school and countless phone calls from my dad and the head teacher, Mark and I decided to return home.

Because of the trauma I had suffered, I struggled to form healthy attachments, so I had a very limited capacity in regulating stress; running away was my go-to option as it enabled me to dissociate. This defence strategy would help me to cope as the relief from the accumulating stress became a powerful reward by bringing me back to a functional state. Whenever I felt negative types of emotions, they would always come represented as highly charged. Without being able to understand what I was feeling, I became scared, so I ran. Learning to disconnect from a young age would become a huge problem for me the older I got, and this caused my internal world to be one of severe confusion.

So, after finally deciding to return home, I went back to school, but I then began truanting. My truanting was based on the classes I had each day, so if I had maths and history, the likelihood was that I would not be going to school on that day. If I had PE, where I could potentially play football, then I would try and make sure I was there. *What was the point of going to school?* I thought. I could barely read and write, which only caused further stressful situations.

At the age of 12, I began to experiment with drugs, and after taking the ecstasy that I used to bury in the loft for my dad, I then decided to start smoking cannabis every day. I would smoke in the mornings, then on my lunch breaks and also when I got home from school. At first, the cannabis balanced me out, but over a sustained period of time, I smoked so much that I became seriously paranoid, agitated, and further confused. As well as smoking, I also decided to sell it, and although I did not make a lot of money, that was not the purpose of me doing it. Instead, it enabled me to smoke for free—so really, it just paid for my habit.

Looking back, I can see that I had now reached a point in life where I needed to self-medicate to relieve myself from the suppressed pain that was accumulating in my body.

Eventually, my dad found out I was smoking when he found cannabis in my bedroom. Instead of shouting or attacking me, which I was expecting, he did the complete opposite and put me in touch with one of his friends; this friend of my dad's would then drive to our house and drop me off cannabis each week. I was surprised one night when I saw this same

29

person turn up at our house unannounced with a couple of his friends. After he and my dad had a discussion, my dad asked me if I wanted to go out with the "boys" for the night. After agreeing, I was asked by these people to direct them to various car parks I knew around the local area—specifically, ones where the lighting was poor, or the flats, for example, did not back directly onto the car parks. Once driven to the locations, these people would then break into parked cars. It did not matter what make or model the car was—their concern was whether or not the stereo detached from the front unit of the car. By just looking through the window, they could gauge if the stereo could be stolen or not.

That night around ten cars were broken into, and each one went as smoothly as the last one did. On one occasion, they did not even have to break into the car because it had been left unlocked. It was a case of just opening the door, removing the stereo, and then walking back to the car we were in. On the last car they did (and I remember it was the last one), they had taken the stereo, but there was also a laptop case which had a laptop and passport inside. After they had taken everything, they said to me that the night was now over, and they explained that they knew a person who paid a lot of money for real passports. After a few hours of "work", I was then dropped off back home. I could tell they had a profitable night because my usual weeks' worth of cannabis was given to me "on the house" that night. This story was one of many I remember growing up. As I was involved and surrounded by crime from such a young age, it became acceptable for me to replicate this type of behaviour the older I got.

At school, I had managed to make some friends, but I went to a poor school where not many people had money. At the time, my dad was indulging in me, he was trying to buy my love through material possessions. He was also doing this to keep me silent due to the continuous beatings I

30

was suffering from. When my dad physically attacked me, he would become upset very soon afterwards, and with the fear of me ever telling on him again, he would then apologise and buy me whatever I asked for. This created another belief, and it consisted of receiving monetary possessions in exchange for abuse and my silence. This belief will become very prevalent throughout my story.

As I progressed through secondary school, I started to have run-ins with various people, which resulted in me being bullied, and the more I was bullied, the more I felt like I had to change and adapt as person to be accepted. On one occasion, I was attacked in a park at night as a bottle was thrown at me, which then smashed over my head. My intention was never to get my dad involved in my business because I knew it could escalate into a more serious matter due to the people I had seen him associating with. When I was younger, I never used to fight back as the thought of violence terrified me since I had seen and been involved with it so much in my home life. Whenever there was violence at school, I would almost freeze, and all of my functions would become inaccessible to me. The feelings that I would then be presented with were exactly the same ones I felt when my dad attacked me; I wanted to run away and seclude myself as I felt frightened and scared, but most of the time, I just could not move, and I became still like a deer facing a set of headlights.

Although I began getting into a lot of trouble at school, football had become a serious part of my life. I had started playing for the school, local, and district teams. Looking back, I now realise that my dysfunctional upbringing, not eating properly, and smoking all affected my ability, which began to influence my performance negatively. Although I was capable of moments of brilliance, I was very inconsistent. Coaches would often try everything to get the best out of my ability, and I would always try my best as

31

I loved playing football, but at times, my mind and body were just not capable of doing what I could potentially do, and this used to infuriate not just the coaches but also my teammates. Eventually, football became very emotionally charged for me, and the higher the level of games I would participate in, the more I did not enjoy playing. This now-added pressure in my life only contributed to my already elevated stress levels.

Despite my inconsistency, I was still being approached by more scouts, and eventually, I decided to go and play for the academy of Watford Football Club. At the time, they were in the Premiership, which is the top league in England. After a few games, my dad finally decided to come and watch me for the first time in my life. I remember we played Tottenham Hotspurs, but with my dad watching, I felt so nervous, and every time I touched the ball, I could not express myself and I made mistakes. I remember the whole time, I felt very anxious, and all I could think about was throwing up. Instead of focusing on the game, I was constantly examining my dad's facial expressions from where he was sitting on the side lines, as I became obsessed that I was disappointing him. After around 40 minutes, I managed to fake a hamstring injury so I could come off the pitch, as the stress had become unbearable. I remember we lost that game, and on the way home, my dad said that he would never be coming to watch me again; he then told me that I was shit and what a waste of time it had been for him. Lastly, he said I should stop putting all my efforts into football because I was not going to become a footballer. After these comments, I decided never to go back, and this further destroyed the passion I once had for football.

Because I held my dad in such high regard, as a godlike figure, which children do towards their parents, I believed everything my dad said and perceived it as factual. A problem I was left with in my future was that I began to find out that everything my dad had taught me was inverted. This then made it extremely hard to change in my adult life, even when I knew the difference between right and wrong. I can tell you from experience that this is why it is extremely hard to work through childhood trauma and also why it is one of the hardest things for anyone to ever overcome. Trauma becomes ingrained and part of your identity when not dealt with correctly, and for a long period of my life, because I had suppressed what I had experienced, I did not have any other point of awareness which would enable me to surrender, release the emotions and begin to heal.

Although my upbringing was turbulent, and a part of me disliked my dad, I also loved him very dearly at the same time. I remember feeling weak about my feelings towards him as I could not figure out how someone who supposedly loved me, could treat me in such a disgusting way. I spent my childhood in a state of internal conflict, and this only ever contributed to me not understanding myself. The confusing nature of my upbringing meant that as I grew older, I made critical mistakes in my life as I did not know who to trust, how to behave and what were the correct decisions to make.

Before we get to the next chapter, I want to make it clear that my dad was not evil because many people will think he was because of how severe my story will eventually become. My dad could be very charming and at times he made me, and others feel important, and this would make me forget any of the unpleasant things he had previously done. My dad's behaviour was not premeditated; instead, it was always reactional and in the spur of the moment. I believe that my dad's upbringing was the contributing factor in the way he behaved, and his problem was the choices he continued to make to not work through his own issues in the correct way. Ultimately, I can now see that my dad did not love himself, and this then caused his life to become one of destruction, addiction, and pain. Unfortunately, due to what I had been exposed to, it was not long before I would also become a product of what my environment had taught me, just like my dad had.

Being constantly shamed meant that I expended all my energy into protecting number one, which was myself. I did this by creating survival tactics; my mentality was that I knew best. There are many studies out there that show how various psychiatric problems that people endure start off as structures for self-protection, and trying to cope and sustain these disciplines eventually becomes an exhausting task to maintain in itself. For me, it felt safer to hate myself rather than to act or do anything else. Human beings are creatures of habit, and my habits at this point in my life had already developed and formed significantly. My mind rationalised the strategy I had formed of hating myself very easily. All I had to do was look for proof, and this was found in abundance in my natural everyday environment by how I was consistently treated.

Due to the ongoing trauma, I was constantly in an environment of intense danger, which meant that I suffered from a failure of imagination and a loss of mental flexibility. This is having the ability to shift a course of action or thought according to the changing demands of a situation. Imagination is critical to survival; without it, there is no hope or chance to envision a better future. With no place to go or goal to reach, I became consumed by my surroundings, and I could not adapt to new demands or conditions which were placed on me. Imagination enables a person to leave their routine everyday existence, but I was unable to do this unless I smoked cannabis because I constantly felt scared, abandoned, and threatened. Eventually, the football I had used as a healthy form of dissociation caused my stress levels to heighten, so football just became another place that triggered me, which again dysregulated me further. Imagination also allows people to make their dreams come true, heightening their creativity levels,

34

relieving boredom, nurturing pain, giving hope, enhancing pleasure in our daily lives, and enriching our surrounding relationships. My way of describing failure of imagination and loss of mental flexibility is like no longer feeling like a human being anymore.

As school progressed, I made a friend called Ricky. Ricky encouraged me to go to school; without him, I would have gone a lot less than I already was. My dad loved Ricky, and when he used to stay over at our house, my dad would always say: "Make sure he goes to school, Rick!" Sometimes he would give Ricky money as an incentive to make sure I went. Ricky loved it at mine because we got to order pizza, play football in the streets, smoke cannabis, and go to bed when we wanted to. Ricky had what I would describe as normal parents who set boundaries, so being at a place like mine must have felt like a dream come true for him.

On many occasions when Ricky stayed over, we had to block ourselves behind my bedroom door to stop my dad from coming in to attack me. Looking back, I must have spent half my childhood barricading myself behind various doors in the house to try and stop my dad from physically attacking me. Ricky tried to protect me as much as he could, but he was only a teenager like me at the time. On one occasion, I remember Ricky decided to jump in front of me to stop my dad from attacking me with a tennis racquet. This then gave me enough time to get up and run out of the house.

Most of the time, my dad never hid his behaviour, and on occasions when Ricky was over, my dad would come home with black bin liners that had thousands of ecstasy tablets in them. I remember my dad would come into my room and show us both. My dad would then give us money to hide the drugs in the loft of our house, which is what we then proceeded to do. My dad was incredibly open about a lot of his life with me, and sometimes he liked to brag about what he was doing. I guess at this point, alarm bells

35

should have been ringing in my head, but I was so accustomed to this type of lifestyle that it became my normality as I knew nothing else.

Due to me burying my emotions and never grassing on my dad again, I had to pay a high price in return; the loyalty I showed left me with a gut-wrenching feeling of loneliness. This would eventually manifest into anger, and I would direct this energy towards myself in the form of my self-sabotaging behaviour and negative self-talk. The reason a lot of people are unable to reach out for help due to childhood trauma is for this very reason, and when I have spoken to various people who have suffered from different forms of trauma, the themes are always the same: they recognise their behaviour and negative thoughts as inherent and normal because it is all they have ever known.

When I was exposed to danger, I could act in a variety of different ways. One way was to shut down my social engagement system. Shutting down and becoming dead to the world at times was the easiest way for me to switch off. Another way I could react, especially as I got older, would be to activate my fight mode, and I found this could make me feel energised and heard. What you will find is that people who have been abused can actually feel more comfortable in fight mode because when they are faced with danger, they begin to actually feel alive by fighting back instead of the usual mundane dreaded numbness.

In order to feel close to another human being, a person must temporarily shut down their defensive system, but this was extremely complicated for me due to what I had experienced so far in life. Many traumatised children cannot enjoy life's pleasures because they are unconsciously on alert, scanning the environment for signs of danger, which can cause a person to never feel relaxed even in environments which are safe. Due to this, everyone, including Ricky, was always kept at a safe distance as it was my way of trying to protect myself.

My existence, which was now my foundation point in life, was one of a very unsafe place. Being violated consistently only made it even harder to get back to where I needed to be, which was a state of equilibrium. Whenever I felt trapped or rejected (which was every day), I was left vulnerable to activating the sequencing patterns which had been encoded into my brain. To restore my body back to safety and relaxation, I needed the activation patterns to eventually come to an end, but with consistent trauma in my life, I was only ever sent back into a dysfunctional mode time and time again. Now when we decide to revisit trauma, there are certain elements we need to consider, and the shock of trauma can be affected by the following:

1. What transpired leading up to the actual event.

2. The trauma in the actual event.

3. The circumstances and impact which follow the trauma, short and long term.

Understanding what had happened to me was extremely important in my future because accepting that it was not my fault, and I was a child became a big step on my road to recovery. Because I was unable to resolve my trauma by addressing what had happened and how it had impacted me emotionally, mentally, and physically, I was left to contend with the manifestation of my suppressed trauma in my future; this would be the devastating after-effects which consisted of my future addictions. Working through my trauma as soon as possible could have helped to eradicate the devastation it would go on to create in my life, and it would have most definitely reduced the impact on me, but that was impossible because I was unable to reach out and trust another human being due to the damage which had already been caused throughout my childhood. Working with trauma is very delicate and complex, so in some cases, it is not possible immediately, but the longer it is left, the worse it will become as it continues to grow and then mutate.

As I was coming towards the end of secondary school, I started to notice that some of the individuals my dad was spending time with were not your average type of people. It was not uncommon to see guns in our house, and several times when I came downstairs, I saw guns on our glass coffee table in our lounge. I never questioned my dad about this or any of his behaviour, I learned to accept it as it was my normal everyday life, and I think my dad knew deep down that I had learned my lesson for telling on him previously. As well as the guns, there were also people coming over to the house late at night, and they were either going out to the garden or into the loft to bury stuff. Despite this unusual behaviour, I liked most of my dad's friends as they were always happy to see me, and sometimes they would bring me gifts, such as computer games and designer clothing.

As I formed my own mind through my teenage years, I saw that my dad made a lot of money from illegal activities, although he also had a legitimate job. When my dad had money, he seemed to always be happy, and when he didn't, he was always angry and irritable, so in the future, I thought that acquiring as much money as possible would make me happy and solve all my problems. The consequence of this inverted belief was that I based all my goals and happiness in my adult life on money which again was another inversion.

Despite my dad having a legitimate job, it could in no way pay for his lifestyle, such as the holidays, the expensive cars, the nights out and the items we had in our house. Everything was state-of-the-art technology at the time, whether that be the huge TVs, expensive stereos, keypad entry system to get into our home or the security cameras outside and inside the house. The funny thing was, though, that despite all these expensive items, we barely had food in the fridge, and I was lucky if there was some milk to make a bowl of cereal.

Although there was not much food available in the fridge, I never had to worry about money as there was always a lot of cash lying around the house. Whenever I had friends over, my dad would often treat them as well. Due to this, everyone thought my dad was the coolest dad in the world, and whenever I said anything bad, my friends would take my dad's side. So again, in the end, I tried to bury what I felt by disconnecting from my emotions. My friends were all envious of my situation due to the freedom I had and being monetarily spoilt, but they had no idea what it felt like to live without a proper family unit or even feel safe. What I needed was stability, boundaries, and discipline—something I was never going to ask for openly. My way of rationalising my dad's behaviour was to accept my friend's statements about my dad. I was spoilt, had money, and got most, if not all, of what I. I just thought the sacrifice for having all this stuff my dad would buy me, which my friends never had, was the abuse I would have to accept in exchange.

My dad's legitimate job was working as a full-time burglar alarm engineer. He had managed to get into the industry when it really began to pick up, around the mid-1980s. Over time my dad's job started to blend in with his social life, and he began spending time with the people whose houses he was working on. I went with my dad to work on some occasions,

39

and I remember being surprised by how big some of the houses were. One house, in particular, was owned by an Arab prince, and I could not tell you how many bedrooms there were in his property. It had an indoor and outside swimming pool, sauna, steam room, and tennis court. My dad would always warn me not to touch or say anything, "Keep your mouth shut unless someone speaks to you," he would say.

My dad knew and made friends with many wealthy people; he had even dated a page-three model for some time. He would also drive around in some of the most expensive car's money could buy, such as Ferraris and Porsches, and he even had a Lamborghini at one point. What I found out later was that my dad had a link in London who used to supply him with cloned cars, and this is why they also did not stay for very long. The cars were stolen, the serial numbers would be scratched out, and the plates would be copied. My dad would be driving a stolen vehicle that shared the same number plate as an exact replica somewhere else in the UK.

When I eventually finished secondary school, one of my teachers had worked out that I had missed three out of every five days in the five years I had been there. This meant that I was only there for 40 per cent of the time I was supposed to be. I also had been suspended a few times and was constantly in trouble for 'playing up' as the school called it, and when the end was in sight, they could not wait to get rid of me. I would have been expelled towards the end, but it was decided that there was no point as there was only a small amount of time left, so an arrangement was made that I would attend to sit my remaining exams, but I did not have to go to school for the last few months.

School saw me as a bad and troubled pupil, so teachers would try and punish me by either shouting, giving me detention, or suspending me. I never listened, and most of the time, I would just tell them to "Fuck off!"

and walk out. My situation at school was that I would go there to get away from my troubles at home, but due to the troubles at home, I was unable to behave appropriately whenever I attended. It was a catch-22 situation for me. School became very toxic, just like my home life, and it was a vicious cycle that just repeated. All this did was contribute to me feeling like I was a "bad child" and not wanted anywhere—and also not wanting to be anywhere. Each place I turned to became a place of rejection, abandonment or punishment.

After finishing my exams, I left school with one GCSE in English, and that was it. I was lucky to even get this as I had given zero effort. I did not think too much about my future, as all I ever wanted to do was play football, but I had turned my back on playing after the criticism from my dad. I had found school tough because of my nonattendance, attitude, and dyslexia. I struggled massively with numbers, spelling, and reading, which made it impossible for me to learn in the way the school wanted me to.

Looking back, I can now see that my dependency for my dad's affection had a real influence on me. He was either totally hands-off—leaving me to fend for myself and giving me no rules about morality—or he was totally hands-on, in an extremely violent sense. My dad had persuaded me that he was all I had in this world, so I relied on him—even though he was hardly ever there. I would spend hours cleaning when he used to go out, in anticipation that he would be in a better mood and happy with me when he came home. No matter how much I cleaned or tried to please him, his moods were not dependent on me, and instead, they revolved around the drugs he was taking himself.

The cleaning which I became fixated on is known as OCD, and it is an obsessive-compulsive disorder characterised by recurrent thoughts that create anxiety, and an overwhelming urge to continuously perform repetitive acts in an attempt to relieve that anxiety. The reason I performed this type of behaviour was to try and gain some control over my destructive life. I thought that the more I cleaned the house, the more I could control my dad's behaviour. At this point in my life, I was most definitely suffering from several undiagnosed mental illnesses.

Human beings are designed to be social creatures, and mental problems occur when we are not able to engage with our environment safely. Everything regarding the human body's design is made to engage and thrive in social systems. Relationships and interactions from the earliest part of a child's life are what then goes on to give meaning to their existence. Because of the unstable nature of my upbringing, I continued to retreat from every positive relationship. Instead, I focused more on the destructive patterns I had now formed. Without the correct direction, I became misinformed about succeeding in life. What you will find in similar instances is that people without direction or purpose will gravitate to areas in their life where they can expend their energy on producing non-constructive results because they do not have the correct blueprint to go on to excel.

Many people in my adult life have told me to "just get over it" in terms of what I have been through. What I want to explain to these types of people who are so naive on the subject of childhood abuse is that it isn't something you "just get over". This poison is something that must be confronted, understood and then worked through to remove the devastating effects it will otherwise continue to cause. Child abuse is usually inflicted by the very people who are supposed to take care of a child when they first enter this world, knowing nothing else. These come from the most important people in a child's life, and this creates such a strong attachment of distrust that is it any wonder why so many people who experience childhood trauma struggle to ever come to terms with what they have experienced. The emotions that I buried did not just evaporate into thin air for them to never be seen again. Instead, they wanted to be heard and recognised at some point, but until then, I was left to find alternative ways to express myself. This would then manifest in my everyday life in the form of severe negative behavioural patterns, and I would eventually go on to become addicted to drugs and alcohol. I suffered from an eating disorder, panic, depression, and many of my relationships were marked with distrust. How suppressed trauma manifests is limitless and like the worst plague imaginable. People who experience such disturbing childhoods as mine do not experience love or safety correctly, and resorting to other means can feel like the only way for a person to rid themselves of the unbearable pain which has infiltrated their life.

Due to the pain I experienced growing up, a barrier had been created and I did not know how to connect with my inner self. This was never taught or explained to me. Children in similar situations by the time they reach adulthood are then cast out, and many end up being incarcerated due to the problems they have been unable to manage. This then creates further pain and suffering as people are placed into cages as we would do with rats, gerbils, and hamsters. They are then no longer accepted in society, so is it any wonder why these people become even more disillusioned with life and more susceptible to re-offend or to resort back to the only means they have had at their disposal to relieve their pain, such as their coping strategies, which have helped them to survive by numbing the unbearable pain in the first instance?!

If we take a look at how the brain works, we can see that when the stress response system is activated, a person will become dysregulated and out of balance, and they will begin to shut down an important part of the brain called the cortex, which is responsible for thinking and problem-solving. When this happens, a person will become dominated by the lower

43

part of their brain functioning which we call the reptilian brain, and when this disconnect materialises, a person cannot access their cortex until they are able to get back to balance and regulation again. Rational communication at this point is non-existent because whatever is being communicated is being filtered away to the lower brain functions. If we use this point when discussing the educational system, I can see that teachers must understand this basic principle because there is no way a child can learn if they do not have access to their cortex. In order to communicate rationally, then, a person on the receiving end has to be regulated, and only then can you begin to engage coherently with them.

The protection of children should be the highest priority, and it is the main reason for me writing this book. Children will become the adults of tomorrow, so getting this right is imperative. I was left to make fundamental decisions for myself as I was too scared, and I did not know where to turn when I was repeatedly abused because of the consequences of reaching out. I should not have been put in a situation as a child where I had to make fundamental decisions in my life—no child should.

If we look at some of the negative aspects of society in general, such as alcohol, drug addictions and violent crimes, we will find that the highest percentage of people who fall under these categories have experienced some form of childhood trauma which they have been unable to work through correctly. What I have found through extensive research is that there is a whole curriculum missing from our educational system; mental health, trauma and addiction, at the very least, are just as important as reading and writing, so why are they not taught or explained to us with clarity and depth? Instead, we ignore these pressing subjects and stick labels on children such as ADHD when they are "acting out". The answer is always, "Let's give them some medication. That will sort them out." I will discuss the negative impact of mainstream medication further on in the book as it's an absolute travesty what is going on today in the world.

What we should be doing is looking at the root causes of why children are behaving as they are. I remember at school in maths, for instance, I would sit there drawing out my football teams, and when the teacher would come over to my desk, I would be screamed and shouted at. Their recommendation was that I had **ADHD** because I could not focus correctly, so now we have a situation where people are potentially labelled with a condition just for exhibiting a positive form of dissociation. What my teacher did not understand was that I was raised in such a volatile environment that my positive dissociation was a way for me to survive, as this kept me regulated as it brought my stress levels back to a manageable level. If I could not dissociate, then the intensity of my environment would have caused me to not survive, and only punishing and trying to label me for doing so ended up creating more distorted feelings and triggers for myself.

Without basic understanding, how can we expect teachers to teach? No teacher should ever be put in a classroom until they understand this basic knowledge. Without this, how can a teacher understand the behaviour of certain children? How can they reach or communicate with children like me who require different needs? Not only does punishing children clearly not work, but it is also disgusting, wrong, and barbaric. Aggressive outbursts, for instance, are a form of traumatic stress; if the school is not offering a safe environment, then further triggers are then created for that child. Temporarily you can stop a child with punishment, but on a physical level, what happens then to the stress hormones that are not laid to rest? I can tell you that they will only be dispelled again at the next available opportunity in a variety of other unhealthy ways. Emotional regulation is essential in managing the effects of trauma and neglect, so it is imperative that this is

45

understood. What is seen as an acceptable challenge in the classroom to most will become an overwhelming demand on a child who has a heightened stress response system due to trauma.

Through my research, I have found that the way to bring a child back to balance is through creating rhythmic activities, and this can be done through what the school classifies as enrichment activities, such as music, dance, and sports. We, as human beings, learn faster when we interact and move with others through somatosensory activation. The somatosensory system is the part of the sensory system concerned with the conscious perception of touch, pressure, temperature, position, movement, and vibration, which arise from the muscles, joints, skin, and fascia. These types of enrichment activities should be strongly encouraged and made more of a priority by any educational system that cares about the welfare of its citizens.

Now, if we do not receive the correct nurturing from our home or school life, another way must be discovered to take care of ourselves in its absence. This then creates an experimental stage, when people search for some form of relief due to the pain they are suffering from. For me, cannabis was the beginning of that journey, but for others, it could be anything from various drugs, binge eating, or people cutting themselves. We must understand that trauma is where the majority, if not all, problems stem from. The drugs and the alcohol I would go on to be addicted to were not the root causes of my problem, they were the symptoms, and instead, it was the trauma I had buried deep inside of myself.

We must understand that children are full of innocence. Do you think that the people we see in prison today for stealing or committing violent offences, homeless people sleeping rough, or even heroin addicts turned around and said one day, "I want that to be my life"?! We are not

46

talking about a few people here; it's millions of people worldwide and having that many affected shows something is fundamentally wrong with the system.

While everyone continuously turns a blind eye to this by treating the symptoms of a failed educational system, people are being made to suffer deeply and unnecessarily. Ladies and gentlemen, I am finishing this book in 2023; I am not writing this in the year 1850—why has this not been fixed already? I hear people constantly talk about how we live in a modern society, but my question to that is based on what? Because you can connect to Google on your phone? I can tell you that we are not a modern society. Instead, we are a primitive, backward and sick society, and once people first realise this, maybe we can then start to focus on the correct issues that need to be fixed. Only at this point will we move forward from the dark ages we currently live in. When new generations form in the future, this period in life will be looked back on as one that was not highly advanced, and instead, we will be viewed as an extremely sick, destructive, and primitive culture.

Let me use the point above to elaborate on this further: what is the point of being able to look at a world map and point out where France is in a geography class if you do not know how to react or respond when you have been treated violently, or you do not understand the emotions you are feeling internally because they have never been explained or taught, or again you do not know how important self-love is? What would you consider more important? Now that does not mean I am saying remove geography from the curriculum; it has its place just as other subjects do, but this topic I am passionately talking about deserves the highest priority above everything else, yet it is still not communicated with clarity, depth and understanding. To me, this is one of if not the biggest tragedies going on today in our generation. Part of me thinks that the system is so dysfunctional that this cannot be a coincidence because how can a system be designed so wrongly? Since I was not taught anything regarding my experiences by my parents or from an educational point of view, I had to find a solution eventually through unhealthy coping strategies, and believe me, these coping strategies became an extremely strong medicine that I depended on, no matter how much they fucked my life up.

The people in charge of these decisions will tell you there is not enough money to implement the change I am describing, or they will claim that the budget won't stretch to accommodate what I have suggested. If we want a healthy society, we need to start by investing in these children and giving them a real chance in life regardless of the cost. The initial outlay will be made back in the future. When we start to heal this diseased society, we all live in. I can contribute an idea that took me all of three-and-a-half seconds to think of: how about we save the billions of pounds we are spending on introducing 5G, and instead, we invest that money in reforming and updating the flawed educational system? Is everyone going to die if we are left with 4G for a little longer? Everything to me in society is backwards, and what takes higher priority in every instance are things that do not warrant it. Technology has advanced so rapidly that the human body and mind have not been able to keep up with it, which is why we see ever-increasing mental illnesses directly linked to technology. I will go on to explain further the impact of technology on humanity throughout my story. Now is the time to produce a healthy society first. As you will see by my story, everything we need to be just that already exists.

Due to everything I had experienced so far in my life, I had now become a consequence of my environment, and as a result, I would have to face up to the outcome of my actions.

Emotional and physical child abuse inflicted on children by their guardians is a learned pattern of behaviour that consists of ancestral debt passed down from the previous generation. The person who is then prepared to break this continuous cycle and remove the poison from within will not only save themselves, but they will also protect and preserve the next generation in line.

—Jamie Gregory

Chapter 3 – Ugly

(Very bad or unpleasant)

DISCLAIMER: The drugs mentioned in this and other chapters, such as crack cocaine, ecstasy, and cannabis, can have harmful, possibly fatal side effects. My past use of these substances does not in any way mean that I endorse their use; in fact, the opposite is true. I am not responsible for any harm to the reader's health relating to the use of drugs that are mentioned in this book.

Was I now damaged by what I had experienced so far in life? The answer was most definitely yes. After leaving secondary school, aged 16, I found myself lazing around the house most days, not knowing where my life would take me. I would now label myself as someone who was ill-disciplined, and I lacked motivation. If I had won an award for laziness, I would have probably sent somebody else to pick it up for me. My dad had now started to pester me about finding a job, and after searching, I managed to find one working in a local convenience store, stacking shelves and serving customers. I remember this job used to bore the life out of me, and the only reason I kept working there was due to the cigarettes I could steal from behind the counter.

One evening I was supposed to be staying out for the night at a friend's house, but we had an argument, so I made my way home unexpectedly after finishing a shift at work. With my dad not expecting me back, there would be the possibility that something untoward would be transpiring.

Upon my arrival, I entered the house through our intercom system. After walking through the front door, I was unsure what I saw at first, but after I focused, I realised that my dad had been taking drugs in the lounge. I found this incredibly strange at the time because while I knew that he took drugs, I had never physically seen him take them before. What I found even more bizarre was that Rob was also there; Rob was my best friend Mark's older brother, and I did not know Rob even knew my dad up until this point.

After my dad had seen me enter the house—I remember what happened next as if it were yesterday—Rob quickly turned round, so his back was facing me, and he whispered, "He's seen us, Tony!" At first, they both tried to hide any evidence, but bits and pieces were falling onto the floor in plain sight. I had just caught them both in the middle of a full-blown drug session.

After questioning them, they explained what they were doing by confirming that they were smoking crack, and it was not as bad as people made it out to be. To justify this statement, Rob decided to do a pipe right in front of me after a prompt. "Show him, Rob," my dad said. After taking a hit on the pipe, Rob could not speak for around five minutes. When I spoke to him, he would nod his head in response as he covered his mouth with his hand.

Despite Rob struggling to speak for a short time, he seemed fairly normal, so this was my confirmation that crack was not as bad as I had previously imagined it to be. As my dad and Rob were both taking drugs in my home, the thought of crack became further acceptable to me. From that moment onwards, my life began to change drastically, and the next 18 months became a blur, so trying to associate timeframes with what was occurring back then is impossible.

After a discussion with Rob, my dad turned to me and said, "Why don't you try one?" I then remember clearly Rob turning round and saying very sternly, "Tony, no!" It was as if Rob was the adult, and my dad was the child. Eventually, my dad allowed me to try a pipe, and this was his way of rationalising his behaviour in an ugly and distorted way.

Before I started, they both demonstrated how to prepare a pipe. First off, they chucked away the old pipe they had been using in the kitchen bin, and they then used an empty plastic Coke bottle that was on the dining room table. Rob then proceeded to stab a hole into the top of the bottle with an empty biro pen tube; this then resided half inside and half outside the bottle. At this point, it was no different from the bongs I used to smoke cannabis with. My dad then went to the kitchen and got some tinfoil out of the cupboard; it was probably the only thing we had in the kitchen at the time because there was literally nothing else. After unravelling and then placing the tinfoil on top of the empty coke bottle where the lid was supposed to be, Rob tightened this with an elastic band by doubling it over, and this then secured the foil. He then used a safety pin and proceeded to stab lots of small holes into the foil. After this, my dad then went into his pocket and pulled out a small piece of cling film. After he unravelled it, which seemed to take an age, I saw a white/yellowish stone which I was surprised to see was incredibly small and similar in size to a small breadcrumb. This is what Rob called a 'ten stone", and the reason for this is because it cost ten pound to buy. The small stone was then broken up into three pieces, and one was handed to me. One thing I noticed straight away was whilst this was going on, there were lots of cigarettes left burning in an ashtray. They were both lighting cigarettes and letting them burn out so they

52

could use fresh ash each time they smoked a pipe. After the pipe was prepared, ash would be placed on top of the tinfoil so the crack could reside on its surface, creating a barrier between the foil and the crack. New ash was constantly needed as the old ash would create blockages, which meant that the fumes of the crack would not enter into the bottle. My dad then gave me an important piece of advice: "It is essential that if you are smoking crack, you must have fresh ash and new tinfoil."

It was now finally time to do a pipe, and I was told exactly what I had to do. At first, Rob said he would hold the lighter and burn it for me. All I had to do was inhale the smoke by sucking through the biro tube. The aim was to keep inhaling until my lungs were on fire and I could not inhale anymore; I was told to only stop once I felt dizzy and my lungs felt full. As the crack burned, the fumes filtered down into the bottle and as I began to suck from the biro tube, the piece of crack on top decreased in size, with all its contents in the form of smoke entering through the bottle and then directly into my lungs.

The first time I took a hit of crack, I did not experience much of a high because I blew the smoke out too quickly as I was scared; however, after a couple more attempts, and a few more explanations, I finally managed to get the hang of it. The first real hit I took—after I blew the smoke out—I felt like I was going to collapse because the rush was so intense. I remember I had to hold onto the dining room table because my legs had turned to jelly as I became very unstable and disorientated.

The feeling I experienced after smoking crack could be described as a rocket exploding inside of me, and I was about to take off and start floating. It also felt like I was connected to something which no longer felt like pain as all my internal issues dissipated within that instance. I would describe the feeling as being remarkably similar to inhaling laughing gas from

53

balloons, which I have also done, or 'hippy crack' as some people call it, but times that sensation by about 100, then you have what is called crack cocaine. As I blew the smoke out of my lungs, everything including my sound and vision, became distorted for around five minutes, and I felt total utter bliss and peace. My whole body tingled—then the experience was over just as quickly as it had started. What I found strange was that after ten or so minutes, I felt relatively normal again. I had taken ecstasy before, and the high had seemed to last for hours, but while crack was much more intense, it only lasted for a very short amount of time in comparison. Because I was able to get myself back to normality relatively quickly, I was able to further rationalise my decision to continue smoking crack.

In my short lifespan, I had already been subjected to neglect, sexual, physical, emotional, and now substance abuse by my father. Addiction is more likely to happen to people who have been exposed to situations that could make their brains more vulnerable to change; people such as myself are constantly seeking repeated highs to make up for the lack of dopamine which is not being produced naturally in the body. With crack becoming an escape for me, the repeated exposure over time enabled my brain to further undergo the necessary changes to fuck it up that little bit more than it already was.

There is a phrase out there that many people use, and this is called 'chasing the hit'. I want to describe to you what this means. The first pipe of the day is always the most intense. After my first pipe of the day, I would go on a continuous search to experience that same sensation I initially felt, but no matter how much crack I put on a pipe, I was never able to re-create the experience of that first pipe of the day. That is where the phrase chasing the hit comes from. I would often put a full ten stone on my first pipe, knowing that this would be the best time to get the maximum out of the hit. In fact, many times, I have smoked crack and done such a large hit that I ended up passing out or collapsing. The aim was never to do either, but as I became more immune to the drug, I wanted to keep experiencing that same sensation, and to get back to the same levels I had done previously, I needed to take more and more of the drug in larger quantities as time progressed. Although smoking crack relieved me of pain, each time I did it, I was seriously harming myself, and looking back, the destruction that was about to follow was inevitable.

Growing up with no internal sense of security meant that I had no awareness of the difference between danger and safety. I had spent the majority of my childhood feeling numb, and a situation such as this made me feel alive.

After I became addicted, a cycle was created. An external stimulus is registered by the limbic system (the part of the brain involved in our behavioural and emotional responses), this then creates a desire, and in my case, it was a desire to smoke more crack. The cortex (the outermost layer of the brain) then registers this as conscious, and a signal is then sent to the body to act and go in search of that desire; on instruction, the body does what it is told to achieve its outcome. The activity of smoking crack would trigger a signal to be sent back to my limbic system for it to release opioid neurotransmitters (these are naturally produced by the body and include endorphins, enkephalins, and dynorphins). These neurotransmitters then raised my circulating dopamine levels, which in turn created a feeling of satisfaction once I had smoked crack and this then is registered within the brain. The crack I was smoking became the key to unlocking the door for my experience to be felt with chemicals that already existed inside of my body.

55

So, when I was participating in smoking crack, we could see that the ultimate goal was to produce neurotransmitters to help alleviate the pain I was suffering from. If we can then apply this as a general rule to society, we can see that most, if not all, people that are taking such hard drugs are using them not because they are bad people, far from it; instead, they are taking them to relieve themselves of their unbearable pain that they are burdened with. Crack sucks the love and life out of your soul, as you are about to see, so believe me when I say that no one is *happily* taking a drug such as this.

Once exposed to substance abuse, epigenetic changes begin to occur; previously inactive genes become alive and fully activated. With these genes now switched on, the brain starts to change how it reacts when exposed to an addictive substance in the future. Brain cells then begin to change and go from being in a normal state to a highly addictive one. The real concerning issue with this is that once these changes have occurred, it is highly likely that the brain will revert back to its now newly formed way of behaving by responding to triggers in the future.

So, what is crack? Crack is the most addictive form of cocaine. Once it arrives in the country, it enters through the borders in various states, and it can then be modified and turned into a rock crystal form. Most people can do this as it is basic chemistry; I am not really too sure of the exact formula, but it goes a little something like this:

Cocaine is put through a process either called "boiling down" or "washing" using bicarbonate of soda. Sodium bicarbonate is a base used in the preparation of crack, although if this is not available, other weaker bases can be used as a replacement instead—but trust me when I say they are never as good. The reason it's called crack is because it makes a crackling sound when smoked, and this is due to the sodium chloride (table salt) being left in the base with baking soda (sodium bicarbonate) in the washing process.

56

This is done with water, and a kitchen spoon will do. Once mixed together and then heated, the bicarbonate reacts with the hydrochloride of the powder to form cocaine, which then creates freebase cocaine and carbonic acid ($H2CO\ 3$) in a reversible acid-base reaction. Freebase cocaine then separates as an oily layer and floats to the top of the now leftover aqueous phase. Oil is then picked up with any type of thin instrument— a metal ruler will do—and this pulls the oil up and twists it, allowing the air to set and dry the oil. At this point, it allows the marker to turn the oil into a rock substance, and then bingo, you have what we call crack cocaine. The formula goes a little something like that.

The street names for crack and cocaine are endless: blow, rocks, bump, coke, dust, flake, big flake, Peruvian flake, pearl, snow, snow white, sniff, toot, candy, dice, cookies, nuggets, and tornado are just a few of them. Visually, the crack looks like candle wax or breadcrumbs with a slightly off-white colour, but colour differences vary from shades of white to dark yellow. The colour signifies the potency and the additives used; for instance, Rob used to always like crack cocaine which was a darker yellow colour, and he would always get this from a dealer called "blue". Rob said, "The darker the stones, the better the quality is." Also, the smell of the drug is very significant; when smoked, it does not smell like roses or perfume. Unfortunately, instead, it is very similar to burning rubber or plastic.

Smoking crack cocaine allows the substance to move faster through the lungs and into the bloodstream. This then produces a quicker reaction than sniffing it. When snorted, it can take anywhere from up to 20 minutes for the effects to be felt at their most potent point, and these effects can then last for around an hour. When injecting cocaine (something I've never done), it can reach the brain within one minute, and the effects can apparently last up to 30 minutes; however, when smoked, it takes anywhere from 10-20 seconds to reach the brain with the intense effects lasting for around 5-10 minutes. Smoking causes the most devastating effects, and when I smoked crack cocaine, I would potentially be setting up a pipe every 15 minutes, so the amounts I used to smoke were truly inhumane, especially if you consider that we would all binge for days continuously.

Destruction of the body soon follows with symptoms such as tooth decay due to mouth dehydration, which causes bruxism (involuntary teeth grinding and jaw clenching). Appetite decreases, so malnourishment becomes prominent, movement disorders, restlessness, irritability, paranoia, anxiety, hallucinations, insomnia, constant nose bleeds, severe increase in heart rate, which makes a person prone to heart attacks, increased body temperature, and blacking out (this happened to me several times). When I read back through that list, it sounds more like a plague to me rather than a drug people would choose to engage in happily.

The devastating effects do not just come from the drug itself either; dealers will mix up the purity to increase the volume to maximise profits. They do this by diluting it with things such as corn starch, talcum powder, laundry detergent, boric acid, laxatives, and flour; I even used to know one guy who would mix his cocaine up with the creatine he used for the gym. This means that when consuming crack, it is impossible to know what you are allowing to enter into your body unless you are getting it from source or if you are prepared to go through the laborious exercise of washing it directly yourself.

Now that we know a bit more about crack cocaine, we will return to the story. Over the coming months, smoking became a very regular occurrence and Mark, Rob's younger brother, also decided to get involved. Mark and I spent a lot of time together, so it was inevitable that if I was smoking crack and so was his older brother, then he would eventually as well. It was not long before Mark, and I became addicted, just as Rob and my dad had. At our peak, I would say we were making the trip to Graham Park estate (more about that later) to buy crack three to four times a day.

Once I became addicted, it began to affect the way I felt, both physically and mentally. The feelings I would be presented with while on and off the drug created a powerful urge to continuously use the substance time and time again, no matter how destructive the consequences became. What then happened is another cycle was created because when you are addicted to something, it causes withdrawal symptoms when not being used, and this then projected out into an unpleasant experience for me, so it became easier to carry on doing what I was so desperately craving for, because the alternative became too painful not to.

As time progressed, my body craved crack to function and survive. I then became violently sick as I began suffering from headaches and fever-like symptoms, some days I had no energy to even move parts of my body, but as soon as I took a hit of crack, I was right as rain and ready to go turbo again. With the pull towards crack being so intense, my life revolved around recreating that internal sensation of peace time and time again because, in its essence, it meant freedom from my pain, if only for a small amount of time. The more I smoked, the more my mental health declined, and as time progressed, I was no longer consciously aware of this because my negative symptoms became so apparent that I was unable to recognise them as alien anymore. They just became part of my identity.

Before we smoked crack, we would all meet up and chip in whatever money we had. We would then drive to Graham Park estate, which was around 25 minutes from where we lived, but we would get there in about 15 minutes as my dad drove ridiculously fast. My dad would always drive, and either he or Rob would always meet the dealers to buy the drugs. After scoring, in the car, before we left to go back home, the crack would be distributed to each of us, and we would then hide it in our mouths in case we ever got stopped by the police. While driving back home, there were countless times when my dad would get very impatient, so he would decide to start smoking a pipe while he was driving down the dual carriageway. It was not uncommon for us to be going around 100 mph when my dad would turn to Rob, as he would always sit in the front and say impatiently, "Hold the wheel, Rob!" My dad would then get a pipe out from the side of the car door and start lighting up while driving. Rob would then have to hold the steering wheel until my dad was able to take control again.

As our sessions became a daily occurrence, my dad eventually stopped working and lost his job. Due to this, money became extremely hard to come by. However, he did have a scam on the go at the time, which he used whenever he needed to get hold of money fast. This consisted of ringing up old clients for whom he had fitted burglar alarms for in the past. This was around the same time that everyone feared the "Millennium bug", and I remember it being plastered all over the newspapers and in the media. My dad used this as an excuse to tell his previous clients that their alarms needed testing. After attending and taking the battery out of their alarm systems, he would state that he had to run certain tests back at his van. After giving the battery a good clean, he would return back to the client's house, stating that he had to change the battery as it was faulty, and he would then put the same old battery back into their alarm system.

Further to this, he would make up some more lies about various other things, and then he would eventually leave with a reasonable amount of money in the region of between £100 to £200. Each "job" would take no longer than 15 minutes to complete. On a good day, my dad would complete two or three of these jobs, and this would then give him the money he needed to pay for his crack addiction. You would like to think, we were all at breaking point, but let me tell you—things got so much worse than this. We are only at the beginning in terms of how fucking bad everything would eventually become.

After old clients started to run thin, the next step was for my dad to empty a bank account my grandparents had set up for me. They had opened this account when I was a child, and this was supposed to be used towards some form of education. I was never going to go to university, as my dad put it, so why not take the money and put it towards a good cause? I then lied to my grandparents, telling them that I needed money for my schooling. It was not hard as my dad muttered some Greek words to them, they then looked and stared at me intensely, and with a prompt from my dad, I nodded my head. "Yes. School," I said to them, not knowing if they fully understood me due to their lack of English. That money did not last us long, so the next step was for my dad to sell some of my possessions, like my signed Arsenal shirt, as well as my games console and PC. As he said, he had bought all of this for me, so it was basically his to do what he wanted with. My dad had a knack of doing this—he would buy and give me gifts, only to take them back if he ever needed to sell them.

As long as this drug-taking lifestyle continued, it was inevitably going to lead to one outcome: we were all going to start committing crime to fund our addictions, and that's exactly what happened. If something was not literally bolted down, I would steal it. Some of the stuff I did, I began having nightmares about. As well as committing crime, my dad started to sell everything of notable value in our house, and things such as the washing machine, sofa, TVs, and his sound system were sold. Towards the end of our 18-month crack binge, our house was derelict, and there was not even a sofa to sit on or a washing machine to wash our clothes in.

61

As my life began to deteriorate, questions began to surface within me. I knew my dad had always used recreational drugs, but I now wondered how long he had been using crack for. My dad had always worked and had money, no matter what the circumstances were, but now, we had absolutely fuck all. This left me feeling frightened, and the consequence was that the more vulnerable I felt, the more I needed to smoke crack to leave my reality.

After the binges ended, I would get feelings of regret and doubt. I would then cry to myself in my room, alone, and ask myself, *why do things have to be so hard for me?* This was the only time when I would consider not taking any more crack, but it did not last long as my pain would re-surface and then intensify the longer I tried to abstain.

Addictive substances such as crack cause highly intensified emotions which fluctuate when intoxication is taking place, and this also occurs in the withdrawal stage. Because a person's emotional and behavioural circuits are closely tied, this causes a mass imbalance, expressed as behavioural patterns, moods, and emotions experienced. Estimated studies show that more than half of people who develop a form of addiction also suffer from reoccurring mental health disorders.

When I became disengaged and lost in the moment, I totally disconnected from reality. The scary thing for myself and other addicts is that this disconnection actually feels like a connection to something that is no longer related to pain. When a person becomes addicted, freedom of choice goes out the window, and the brain becomes impaired because of the toxic effects which are brought on by the substance abuse. The addiction will then only escalate over time, as it did in my case, because the body's tolerance level rises, which means there is a requirement for more of the drug to satisfy the ever-increasing demand.

So, what is addiction? Addiction is a state of being so dependent on something that it becomes difficult or impossible to do without for any significant period of time. Whatever the addiction, the person can no longer control it. Addiction is a disease of the brain due to the genetic changes which take place, environmental conditions, and the psychology of the mind. Addictive substances, for instance, affect the brain by making it act in the same way as it does towards pleasurable experiences by increasing the release of neurotransmitters. Genetic susceptibility is also a factor in why some people are more likely to become addicted than others, but I can tell you from experience that your environment plays a very prominent role. Once you are in this shitty cycle, the effects are devastating. Physical and mental health are destroyed, emotions and sensations become disturbing, and relationships become volatile, destructive, and painful. Selfish behaviour patterns begin to form, which have no regard towards friends or family, and the negative mindset of addiction leads to one that heightens the already negative feelings that someone could feel, such as shame, guilt and apathy.

Addiction eventually becomes driven automatically by the substance through the brain and not by the individual's intelligence, integrity or willpower. Maintaining patience and compassion for people who are suffering and separating them from the addiction is imperative, as the behaviour displayed is the symptoms and not the actual person. When you are able to do this, you will see a human being inside who is hurting and in extreme pain.

The basic foundation of addiction went through three stages in total for me.

1. Experimental use: This is when I first began using a type of substance.

2. Regular use: I began to rely on a drug and became dependent on the effects to help me manage and get through my everyday life.

3. Addiction: At this stage, my life became solely focused on my addiction. Without the substance, I felt like I could not proceed through life. Safety and well-being were things I would now sell if I could turn them into a commodity of some value because I no longer had any use for them.

When I became addicted and went through these three stages of my addiction, I became extremely selfish. The drive within me to obtain more of the substance was so disgustingly intense that my only motivation was to get more of it, regardless of whom I hurt along the way. At this point, the lengths that I and other addicts would go to in an effort to fulfil that addiction are shocking, extraordinary, and do not belong in this world.

An important point I want to reiterate is that people suffering from addiction are sick people who need to get well; they are not what society portrays them as, which is awful and disgusting people who need to become good. The family unit is the most important social environment we have, and a person's quality of life depends to a large extent on how well that person interacts within that system. This is why if we look at the lives of people who suffer from addiction, we will find that a high percentage of them come from broken, families like mine.

An incredible number of people who go through trauma resort to some form of substance abuse due to the constant negative feelings that they are presented with. The brief relief that can be acquired from addictive substances can become a repetitive behaviour, which in turn can develop into a full-blown addiction. When using a substance to cope, it is referred to by psychologists as escape/avoidance coping, and the reason for this is that people are resorting to drugs or alcohol, to numb themselves and escape from their everyday existence by getting a temporary fix. Of course, this way of coping is delusional because by trying to avoid the inherent problem, all the person is doing is continually making it worse, which, in turn, solves nothing.

So now we know a little more about addiction, you can see how things had now escalated in my life. These were now some seriously dark times, and I would spend days constantly in the kitchen of my house, never talking, just searching for, preparing, or smoking crack. Although we took it as a group, we were always secluded in separate rooms of the house once we began to smoke it. At this stage of my addiction, sanity had most definitely disappeared from my body.

On one of the last occasions, if not the last, we all drove up to Graham Park estate to buy some crack. It had now become very risky driving into the estate due to my dad's car constantly being seen driving around the area. On this occasion, we had driven into a petrol station located on Apex Corner, and I could not tell you what day, year, or planet I was even on. I had decided to go inside the petrol station to buy some Milky bars because we needed the tinfoil to smoke the crack once we got home. Within seconds of me being inside, armed police surrounded the car. The police then forced us to the floor as they searched everyone. After not finding anything, we were all let go; As I mentioned earlier, my dad always told us to hide the crack in our mouths. That night, we drove back home to London Colney with all the crack we still had on us, and I remember we spoke about how the car was now marked as the police had identified my dad's number plate, this meant that we could no longer drive into Graham Park estate anymore. This part of the story will become very prevalent the further we delve into the book, as I will explain where my dad's car was found when he was killed.

The final straw was now here. Our home was repossessed as my dad could no longer keep up with the payments, and we were then moved into temporary accommodation in the form of a mobile home in Chiswell Green, on a caravan site.

The last time I smoked crack was when I had been smoking for several days straight—I had collapsed and banged my head on the toilet in the mobile home we were now living in. When I awoke, I felt like I had been asleep for ages. I then went into my dad's room and saw that he was fast asleep in his bed. For some reason, it was this event that scared me enough to finally make the decision to leave him. I remember walking outside of the mobile home, and my body filled up with dread. I then ran to the phone box down the end of the street, and I called my mum after not speaking to her for what felt like an eternity. I explained to her on the phone that I needed help, but I was not willing to discuss in depth what sort of trouble I was in.

My recent passing out and hitting my head on the toilet was not the first time I had collapsed. My lungs constantly felt on fire, and my breathing was very heavy and unnatural. When high on crack, I lost all sense of time and reality. Sleep became near impossible due to the buzzing and high sensation I constantly felt, even hours after finishing my last pipe. I had now become painfully thin, and I would classify myself as anorexic at the time. I had eating problems, as explained prior to this, but now I was not eating at all. At my lowest point, I went down to 7 and a half stone in weight. If you bear in mind that today after finishing my book, I am a fit and healthy person who weighs around 12 and a half stone. Looking back at the very few pictures I have of me then is truly horrifying because I looked—and was—seriously ill.

Leaving my dad was one of the hardest decisions I have ever made. I never told him I was going, and I knew that this would potentially be one of the last times I ever saw him. I made a selfish decision, and that decision haunted me for many years afterwards as I felt like a coward, even though I knew it was the right choice to make. It was time to put myself first because things were so severe that if I was lucky, I would end up in jail; if not, I would wind up dead. I genuinely believed that my dad was all I had in this world, so the amount of courage I mustered to achieve this still amazes me to this day. In the end, it broke my heart to see the level that everything had escalated to. As I grew older, I never felt this pain because I learned from a young age how to bury anything that I could not handle or even begin to understand.

Hopefully, I have shed enough light on the devastating effects of drug abuse for you. When you encounter a drug addict, instead of judging or looking down at them, you should maybe think for a second with your heart. What a lot of people are unaware of or do not understand is that pain can be so intense in life, that a person can feel like they do not have any other alternative available to them. No one enjoys this type of life; who grows up saying they want to be addicted to a substance? Without giving people the correct education or the tools to progress through life, how do we expect people to change? By throwing a £1 coin on the floor into a hat that a person has laid out next to their bed if they are sleeping homeless? By telling them to stop taking the drug because they will destroy their lives further? If the brain is diseased and not working correctly, how can these people make rational decisions without rational brain functions? By the time some of these people seek help, their addiction has destroyed the brain to such an extent that the substance has sucked all of the life and soul from their bodies.

Life can be so cruel sometimes, but I believe that if we all came together, it would not take a lot to make a change for the better. With a collective effort, we can all contribute towards a fundamental change and raise the consciousness of people, and this can be done by introducing information on the effects and consequences of trauma into the educational system as part of the curriculum. In my opinion, secondary schools should be integrated with alcohol and drugs groups, the prison system, mental health organisations and hospitals. Instead of treating each establishment individually, it would be beneficial if they were all combined, with each organisation supporting the next and working together collectively. Part of that curriculum would be exposing teenagers to the drastic effects of what can happen when trauma is not dealt with correctly. Teenagers should visit these places so they can experience exactly what is going on in the real world, and this will then give them a realistic expectation of what life could potentially be, and not what they currently teach in schools which gives no one any real-life skills.

When I left school, I did not know how to approach life. I was left trying to work out how I could use the algebra and chemistry that I was taught! *Where am I going to use this in my everyday life? How is this going to help me now?* I mean, the chemistry may have helped me to cook a bit of crack, but that did not turn out to be constructive for me. Instead, I was exposed to a world that I did not have the tools to navigate through. How is algebra going to help anyone when they have been neglected, abused, or exposed to danger? Most people don't even understand algebra. I mean, maths is numbers, right? When they started introducing letters, that was when I became confused. My teacher would say, "So, Mr Gregory, what is

3x + 4?" My response would be, "Fuck knows because you have started adding letters in there now, remove that stupid x, and I will give you the correct answer." Has anyone ever used algebra to help them get out of a life-threatening situation? I certainly haven't. Has the cashier at Tesco ever said to you, "Here's your change, it's £3.50 x, don't forget your x"? The point I am making is this: we are sending kids out into the world without equipping them with the tools they need to survive. Yes, algebra can be used by some people, and so can chemistry, but we learn subjects at school that do not have anywhere near as high importance as what I am openly discussing with you. What's the alternative to not introducing this education? Turn on your tv and go to the news channel and you will see. So many years of an inverted and failed educational system, and yet still no one has taught us how important truly loving ourselves is.

At this point in my story, at the age of just 17, I had finished smoking crack. I wish I could tell you that my life was about to improve, but sadly it would only continue to get worse, and the darkest days had not even arrived yet.

Before we move to the next chapter, I just want to use this opportunity to apologise to anyone I have hurt along the way. I never set out to commit crime—that was never my intention. I was so addicted to crack that I became sick, and the reality I had embroiled myself in had become a completely distorted one. This is not an excuse for my behaviour, far from it. I have taken full responsibility for my actions, and my conscience is now finally clear. If it helps anyone to know that I suffered massively, then, believe me, it nearly cost me my life.

"Addiction starts with pain and ends in pain."
—Eckhart Tolle

Chapter 4 – Temporary

(Continuing for a limited amount of time)

Always me, I thought! That was my attitude now, and I felt like I had a big target positioned right on my back. Deciding to confide in my mum was a clear apparent sign that I had no other options in my life.

After leaving my dad, I arrived at my mum's house; she had now remarried her new partner, who was my stepdad, Ian. As soon as I arrived, the culture shock hit me straight away. Looking back from a place of balance, I could not see how severe my situation had become at the time. This actually sounds ridiculous me saying, but I had become so accustomed to a life of struggling, pain, and dysfunction that it had become my normality.

I was now approaching the age of 18, and I was coming off a very intense 18-month addiction, but just because I had decided to stop smoking crack, it did not mean that I became instantly healed. Due to the consistent damage my brain had been subjected to, my prefrontal cortex (the part of the brain that makes up the frontal area of the frontal lobe, which is thought to be involved in higher cognition, planning, personality, and social behaviour) began to falter drastically. This part of the brain enables a person to observe what is happening, predict a reasonable outcome, and then make a rational conscious decision. Being able to think calmly and feel emotions will allow a person time to respond rationally, but with my brain configured to be in constant fight or flight mode, coupled with my lack of nutrition and disrupted sleep patterns, trying to control my impulses and emotions became like trying to play tennis at Wimbledon with a kitchen spoon instead of a racquet.

The pain I began experiencing from the cravings became so intense that I would wake up from sleeping and find myself panicking and covered in sweat; I would then start sobbing to myself. Because I was struggling to sleep, I spent my life feeling exhausted. I would then try to manage my predicament by using my willpower, and I would resort back to this tried and tested method every time as I refused to discuss what I was experiencing internally with anybody. A big problem I had was not confronting the true nature of my reality which was composed of not feeling wanted or loved and not being allowed to speak my truth throughout my childhood. All this did over a sustained period of time was disconnect me further from my internal state.

About a week had passed after arriving at my mum's, and I was now expected to find a job and start paying my way. I had decided to apply for work in the nearest town, Petersfield, which was seven miles away. Petersfield was not the easiest place to get to as it was too far to walk, and because I did not drive or have a car, my only means of transportation was to get a bus, but the bus only ran every hour and not past 6 pm.

The first job I managed to find was working in a perfume factory. *I am not sure why they hired me as a robot could have done this job,* I thought. After starting work, I was required to put perfume lids on the top of bottles that came through on a conveyer belt. The conveyer belt would bring bottle after bottle after bottle after bottle after bottle after bottle (you get the picture?). I can honestly say that I had never been so fucking bored in all my life, and to top it off, there was nothing worthwhile to steal, so this was only ever going to be temporary. Eventually, after no longer than a month, I decided to quit. Due to the mundane nature of the job, I was left to distract

71

my mind from stopping unwanted thoughts which would appear, and these thoughts were coming from deep inside of me; my inner child was crying out to be healed. Because these thoughts were so damning, negative and emotionally charged, I further suppressed them by smoking cannabis as much as I possibly could.

My next job was working in a petrol station, I had worked in a convenience store previously, so I knew how to serve customers and operate a till. However, the first bus in the morning did not arrive in time to get me to my early shifts, so Ian kindly lent me his push bike to cycle to work. I would then set off at around 4.30 am to arrive at my morning shifts, which would start at 6 am. I knew immediately that this job would never last more than a few weeks at most, as the energy required to ride the bike each morning left me feeling further exhausted, stressed and agitated before I had even started my shift.

On one of these journeys, in a fit of anger, I stopped on the side of the road, picked up my stepdad's bike and threw it into a bush in frustration. I could not believe what my life had become, and I could not see a way out of the situation I had now found myself in. Although I was safe and living what most people would classify as normal everyday life, it felt so unnatural and unnerving for me. At the time, I most definitely did not feel mentally, emotionally, or physically ok, but I tried my best because I had no other alternative; my mum had also given me an opportunity, and I did not want to let her or even myself down, but by not reaching out and fully accepting the urgent help I required, there was always going to be another disaster around the corner.

As time progressed, I declined further, and this meant that I tried even harder to bury all of my clear evidential issues, but the harder I tried, the more prominent they became. My nightmares became more consistent, and my dad would appear vividly, and this became incredibly uncomfortable for me, especially as I felt shameful for leaving and not trying to help him overcome his addiction. Some days I would go to work without sleeping, and this only ever heightened the negativity which was beginning to accumulate in my surroundings. Unfortunately, I had not acquired the necessary tools at this point to confront the demons that had turned my head into hell.

On top of my many mounting issues, trying to eat anything substantial and consistent was still a massive problem for me. Whereas before I had not been eating, now I was, but on the occasions when I did manage to get some food down me, it usually resulted in me vomiting it back out in secrecy. The taste of food was too awful to stomach, and a contributing factor was that my mouth had been seriously eroded by the crack I had smoked. I remember when I eventually visited my dentist at the age of 20, I was asked if I had suffered from bulimia and was told that my teeth and gums appeared to be that of a 40-year-old man.

The only way I was ever going to be able to start healing was through love, but my version of love at this point was based on my childhood experiences. The more guilt I felt for not helping my dad, the more I thought I should have been the one to stop what was going on. How could I love myself if the guilt I felt ultimately created a need to punish myself further? I felt that I did not deserve or warrant anything good in my life due to my selfishness. By thinking and then feeling various negative emotions, I projected my internal negativity out into my external reality, and this made it impossible for people to help or show me love.

My life was now falling to pieces at a very fast rate, and after deciding to quit my job once again, my mum had decided that it was time to take me to see a psychologist. After no longer than ten minutes into the session, I lost my temper, which resulted in me storming out of the psychologist's office and walking back to my mum's car. On my way out, I had told this psychologist to "go fuck yourself," which back then was a fairly calm response from me. His ten-minute diagnosis was that I had a "personality disorder...like a football hooligan." *He must be good, this psychologist,* I thought. *I wonder if he charges by the ten minutes instead of the full hour.* This 10-minute episode became imprinted on my mind and contributed towards me refusing to have any form of therapy for a further 12 years.

The psychologist and my mum had pushed my buttons almost immediately, which meant that I had gone into a defensive state. When a person goes to see a professional for help, trust needs to be built slowly with the professional they will be sharing intimate details about their life with. I remember this session clearly when I look back. When we sat down, my mum began reeling off a list of my behaviours. She said, "He smokes, takes drugs, fights, can't hold down a job, he's abusive." My mum had used the session to get everything off her chest, which ultimately was not going to make the session constructive for me. I cannot blame my mum for this, though—she had got to her wit's end with me, and this was the only way she knew how to approach a situation such as this. There was not exactly a manual you could buy for the type of behaviour I was displaying.

Trust and feeling safe are the most important components of any type of therapy one wishes to have, but I did not even trust my mum at this point, and with her being there in such close proximity, the session was fundamentally flawed from the get-go. At the time, it felt too soon to be pushed by my mum into a situation such as this, but I can now understand my mum's thought process when I look back, in her wanting me to accept help because she loved me. However, one thing I have learned through my life experiences is that a person must desire help, it must come from within and not because someone else has forced them into it. The flip side of the coin, was that in this instance, I was living under my mum's roof, which meant that I had to accept the decisions she was making.

Although my mum and Ian tried to help me, I would only ever see their actions as some form of punishment. The main motivator for a person's brain to learn is based upon behaviours that incentivise us with rewards; this is known as positive reinforcement, and after an action, the behaviour becomes reinforced. It also works the other way around with negative reinforcement, and after a behaviour has been produced, which is responded to by punishment, we then learn to avoid that further. At this time in my life, positive reinforcement was taking drugs because this relieved me of the pain I was inherently feeling. Still, whenever my mum offered me any form of help, I would only reject it because everything that had been associated with her from my childhood experiences was based upon negativity and punishment in my distorted perception of reality.

After the brief ten-minute session with the psychologist, I remember trying to process how quickly my life had changed, but it had happened too fast for me to fully comprehend. Not too long ago, I was smoking crack and committing crime—then, within what felt like an instant, I was trying to work a normal job, cycle to work and eat dinner at a set time with my mum and stepdad. The dinners always came with vegetables, and every bite of a carrot or pea took me straight back in time to the dread and horror which was my mum's house when I was a child. Situations involving vegetables, for instance, became triggers. Once these triggers were activated, I would then experience negative thoughts and emotions; at this point, all hell could break loose over a piece of veg. Looking back, I am also sure that my mum must have been experiencing her own triggers as well; she has told me on many occasions that I remind her so much of my dad. Living at my

75

mum's was just a recipe for disaster, especially since I was unwilling to accept the urgent help I required. Our constant battles gave me feelings of unsettlement, disappointment, and anger. Her house did not feel like my home, and no matter how long I lived there, it never would be. In my mind, I was living with enemies on the frontline of a war that was taking place every single day.

Living at my mum's felt worse than living at home with my dad and a contributing factor to this was down to the indoctrination I received from my dad, and I also never developed enough consistent patterns of feeling safe around my mum. The more positive experiences that are had with a person, the more the brain categorises that person as safe and familiar. My mum had very set basic rules, and I had never lived a normal structured family life before, so it felt very unsettling for me whenever she tried to set boundaries, rules or give me discipline. As a result, living at my mum's was never going to work or last long—and eventually, it all came crashing down, big time, one evening.

Finally, after several huge rows and my mum finding cannabis hidden in the chest of drawers in my bedroom, I was kicked out onto the streets by her partner, Ian. Having nowhere to live devastated me, and this only reconfirmed what my dad had said all those years ago—that my mum did not want or love me. The cannabis I was smoking was not going to cure my trauma, and when I smoked, all it did was fuck me up further; yes, it helped me to block out my feelings temporarily, but this came at an extreme price because it blocked my chemical systems that regulated engagement, motivation, and pain.

Finding drugs in my room was the final straw. On top of this, there was a mounting list of other negative behaviours I was displaying, which included the many physical fights I was starting to get into with various people, and my clothes were constantly stained in blood, which my mum would find. I was now getting into trouble with the police on a regular basis, and this had started to affect my mum's reputation in the village. My sister Alexandra was only a young teenager at the time, and my behaviour was now impacting on her as well. She had to suddenly live with a brother for the first time, and this exposed her to my drug-taking, fighting and dysfunctional existence. Removing me from the equation was my mum's only way to save not only my sister Alex but her marriage with Ian; the impact of having me living there was causing every single person harm.

The pain of becoming homeless only made me dissociate further. Fundamentally, human beings are social creatures, and our brains are wired to engage with people, but now totally on my own, I began to retreat even further into my perceptions. The trauma that I had been exposed to in my childhood had devastated my social engagement system, and it interfered with my cooperation, nurturing capabilities and ability to function in social situations, which meant that I became like a time bomb.

At this point in my life, images, emotions and thoughts just became sporadic pieces of information that had no correlation with one another. I could now be triggered by anything, such as the slightest negative thought, and this could then set me off into a full rampage as I struggled to control my anger as it spilt out of me. The trauma I had experienced and then suppressed had now mutated and taken on a life of its own. Looking back, I have no idea where my soul was at this stage of my life because I was most certainly not present.

I was now suffering from post-traumatic stress disorder (PTSD), which is an anxiety disorder caused by very stressful, frightening, or distressing events. There is also a close relationship between PTSD and substance abuse. My stress hormones would keep circulating to help my body protect itself, but the feelings, flashbacks, sensations, and nightmares eventually became much worse than the actual trauma itself. When it comes to life-disturbing symptoms, then PTSD is the Manchester United of the league, the good Manchester United of the past, not the shit one now. Shutting myself down caused me to develop tunnel vision, and the substances I was taking enabled me to find momentary relief from the everyday pain that I was suffering from. The problem I had was that once I withdrew from these addictive substances, the emotions and sensations which I would be presented with became extremely intensified. I will go on to explain further about PTSD as we go through my story, as what I was suffering from at this moment in time ended up being like a teardrop in the Pacific Ocean in comparison to how bad things became.

I was now unable to understand my emotions, sensations, and why these flashbacks were intruding into my life, especially because they became very inconsistent. There was never a conscious sign available to me when these problems would appear, and when they did, there was no telling how long they would even last. Due to this, I could not make sense of the world around me, and I started to think that I was going insane. Each terrible feeling that appeared would continue in me believing that what had happened so far in my life was my fault and that I was indeed a "bad child". None of this could be eliminated by understanding or reason, despite me being the one who was now creating more difficult situations for myself by my erratic, unconscious behaviour.

Because I had grown up disconnected and not in rhythm with my body, I began suffering from alexithymia. This is a subclinical phenomenon involving a lack of emotional awareness or, more specifically, difficulty in identifying and describing/ distinguishing feelings from bodily sensations of emotional arousal. When the brain shuts down, it invokes the structures that

78

enable us to feel and takes further actions to prevent harm to ourselves. When the brain's structures are subjected to serious trauma, such as in my case, emotional detachment, confusion and irritability become seriously prominent and just like breathing air.

So, I was now sleeping on the streets, and winter was fast approaching. Luckily, I had found another job, working at a Little Chef, a few weeks prior to becoming homeless, and on occasions, my manager would let me stay at his flat in Petersfield. I also made several friends in the village where my mum lived and also in the town of Petersfield. These friends used to help me out with somewhere to sleep on occasions as well, so at this point in my life, I was not fully homeless just yet. Some nights, though, I had nowhere to stay, so I would end up sleeping in a bus stop near my mum's house or at the back of my mum's garden on the other side of the fence without a blanket. I remember the nights being so cold, and my hands and feet used to become so numb that I thought they were going to fall off. I remember it was especially hard when it rained, and I would try to seek cover under some large trees to stop myself from becoming soaked wet through. When I did get wet, I used to shiver and cry to myself, wondering how much harder life could become. Little did I know it still had many further darker places to get to yet.

Because I was so concerned and focused on my outside environment, I was unable to redirect my attention to where it needed to be, which was inwardly, and only when I could begin to focus on my internal state could I start to change the devastating and destructive patterns I was continually creating. All I saw were situations and events that kept occurring, and in my mind, they were all random, unconnected and stemmed from the influence of other people; I just could not understand the impact I was having on anything that happened around me as I was so concerned in trying to contain my inner turmoil.

As the days and weeks passed, I knew my situation was becoming more extreme as options for places to stay became limited, which meant that I was spending more time sleeping on the streets. I could not afford to rent anywhere as I did not have enough money saved up to pay for a deposit on a room or a flat. In my mind, I still believed I was strong enough to get myself out of the predicament I was in with my willpower and without any outside help.

Living in complete survival mode meant that I focused on short-term day-to-day thinking and behaving. I did not know how to plan, so I just lived off the emotions I felt each day. This only made my behaviour unstable at the best of times, and this contributed towards my suffering from severe depression. I will first give you a definition of depression, and I will then explain what it felt like for me.

Depression is a very common mental disorder affecting more than 264 million people worldwide. It is characterised by persistent sadness and a lack of interest or pleasure in previously rewarding or enjoyable activities. It can also disturb sleep and appetite; tiredness and poor concentration are also common. Depression is a leading cause of disability around the world and contributes greatly to the global burden of disease. The effects of depression can be long-lasting or recurrent and can dramatically affect a person's ability to function and live a rewarding life.

The causes of depression include complex interactions between social, psychological, and biological factors. Life events such as childhood adversity, loss and unemployment can contribute to the development of depression.

Psychological and pharmacological treatments exist for moderate and severe depression. However, in low- and middle-income countries, treatment and support services are often absent or underdeveloped.

Now we know a little more about depression, I will explain in detail how it affected me. Depression meant that I wanted to cut myself off from everyone so I would not have to communicate with another human being as it felt too painful for me. Food has always been a big problem in general, but when I felt depressed, I could go for days without eating as I just did not have any appetite. Finding enjoyment in anything was near impossible, no matter what it was—even football, which I used to enjoy playing and watching, held no interest for me. Waking up each day would feel like running a 20-mile marathon, and when I closed my eyes, I finally found some form of peace. Sleep was all I looked forward to because it enabled me to disappear out of my destructive reality. My body would ache for no apparent reason, and I felt like I was constantly bruised or in pain; I would walk around feeling like I had been in a serious car accident but with no visible physical injuries. I would often either experience severe numbness or I would suffer from the complete opposite, which was intense sensitivity. This could then cause me to break down crying in isolation. Sometimes it just took something insignificant for me to cry spontaneously. I was so fucked up at this point that my emotions were trying to escape in any way they could. Whatever I tried to do resulted in obstruction, volatile situations, and failure, so I felt hopeless, and part of me wanted to give up. At the time, because I was too scared to end my own miserable fucking life, I was left with feelings of being a coward and weak.

Depression for me was caused by the distressing childhood trauma I had been exposed to, then tried to forget about by suppressing and hoping it would vanish. If you add in taking drugs, not eating, not sleeping, and

81

generally just not taking care of myself or my needs, I mean, if you wanted the most potent recipe guaranteed for depression, then my life up until this point would give you a 100 per cent success rate every time you rolled that dice.

Biologically, depression was always going to happen to me because various biological abnormalities have been found in the brains of depressed people, such as decreased levels of the neurotransmitter serotonin, which is the key hormone that stabilises a person's mood, feelings of well-being, and happiness. This hormone impacts the entire body, and it enables brain cells and other nervous system cells to communicate with each other. Where depression is found, there are abnormal patterns of neural activity in parts of the prefrontal cortex. As explained previously, this part of my brain had already been smashed to pieces with a sledgehammer due to my childhood experiences. Depression was a natural consequence of where I was now in my life.

For me to finally overcome the situation I was in, I would need to face up to what I had experienced in my childhood. The real test is what each of us do when we are in solitude, as this gives a person the opportunity if used correctly, to face our demons, learn then evolve. Many people spend their entire lives trying to avoid the ill effects of solitude, when in fact, it should be embraced as this is the key towards transformation for any individual.

Controlling the mind to act in a way conducive to your needs is no easy feat. The reason for the complexities of this challenge is that, as human beings, we do not want to ever feel pain, and this means that a person will go to great lengths to mask any form of discomfort with as many superficial experiences as they can find—and believe me when I say, I eventually found every single one of them.

82

Retreating from my environment really destroyed me, and if we go all the way back to the evolutionary stage of human beings, we will see that we are designed in such a way that we can learn and survive when in a social community. My community, however, consisted of myself and whatever I could find to smoke or shove up my nose. For me to eventually start the process of healing, I would need to reach out and trust another human being and go on to have hypnotherapy in my future. I will now explain why that is and how it benefits any person who is suffering from their childhood experiences.

The period between the ages of two and six are important as a child spends a large amount of time in what we call the theta waves stage. During this time, a child is able to download an incredible volume of information which they can hopefully use to excel in their environment or, in my case, falter. During the early development years, a child's consciousness has not evolved enough to critically assess that those parental pronouncements they have received were not true characterisations of the self, so once programmed, they then become defined as what we call our core beliefs. These beliefs then unconsciously shape the behaviour and potential of each person. What this means is each caregiver's behaviour and beliefs will transfer over to the child. These behaviours and beliefs are then hardwired into the brain as synaptic pathways through the subconscious mind. Once programmed, they begin to control a child's biology until there is an effort to eventually reprogramme them, and this is what hypnotherapy can help a person do.

Now, when a patient goes to see a hypnotherapist, their brain waves are dropped into a theta state which is the same stage we have discussed when a child is between the ages of two and six; the reason for this is because the low-frequency brain wave puts the person into a more suggestible and

83

programmable state again. The patient is able to make their unconscious mind conscious, and then start to construct new beliefs, which over a sustained period of time, become more prominent than the old ones. The resulting factor is a complete change in a person's reality.

The subconscious mind is the key in the process of change. So, what is the subconscious mind? It is essentially an emotionless database whose function is to read environmental signals and respond with hardwired behaviours. Behaviour-activating stimuli may be signals the nervous system detects from the external world and/or signals that arise from within the body, such as emotions, pleasure, and pain. When a stimulus is perceived, it will automatically engage the behavioural response that was learned when the signal was first experienced. So, in my case, I had to relearn so much because my worldview was an inversion and very far away from where the real truth lay.

So, if we take a minute to look at how this played out so far in my everyday life, we can see that my subconscious mind was the one on autopilot while my conscious mind was my manual control. In addition to facilitating habitual subconscious programmes, the conscious mind also has the power to be spontaneously creative in its responses to various environmental stimuli and in its self-reflective capacity, the conscious mind can observe behaviours as they are being carried out. As a pre-programmed behaviour is unfolding, the observing conscious mind can step in, stop the behaviour, and create a new response, which means that the conscious mind offers us all free will, so we are not just victims of our programming. Being fully conscious to not allow the programme to take over is where the game begins, and this is because the subconscious mind takes over the second the conscious mind is not paying attention. The conscious mind is the self and the voice of our own thoughts; it can have great imaginations and plans for

84

the future, but the subconscious mind is the one that is really running the show behind the scenes and how it runs this show is exactly how it was programmed to do so.

When I look back and evaluate what happened to me, especially as a child, I can see that I had a lot taken away at crucial stages of my development: my mum, Tracy, my cat, and both my sisters—all of this was before the age of six. This sense of abandonment transferred itself into my adult life, and the older I became, and the longer I would continue to bury my issues through escapism behaviour, the more problems I would go on to encounter, and the more severe they would become. Hating the world and myself was not benefitting me, and until I was finally able to forgive myself and look inwardly by creating solitude in my life, I would never be able to change the consistent patterns of failure, destruction and pain that were now dictating the direction of my life.

At this point, I was clearly on the brink, so you would like to think that now would be the catalyst for me to start moving forward by repairing some of the damage and devastation caused. Unfortunately, that was not the case, and things were only ever going to escalate further.

"*Be the change you want to see in the world.*"

—Gandhi

Chapter 5 – Hurt

(To feel physical pain)

Tough would be a way to describe my life if I had to use just one word. One morning in November 2002, I had turned up to work at the Little Chef, and on this particular occasion, the office phone rang, and I remember finding this strange because I had never recalled the phone ringing so early in the morning before. My manager then proceeded to answer the phone in his office while the door was left wide open. I was positioned in the room opposite, and my eyes became fixated on him as I felt a cold chill shiver shoot down my spine. After answering the phone, my manager turned to face me and said, "It's your mum on the phone." He then left the office. I will never forget the expression on his face that day. It is something that will forever remain with me.

As I approached the phone, I began to tremble. I knew before I had picked the phone up that my dad had died; it was a sixth sense feeling that had overcome me. After picking the phone up, I said, "Mum?" in a trembling voice. At first, she was crying, and I could not make out what she was trying to say, but then it became apparent as she composed herself and said, "Jamie—your dad was killed last night. He was hit by a motorbike, and the person riding the bike has also died." After hearing this news, I felt physically sick, and I began to have a panic attack. After the brief phone call ended, I rushed outside of the building through the fire exit door. I could not believe what my mum had just told me, never mind understand or even begin to deal with the emotions that came rushing to the surface.

I had only spoken to my dad a few weeks ago, and I remember he was in a much better place in his life; he also sounded positive, which came as a relief to me at the time. My dad had said that he was going to visit both my sisters and me, and he also said that he missed me very much. This conversation had given me a glimmer of hope at the time; if my dad was finally turning his life around, then maybe I could potentially move back to live with him in the not-too-distant future. Thinking this had given me extra motivation over the coming weeks to wake up each day, and I felt like I had something to work towards. Hearing my dad sound positive on the phone made me feel justified in my decision to leave him, and although a part of me felt apprehensive, I was also looking forward to seeing him again under different circumstances. Regardless of what had happened in the past, my dad was still my dad, and I loved him despite the conflicting anger I also felt.

The second my mum broke the news of my dad's death to me, everything changed instantly, and I would further detach myself from where love was. The guilt I felt for abandoning my dad felt like being smacked in the face with a cold brick. I now thought I could have saved him if I had stayed instead of leaving. Due to my sudden shift in perception, I doubted my thought processes and sanity even further. In my mind, I was now responsible for my dad's death, he needed me, and I left him—and now he was fucking dead. My only way of dealing with this added pain I began to feel was to bury it deep inside of myself. I then tried my hardest to hate my dad, as this made his death easier for me to accept.

My feelings towards my dad are far too complex to try and describe to you with words, but I do know they were always very divided. The anger I felt towards my dad was my way of protecting myself, and this is a very common response, especially from people who feel hurt, threatened, or scared. Felling angry then escalated into rage, and this then infiltrated all of

87

the relationships in my life, which, prior to my dad's death, were already fucked. With my dad now dead, I was pushed that little bit further towards where the darkness was.

What I would eventually come to realise through therapy in my future was that I was 17 years old when I left my dad. He was a full-grown man who made his own choices in life, and what happened to him was not my fault, and I could not continue to blame myself. The problem I had was the older I grew and the more I was unable to feel this, the more I buried my pain, resulting in further volatile situations. Ralph Waldo Emerson summed this up perfectly when he said, "For every minute you are angry, you lose 60 seconds of happiness."

My dad's death had now broken me, and looking back, I can see that a further significant change occurred from that moment onwards that was very scary. I was already emotionless, distant, and cold, but I became even further detached, and I then began to hate myself, my life, and the world that little bit more than I already did. Many people had said to me that I was going in the direction of someone who would be dead or in jail by the age of 21, and at this point, I thought, *Fuck it, I will prove each and every one of you right.*

Not too long after my dad's death, I was told that his car had been found parked close to Graham Park estate, where we all used to buy crack cocaine. We had stopped driving into the estate towards the end, and this was because it had become too risky as the police had started to recognise the number plate of his car, as explained earlier in Chapter 3. I believe my dad had parked where he had, so he could jump the fence to get into the estate and score crack without his car being noticed. My dad attempted to cross the road when he was high on drugs (they found a high level of cocaine in my dad's autopsy report), and with his judgement being impaired, he got hit by a motorbike. It was all very sudden and tragic at the time, but looking back, it was inevitable, given the life choices he was continuing to make.

Around a week had passed when I attended my dad's funeral with my mum and sister Alex. Although I was homeless, my mum and I had decided to bury our differences as she wanted to be there to support me and my sister. I think my mum also felt a duty to be there; although she and my dad had divorced, and no matter what destruction he had caused, my mum had reached a place in her life where she felt sorry for him as she knew he was a very sick man. All of my mum's three children were conceived with my dad, so I believe there must have been a time in her life when she loved him.

This was my first-ever funeral, and I found the experience very distressing. As they were burying my dad's coffin, my grandma tried to jump into his grave as she was held back by several people; she was uncontrollably distraught at the time. As a parent, you are not supposed to see your children die; naturally, it is supposed to be the other way around, so I cannot imagine what both my grandparents were feeling and going through at that moment in time.

When I left my dad, the situation was dreadful, and I remember my dad had visited his brothers to borrow money. When I was younger, we used to see the Greek side of the family very regularly, but when we were smoking crack, we completely stopped seeing them. Looking back, I am sure they must have known something was going on, but they would have had no idea to what extent. I am sure my book will come as a shocking revelation to any of the family who decide to read it.

After my dad's funeral, the feelings of abandonment, rejection and fear had fully set in. My dad was now dead, the Greek side of the family wanted nothing to do with me, and I was still homeless, sleeping on the streets. I had now turned 18 years of age, so I was deemed an adult, but deep down, I still felt like a vulnerable little child who just wanted to be loved but believed I was unlovable. The only way to describe my situation at the time was to say that I felt like I was all alone and entering through the gates of hell. The alarm bell of my emotional brain kept signalling, informing me that I was in danger, and no amount of insight would silence it because I was not in a safe situation. To make matters even worse, I had decided to quit my job working at the Little Chef as I could not face going to work, so I was now jobless and fully homeless.

My days and nights then became filled with many negative emotions from my past, which began surfacing relentlessly. My life was now flashing before me, and I did not know how much more I had left in the tank to keep carrying on with this pointless existence. Gradually, as time progressed, my memories no longer had visuals attached; once triggered, I was left with emotions and sensations I had no understanding of. This meant in the future, when I tried to trace everything back to where it had originated from, it became impossible without professional help, especially as many of my memories were dissociated ones from my childhood.

My past and present drug addiction further contributed to my continual decline. My current life activities had degenerated to the point where I was only using my brain to survive. My brain was so focused on suppressing my inner chaos that there was no time to pursue anything constructive. With my brain not engaging in learning, problem-solving or other types of brain activity that would promote growth, I was unable to strengthen my brain's ability to function in a productive way.

At our core, human beings are social creatures, and because of that, we are tuned in to other people to seek comfort. Part of the human brain is continually monitoring others as it tries to make sense of and understand other people's intentions. We then sense and absorb the emotions of people around us. Due to the negative behaviour emanating from me, any person with whom I came into contact would always react negatively, and I would absorb and then project this back into my reality; it was just a vicious cycle I was unable to break. The capacity to love is the core success of human beings, and the reason we have survived on this planet for so long is due to humans being able to form and maintain effective groups in harmony with one another.

Several times after my dad's death, I tried to go back to my mums, and she would always give me another opportunity, but the outcome never changed. The last time I was kicked out onto the streets, I ended up sleeping homeless for about six months. On the last occasion, I remember seeing my nana becoming terribly upset as I walked away from the house. My nana had begun to cry, and this made me tearful. I then felt physically sick because I have always had a soft spot for my nana, and the last thing I wanted to do was to make her upset as well. Deep down, I wanted to be part of my mum's family, but I could not. I was just too traumatised by everything that I had experienced so far in my life, and there was no way I could build a relationship with anyone until I sought the urgent help I clearly required.

My time being homeless became extremely difficult. I mean, I have had to go through some tricky situations in my life up until this point, and there were many more to follow, as you will go on to see, but this was definitely up there with the best of them. I now had zero money to my name, so my only means of feeding myself was to steal, so I used to wait for a man who worked in the local village shop to go behind into the stock room each morning, to take deliveries. The door would always be left open, so I would walk in and steal whatever I could get my hands on to eat for that day.

Everything at this point appeared to me as a life-or-death situation, and I was not prepared to die just yet.

Sleeping rough brought about a different set of problems which I had not even considered at the time. I took warmth, shelter, food, and clean water for granted, but these became real everyday difficulties when I was homeless. Some nights, I believed I would freeze to death because I had no blanket, and I could not stop myself from shivering. I was now sleeping outside in the village, where there was no shelter or heat, and the temperatures were frequently dropping below freezing point as it was winter. Putting up with the negative thoughts that would surface at the forefront of my mind each evening became harder as time progressed, and these thoughts further increased the depression I was suffering from at the time. No matter how hard I tried to force these thoughts to stop, they kept reappearing ruthlessly and consistently.

Homelessness is devastating, dangerous and isolating. When I was on the streets, I was frowned upon and treated in further disgusting ways. Through research, I have found that people sleeping on the street are almost 17 times more likely to become victims of violence. More than one in three people sleeping rough have been deliberately hit, kicked, or experienced some other form of violence whilst homeless. Homeless people are also over nine times more likely to take their own life than the general population. Rough sleeping is the most visible and dangerous form of homelessness, and when most people think of a homeless person, they tend to think of someone sleeping rough on the streets. The longer someone experiences rough sleeping, the more likely they are to face challenges around mental health and drug misuse.

At this point, I was expecting a predictable response from the world, and predictable for me was further punishment, feeling terrified and excluded. I was constantly scanning my environment for evidence that my world view was accurate, that the world was indeed a dangerous place, that people were not trustworthy, that I did not belong anywhere, and that love was not real, it was just a word people used that had no meaning; again, all the evidence I searched for was found in abundance in my everyday environment. Whenever I experienced care, nurturing and love from my mum, for instance, it would challenge the worldview that I had formed and held so dear to me. My mind would then think *What the fuck is this? This is not familiar; I want familiar back!* I would then start acting out to create chaos wherever there was order, and I could then gravitate back to my comfortable natural habitat, which was my dysfunctional familiarity. People in similar situations such as mine need patience, understanding and sufficient new experiences which are consistent to enable them to shape new world views. This does not happen overnight, and it takes an extremely long time to create new neural networks; it takes years of new opportunities, cognitively learning new things, new relationships plus a lot of push and pull resistance. Only after this can the old-world view be modified and then responded to in a different manner.

So, I was now completely detached from life itself, which increased my negative symptoms further. I wanted to feel safe, connect with others and receive love, but because I was trapped in my mind, I was susceptible to the lure of self-medicating as it promised me a brief release from my pain. As ACE (which stands for *Adverse Childhood Experiences)* studies have shown, child abuse and neglect are the single most preventable cause of mental illness, the single most common cause of drug and alcohol abuse, and a significant contributor to leading causes of death such as diabetes, heart disease, cancer, strokes, and suicide. The longer my situation continued, the harder it would be for me not to become just another statistic.

Despite my terrible start in life, there is hope due to neuroplasticity, which means the changeability of the brain. One of the key functions of neuroplasticity is that the pattern of activation makes a big difference in how neural networks change. When we have predictable and controllable activation of our stress response system, we begin to form flexible and stronger stress response capabilities, and we are then able to demonstrate resilience in the face of more extreme stressors. The more a person can face moderate challenges and succeed, the more they can do the same with bigger challenges. Let me make this clear, stress is not something to be scared of or even avoided; what causes the detrimental problems is the controllability, pattern, and intensity of stress. In my case, the problem was my stress activation being so unpredictable, extreme and prolonged from the earliest parts of my childhood. Now, this is the part where there is some good news; as the brain is changeable through trauma, for instance, the correct nurturing and consistent positive interactions will cause positive change as well. Once challenges begin to change along with a person's environment, so does everything else. When a person begins to stay in a healthy balance, ultimately, so does their physiology.

This then leads us to epigenetics, which gives us an understanding of how life is controlled. Epigenetic research has established that DNA blueprints passed down through genes are not set in concrete. Environmental influences, including nutrition, stress, and emotions, can modify our genes without changing their basic blueprint. Biological and gene activity is dynamically linked to information from the environment, which we then download into our cells. These cells are like programmable chips whose behaviour and genetic activity are primarily controlled by environmental signals. What this means is once I was able to change my environment in the future, I could then begin to experience a different reality

94

from the destructive one I was now accustomed to; but until then, not much would change for me.

Eventually, after sleeping on the streets, a friend of mine in the village managed to get hold of a tent, and this kept me warmer at night. I remember I would go to sleep thinking about how I was going to survive the following day. I did not have a plan, and I believe this is a big problem with people who are homeless in general. How can these people plan for their future when they are so busy trying to survive the outcome of each and every day?! Once you are in this situation, it is very hard to overcome, and as each day passes, the odds are stacked up against a homeless person ever managing to create a secure, balanced, and healthy life.

After spending my time homeless for several months, I then managed to move to Petersfield, where I stayed with a friend of mine called Liam. An opportunity arose when his mum helped me to get a job stacking shelves in Sainsbury's with her. I was very grateful for this opportunity but being grateful and having all the willpower in the world to overcome what I had been through, was not going to be enough for me to try and fix the devastation in my life. Transitioning from sleeping on the streets to having somewhere to live, a job, and money brought a certain amount of comfort in my life for a short period of time, and this made me feel like all my problems would vanish into thin air. The reason for this was that I based success on having money because, as a child, when my dad had money, he was happy, so I looked for my happiness through monetary means; it was one of my ingrained core beliefs. Basing my happiness on such an inversion from where the real truth lay enabled cracks to appear very quickly, and when they did, I decided to leave my job working at Sainsbury's, and I ended up with nowhere to live yet again.

Drinking around this time in my life became very prominent, and although I did not drink every single day, there were times when I was drinking on more days than I wasn't. All this did was affect me negatively, and instead of alcohol suppressing my emotions, it did the complete opposite, and it became a toxic release for me. My suppressed feelings would then explode, and they would be released in the form of anger and hatred towards myself and the world, which then caused further mayhem. My behaviour became extremely erratic, toxic, and violent, and every time I lashed out, I physically began fighting with various people; I would then find myself being projected back into my childhood. In my mind, these fights consisted of me battling against my dad, and I was fighting all of those scenarios that I was unable to when I was a helpless child. My view at this point in my life was very clear. I did not have an anger problem. Instead, I thought people just had to stop making me fucking angry.

Getting in trouble with the police became a regular occurrence, and this resulted in me being charged and convicted with multiple thefts, several criminal damage charges, theft by employee, affray, several breaches of community punishment orders and a couple of failures to attend court and bail. If I were to estimate, I would say I had been arrested easily over 30 times before the age of 24. On top of this large list, I would also skip bail and flee the country, resulting in a warrant being issued for my arrest and me becoming a fugitive, but I will elaborate on this the further we get into my story. Looking back through my criminal record, I can now see that all of my convictions spanned over a period of four years after my dad's death. This was a very intense grieving period in my life, and I did not know how to come to terms with what I felt internally, so I lashed out with no remorse or consequence for my actions. The biggest problem I had was my thought processes. While as a child, you can be forgiven for what is not in your control, that all changes when you become an adult, and unfortunately, I just did not have any other point of awareness available at the time to understand this, and I just saw myself as a poor victim.

As the police dramas unfolded, I managed to start seeing a girl. Her name was Charlotte, and I would say that she was my first real girlfriend. Although the relationship did not last long, it didn't end on bad terms, and we both still speak today. Although I did not let Charlotte fully in, she was someone who I felt comfortable around as she was always kind, considerate and gentle towards me.

Through Charlotte, I met a couple of her male friends who were brothers and living in Winchester. They were both from London originally, so straight away, I struck up a connection with them as we had similar accents. I remember one night being in a bar in Winchester town centre, and there was an altercation between both Charlotte's male friends and some people they did not like. Due to this, I decided to walk over and start fighting these people on their behalf, and the bouncers of the bar eventually threw me out. Back then, I did not need an excuse to have a scrap. After this, Charlotte's male friends offered me a place to stay, as they knew I was going through some difficulties; little did they know how severe these difficulties were. They had both said I could stay in their caravan until I could sort something more permanent out. It also turned out that their mum knew a person who worked at a local convenience store, and she had been so kind to help get me a job working there as a supervisor. I remember after sleeping in the caravan one night, I woke up and knew from that moment onwards that I could not stay there a day longer. I now had a strong desire to return to London Colney as it was familiar to me, and I just felt an intense feeling of being lost in this place that had no significance. The thought of working a job also began to fill me with intense dread as I was still trying to come to terms with my dad's death.

Not for the first or last time, I found myself in desperate need of money, so on my first shift after starting my new job, I cashed up the till and instead of putting the money into the safe, I switched the pods that contained the day's takings and put an empty pod inside the safe instead. I then stole the pod with the money in it and left the building. Within 24 hours, I received a phone call from the manager of the store, and he explained that he knew that I had taken the money, and if I were to return it, they would not call the police. I remember then putting the phone down, and I just ignored what I had done. I had absolutely no regret, remorse, or intention of taking the money back. Looking back, I had most certainly developed narcissistic tendencies and had no empathy or compassion towards others.

I would like to say that I needed the money to better myself because, morally, it would make my story sound better, but instead, I just used the money to buy more drugs and alcohol to get myself further fucked up. Because of my selfish behaviour, I ended up getting everything I deserved that would eventually come my way. The woman who had helped me to get this job had stuck her neck out on the line for me, and like her, Liam's mum, and my mum before them, I had destroyed any trust and help they were prepared to give me.

Inevitably I was arrested for this crime and charged with theft by an employee, which I found out was much more serious than just theft. I had stolen money from my workplace when I was in a position of trust. When I attended court, I still did not know the severity of the crime I had done until I saw a solicitor; I was then explained that the offence I had committed carried a custodial sentence and I should now prepare for jail. After sitting in front of the judge, my solicitor read out all my mitigating circumstances, such as the fact that I was homeless, I had been addicted to crack, and my dad had recently been killed. At the end of hearing all this, I believe the judge felt sorry for me, so instead of sending me to prison, he gave me an opportunity to turn my life around. I was then given 200 hours of community service, and I also had to pay a fine for the cost of the money I had stolen. After leaving court, I felt mightily relieved as the thought of going to prison frightened me. I had every intention of paying the money back and completing the community punishment order, but I did not know how I would ever do it.

At this point, I now blamed both my father and mother for the predicament I was in. I had managed to use this as an excuse, and I played the victim card as much as I possibly could to others, but more worryingly, I had also convinced myself. The problem which I could not see was that if I continued down this path of blaming everyone else and looking at my problems outside of myself, I would not be able to take the necessary steps in my adult life to begin to change, heal and become a better human being by looking inwardly.

This topic then leads me on to a huge problem that I see today, especially with people I have spoken to and met throughout my life. Some of these people have used some form of excuse to justify why their life turned out the way it did, and I have encountered many people who show severe hatred towards others with no empathy for what that person must have been through to project that behaviour initially in the first place. Of course, it does not make the initial behaviour correct, but forgiveness and acceptance are the only way to cultivate a new set of circumstances for the future; otherwise, that hatred will eventually eat you up from the inside out, as it did me. I really understood this type of mindset as well because I felt exactly the same way before I eventually began to change my life around. Your past is not an excuse, but instead, it's an explanation that offers insight into so many questions we all ask ourselves: why do I behave the way I do? Why do I feel the way I do? Very often, what happens to a person takes many years to unravel. It takes a huge amount of courage to eventually confront our actions, but by starting to peel back and dissect the trauma in our lives, we will expose the real truth about our past. Only then can healing truly begin.

The defining moment for me in the future to gain control was to recognise that, due to my childhood, I had deep-rooted issues that I had suppressed and needed to face head-on, but like most things in life, when stuff is hurled at us from all angles without warning or understanding, and we are being affected negatively, we must reach out and seek help.

Deep down, I could not stand the situations I kept creating, and believe me, I wanted to change at this point in my life, but every time I attempted to do so, I ended back in the same ingrained patterned responses. I only viewed the world through my dominant emotions, and mine were always being projected from a negative viewpoint. Suffering with fear made me feel frightened and on guard. Being an angry person meant that I began to lash out and live in an angry body, and being a child abuse victim made me believe I was a victim with no control over my circumstances.

Although I kept moving forward, there was always going to be further trouble until I reached out and accepted some form of help. This point would come for me, as you will go on to see, but I still had a long way to go.

Emotions can be so intense in life that temporary burial of them is a way to manage and feel nothing instead.
Only when a person can break through their suffering and feel emotion again can they learn, heal, and begin to love once more.

—Jamie Gregory

Chapter 6 – Label

(To put a word or name on something to describe or identify it)

Only at this point had I decided it was time to move back to London Colney, and I did this with the help of my friends Mark and his brother Rob. After returning, Rob allowed me to sleep in the back of his car while I looked for a job. Both of them still lived at home, so there was no way I could stay inside their house because their mum Michelle knew what had happened previously regarding the crack and crime, we were all involved in.

When I returned to London Colney, Rob and I decided to start doing some cigarette runs to Spain. On one of these occasions, we had spent all the money we had on buying cigarettes, so we had nothing left over for food. When we finally arrived at the airport in Spain, we were starving, and I remember the upstairs shops where we could get food from were all closed—but we were still able to walk in between them. After going for a stroll, I managed to find a small café, and through the window, I could see muffins and cakes. In frustration, I slammed the door, and to my amazement, it slowly opened. We both then entered this café, and at first, we were going to steal some food, but then we discovered a till on the right-hand side of the door. Straight away, it went from us trying to steal food to "Rob, let's see what's in the till." After opening it, we discovered hundreds of euros. We both then decided to put the money into a black Nike string shoulder bag that we had on us. At no point during this had it dawned on me that we were in a Spanish airport, where there were armed police walking around casually.

After boarding the plane, the engine started then after no longer than 5 minutes, the engine was turned off again. I remember there were lots of discussions going on between the staff on the plane, and they were rushing around between the aisles. I fully expected at this point that the Spanish police would walk onto the plane and arrest us both, and the severity of what we had done had now only kicked in.

Because I had no sense of danger, empathy, or remorse, I would find myself in reckless situations time and time again without understanding the consequences of my actions. What transpired on this occasion, though, was vastly different from what I had expected and feared. I found out, through asking, that the plane was missing a passenger. Once this passenger eventually boarded, the engine restarted, and we took off and flew back home to England. At this point in my life, my behaviour more than warranted a prison sentence.

After a week or so of sleeping in Rob's car, Michelle found out and said I could stay on the couch in Rob's room. Michelle's partner at the time, big Mark (we called him this to not get confused with Rob's younger brother Mark), also gave me a chance to attend an interview for a company where he worked as a manager. I was extremely grateful for this opportunity, and once again, I could envision a path which would get me out of the dire situation I was in.

After attending the interview and then getting the job, I began working, and I met a person there called David, who would become a friend of mine. My life then settled down for a time, and I began playing football again with David for a local team on the weekends.

At my new job, I was required to work night shifts and drive a pallet truck. I would spend each evening picking and then packing items that would be distributed to various supermarkets around the country. As time

103

progressed, I managed to save up enough money to go on holiday to Kavos in Greece with Rob and some friends. After I returned, I stayed in contact with some workers I had met that lived out there, and I said I would come back for another holiday sometime in the future. Going on holiday, having a stable job and somewhere to live, felt like a world away from what I had been accustomed to, and finally, my life was going in a positive direction, or so I thought.

One night shortly after my holiday, David and I decided to go to a nightclub on our lunch break. There were no rules regarding leaving the premises, but what was not allowed was drinking alcohol. When the nightclub closed, we both returned to work drunk, and within minutes of entering the building, our names were called out over the speaker system, and we were both told to head to the main office. Once I arrived, I was suspended immediately by a shift manager, and a few days later, I was sacked.

Losing my job meant that I once again had to uproot, and I remember feeling so disappointed in myself, and I could not understand why I could not hold down a job like everyone else around me was doing. Because I had buried my issues instead of facing them head-on, I was still struggling internally, and when I needed to contain what would try to surface, I would then do what I was accustomed to doing, which was self-medicating with whatever I had available at my disposal. Taking drugs or drinking alcohol just became like breathing air for me, and I needed them to survive.

When the brain is healthy, the dopamine system rewards our everyday behaviours, and this system brings us happiness when we accomplish something as small as drinking a glass of water when we are thirsty. This system is in place to ensure that we look for and carry out activities that we need to survive by giving us feelings of pleasure; however, when using addictive substances, they flood the brain with a much larger hit of the reward system, so it provides a quick shortcut to feelings of elation by filling the brain with extreme amounts of dopamine. When I returned to my normal state and was not abusing substances, my brain had been affected so much that it began to produce less dopamine, so depression and lack of energy became very prominent.

After being sacked, I had also thrown another spanner into the works for myself. I was still on a community punishment order, but I kept breaching it because I had no fixed abode, and a warrant had now been issued for my arrest. Now facing a certain prison sentence, I decided to skip the country and travel back to Kavos in Greece. The troubles in my life had escalated once again, and I was now a wanted person by the police back in England. The consequence was that the more I ran from my problems, the more they increased.

My thought processes at this time were based upon denial and dissociation because I could not tolerate my circumstances; I would then shut myself down and, very similar to how I had run away to Bognor Regis as a child because I could not face my dad, I had run to Kavos in Greece because I could not face the situation I had now created. Running was a tried and tested way of not having to face the world or myself, and it also brought my stress levels back to a functioning state.

Eventually, I decided to come back to England, and once I arrived, I needed to catch a train which I did not pay for, and the police then caught me. After being arrested, I was remanded to court without bail. I had been so sure I would go to jail this time, but it no longer bothered me as much as it once did because I felt exhausted, and the energy required to sustain this lifestyle of running from everything was impacting negatively on me.

105

The following day I was placed in front of a judge, and additional charges had been pinned on me, which turned out to be for criminal damage from when I had smashed three windows while living in Petersfield. I had been arrested and bailed for this some time ago, but due to moving back to London Colney, I had totally forgotten about this and hoped it had just gone away.

So, I was now in court for God knows how many breaches of my community service order, criminal damage I had committed by smashing three windows, as well as failing to surrender and going on the run. After I sat down in the court, my solicitor began to read out my mitigating circumstances, and it felt all too similar to the last time I was there. He explained about my crack addiction, being homeless, and my dad being killed—and once again, the judge took pity on me. *How many lives was I going to keep getting?* I thought. I was then sentenced to pay more than £5,000 in compensation to the court, I was put back onto the community service order, and this time I was told that if I were to breach my order again or end up in any court in the country, I would receive a custodial sentence. This was now my last chance, and I was determined to take my opportunity.

After finally attending community service, I was pleasantly surprised to see a few people I knew there. At the same time, I moved into a shared house in Hatfield, and a good opportunity arose for me. Rob had started hanging out with a couple of new friends, and after speaking to one of them, I found out that he worked for a company that took apprentices on every year, so I decided to try my luck by ringing them. After a lengthy process, I eventually secured myself a role working as an electrical apprentice, and I was accepted for enrolment in college.

To get this job, I had forged all my references and lied about my past experience. I stated that I had electrical knowledge because my dad was an alarm engineer, and I used to work with him on the weekends; although I went to work with him on occasions, I could not even change a light bulb, let alone carry out any alarm work. I just sat in his van the majority of the time eating McDonalds. One thing I was missing, which I could not lie about, was a GCSE certificate, and they required me to have a minimum of a C grade in maths, but I had failed maths at school and had not even been graded for it. I then decided to go to an external company in St Albans, and I booked an exam, three weeks then passed, and after studying every day, I got the C grade that I required. As I would find out later in my life, what was always holding me back was the trauma I had buried deep inside of me and refused to face.

Did I feel bad for lying on my application form, forging my references, and stating that I had electrical experience? The answer was a firm no. In my predicament, no one would have hired me if I had been honest, and in desperation, I had done what was required to get this job. Telling the truth, in this instance, was not going to get me very far, but all this did was reconfirm to me that lying and being deceitful was the approach I needed to take if I wanted to succeed in life.

Finally, after I started working, I began earning between £500–£700 a week as an apprentice. I was paid for 12 hours of work, although I only worked when the electricity on the track was turned off between 1 am and 4 am each night. This meant that I never worked more than three hours, and it was rare that I ever worked the full three hours. Although I now had a good job that offered me a secure and promising future, a steady income and a potential qualification, I could not understand why I was still feeling so low and struggling with my mental health.

At the time, I had still not passed my driving test, but I decided to buy a car which I had managed to get finance on with the help of a girl I was seeing at the time. I would then drive into London to work some nights, although a lift was available in the company vans. One early morning after finishing work, I was driving back home when I was stopped by a police car. My car was insured with provisional insurance because I had a provisional licence, so my vehicle showed up as being insured. When the police officer came to my window and asked what I was doing and why I was out so late at night, I explained that I worked for the London Underground, and I had just finished my shift. I then showed him my work identification, which had my name and photo on it. The police officer looked at it, and then he got a radio call which turned out to be an emergency, so he left sharply, saying to me, "Have a good night and drive safe." This situation further confirmed to me that I was above the law, and I did not feel the need to pass my driving test. Having no boundaries growing up meant that when I became an adult, I would do what I wanted, and although I had managed to find a stable job, I was still making irrational decisions based on my upbringing.

While I worked on the London Underground, I started seeing a girl, but the relationship turned sour after not too long. This girl loved me at the time—I do not doubt that—but I did not want to be with her, and I felt that I could not breathe the closer we became. My attitude was selfish, and my mindset back then was: if you want breakfast in bed, then sleep in the kitchen. I only thought about myself and no one else's feelings.

Social support is not the same as merely being in the presence of others; the critical issue is reciprocity, being truly heard and seen by the people around us. For a person's physiology to calm down, they need the visceral feeling of safety. No doctor can prescribe friendship or love; even when presented with love, I would only reject it because it was unfamiliar to me. Being so close to another human being made me feel unsafe; I just did not know or even understand how to be in a relationship because, fundamentally, I was incapable of loving myself, and until I did, I could not love anyone else. At no point did I consider this girl's feelings, and the promise she offered me in terms of closeness evoked further fears of getting harmed, deceived or abandoned. My shame played a prominent role in this; I would think to myself that as soon as this girl found out how awful and disgusting I really am, I was sure she would get rid of me at the first opportunity. Once again, I was further detaching myself from love. Because my heart was totally destroyed in my childhood, I could not form intimacy with anyone, so I became preoccupied with trying not to get hurt. Trying to hurt this girl first by pushing her away became a scenario of self-protection in my distorted version of reality. What I was doing was self-sabotaging anything that represented love and safety because I never understood either. My subconscious mind was programmed with misconceptions, which further helped me to partake in limiting and negative behaviours. I was taught that people are dangerous and not to be trusted, so whenever a person got too close to me, I would unconsciously engage in a protective response, which was my defensive mechanism kicking in.

Two important areas in recovering from trauma are learning to accept the past without being incoherent in the present and reconfiguring the already damaged brain system that was constructed to cope with the trauma in the first place. Revisiting, reliving, and understanding my past memories were required for me to view parts of myself that had originally formed my defensive habits to survive. Eventually, I would have to relinquish my unhealthy coping strategies, which was not easy, however, as I had used and relied on them to keep me alive.

After this girl and I finally split up, I decided to move in with a person who I had met on community service. He lived with his girlfriend and kids, and they had a spare room that they rented out to me. This person was also Greek and reminded me very much of my dad because of his criminal traits. Due to my childhood, I felt very comfortable around people who were involved in the criminal world, as that was what I had become accustomed to. Until I could reconstruct my beliefs, I would never be able to form any healthy bonds which consisted of love, and instead, I was left with making connections with people that would further hinder me.

After moving in with this person, 18 months or so had passed, and I had begun the process of severely declining, and it was now only a matter of time before I was either sacked, or I quit my job. Although things were not going in the right direction with work, I did manage to pass my end-of-year college course exam, which now gave me a City & Guilds Level 2 in Electrical Installation; I still, however, could not change a light bulb. I was constantly getting into arguments with people at work, and as an apprentice, you have to accept that, at times, you will not be spoken to in the best possible way. Every time this happened, it felt very personal, and it would trigger me. Every criticism I received felt like it was coming from my dad, and how I was spoken to evoked familiar negative experiences.

A person's brain is designed in such a way that it will use shortcuts, and I can tell you that they are far from accurate at times, as they make each of us vulnerable to stereotypes and generalising attributes of people based upon the broad categories they fall into. The most powerful categories in the brain come from our first experiences in life, and this is what contributes towards tendency for bias. The fear I would experience alerted me to potential danger or harm even when it was not present, and this driving force contributed further towards my psychological disorders, such as anxiety, depression, and obsessive-compulsive disorder. By projecting these insecurities out into my everyday environment, I became outcasted at work just like I had at school and also in my childhood; I then became easy to label as various people just saw a young man who wanted to leave work as soon as possible, who did not want to engage and who did not have any real interest invested in the job.

Traumatised individuals such as myself are often afraid of love and feeling anything because their physical sensations become their enemy, and this then causes fear of being hijacked by their sensations, which keeps both the body and mind frozen in time. Even though my trauma was a thing of the past, my emotional brain kept generating sensations that made me feel scared and helpless in the present moment. Looking back, I cannot blame anyone at work for how I was treated, and ultimately, I would subconsciously create the situations that I would keep finding myself in.

The end was now in sight, and an HR woman from work had driven to the college where I was outside smoking a cigarette at the time. She then pulled up beside me, wound her window down and began screaming. She had found out that I had been driving around for the last year without a driving licence. At the time, I could not see what the big issue was. Okay, if I got caught, then so be it, I would deal with the consequences, but I thought at the time: *What the fuck has this got to do with you and that big nose of yours?* On reflection, I can now see how distorted my thinking was. By driving around without a licence, I was putting other people in danger as well as myself, and if I had hit and caused anyone damage without any valid car insurance, there would have been serious implications for everyone involved. Again, my narcissistic tendencies were shining through. At the time, I would rationalise each singular negative event that occurred in my life, by blaming everyone else apart from myself, just like my dad did, and again, I was re-enacting everything that he had taught me directly and indirectly.

111

After this argument with the HR woman, I decided to leave the job and went to work with the person I had recently moved in with. This person was already working for himself in the oil industry, so we both decided to join together and start a new business. Before I started, though, I had to set a few things into motion. With the amount of driving involved, I now needed to pass my driving test. Luckily, I had passed my theory test, so I booked a driving cancellation test and passed it within a matter of weeks. I then went out and bought a van with legitimate insurance, and lastly, I went and got myself certificated by the Environmental Agency, as this enabled me to legally carry the oil on the van that we would be collecting.

Once I started this new job, I decided that I wanted to branch out instead of just covering the local area. Each time we travelled into new locations, I would spend my evenings obsessively drawing maps, planning routes then googling the addresses of restaurants, hotels, and pubs from where we could collect the oil from. Eventually, we would both travel to pretty much every city in the country in search of used cooking oil. This job was just what I was looking for, and because it was so fast paced, it enabled me to stop any unwanted thoughts from appearing in my mind as regularly as they once had. I now had the distraction I was looking for, which also meant that I did not have to rely so much on my other means of self-medication anymore.

In this new job, I found out that restaurant establishments had to get their oil collected by someone who was registered with the Environmental Agency, and that company must dispose of the oil in a correct manner by being certificated to do so. We had now begun providing a free service to collect and dispose of oil, and once we arrived at these various locations, in the beginning, 99 per cent of the time, each establishment were happy to let us remove their old oil. Although a very high percentage of places had contracts with other companies, they would often not turn up, and there would be stacks of oil left, causing a mess.

The oil we began collecting was either stored in 20-litre cans or blue barrels, and these ranged from 60 litres all the way up to 200 litres. I had now invested in 20, 60-litre blue barrels, and these were the same as the ones we came across daily. This then made us look familiar to the companies these places had contracts with, especially when we would replace their barrel with one which was an exact replica.

On average, we would aim to collect around 1,000 litres a day. Monday was always the best day of the week to work because that was when the majority of restaurants would empty their fryers after a busy weekend. As the week progressed leading up towards Friday, it became harder to find oil, so we very rarely worked past Thursdays, but I would then spend my days off planning further routes to keep my mind preoccupied.

By diversifying and travelling all over the country, we could avoid going to the same places for long periods of time, and this meant that there was less chance of us getting caught or noticed. Although we were arrested countless times, I was able to sustain this job for around four years in total without getting a conviction. When I started this job, we would always ask for permission to take the oil, but over time, and after returning to the same locations, I started to memorise where the oil was kept. It was always easier if you could just pull up to the back of a bin area and take the oil drums without having to ask permission. However, as time progressed, more and more establishments did not want us to take their oil because they started to find out that we were not their designated company that was contracted to collect it.

Eventually, after an argument with the person I was working and living with, mainly due to him constantly letting me down, which meant I could not work, we went our separate ways, and I then decided to get a few people I knew who were reliable to work with me instead.

After expanding, I ended up with various locations where I could take the oil and get cash on the day. Some of these places included a farm in Maple Cross in London, which was the first place I had used, another place was Maidstone, in Kent, and the guys there got me everything I wanted. They would sell me Viagra in huge quantities, cigarettes, and counterfeit money, which I could then sell on to various people that I knew. Another person I used to take the oil to was Bernard, who lived on the outskirts of Bath. I also used a person in Widnes, and he had made a petrol station on an industrial unit. Lastly, I had a few people that I did not use as often, as the price was not the best, but these people were handy when I was in their areas.

Towards the end of working in the oil business, it had become very risky as everything had started to change, especially with how the police regarded and then dealt with the matter. With it becoming harder to obtain the oil, I would come up with more devious ideas for how I could prolong the business. A great one I put into practice was putting the Environmental Agency badge and logo on my van in huge green font. I then had a uniform made as well as ID badges, I created waste transfer notes, which legally I could do, but these were template replicas of the same one the main contracted company were using at the time. I then removed anything that had their name on, and then, in small print at the bottom of the transfer note, I put my company's name. Whenever I was arrested after this point, I would produce a waste transfer note which I would get signed, and the police had no alternative but to let me go as it had my company name on it.

Putting the Environmental Agency logo on my van became a game changer. When we used to pull into places to collect the oil, management

114

would usually assume that we were there to complete an inspection. I would then say, "We are here to make sure that the oil is being disposed of correctly, and we need to take samples with us to test." Not only were we then given the oil without any fuss, but we were also offered free food and drink. There were many times when we would sit and eat in the restaurant for free, then steal their oil afterwards. Some of the places we took oil from included the millennium dome, most of the football stadiums, and the NEC in Birmingham. I even tried Buckingham palace, but they wouldn't let me in. I think the queen was busy that day counting her money.

Over time I did build up a small legitimate customer base, especially around the Hertfordshire area where I lived. After introducing so many people to my line of work, each person ended up going off and doing their own thing, and the oil from my regular customers started to disappear. When I used to turn up to collect the oil, a chef would usually come out and say, "Ahhh, your friend who works with you came last week for it." All the people I had introduced knew my locations and were stealing the oil from the places I was stealing it from.

As the oil became more difficult to obtain and with the police clamping down harder, I recognised that the borderline I had created was getting thinner and thinner each time I went out to work. In the end, I just got tired and fed up with the drama associated with the job. I had now started to feel constantly anxious, and with the end in sight, I decided to call it a day. After quitting, I began to feel relieved as I had started to gravitate away from the job and the people with whom I had been involved and was working with.

My perception of money, coupled with the criminality that I had been exposed to from a young age, meant that I had now become a seasoned, educated criminal with no boundaries or limits regarding how far

I was willing to go to earn. Oil, Viagra, cigarettes, fraudulent money, you name it, I was selling it. Because I was never short of money, I could always afford new clothes, food, holidays, and nights out. The mind works in many complex ways, and one of these for me was creating an environment to keep myself preoccupied from ever facing the true nature of my reality. My limited awareness believed that because I had money, I was now finally healed, and whenever I felt frail or darkness would appear, I had acquired enough money to get that temporary fix time and time again.

Finally leaving my job working in oil coincided with me playing football regularly for fun, and this also helped to regulate my stress levels; I always made sure I was available to play on the weekends whenever we had a match for my local team, and the reason I was able to leave the oil so easily was that an opportunity had arisen for me to go to Texas, America, with my friend David, on a soccer scholarship.

David and I had been in regular contact with an agent who had helped to facilitate the move to America for us. We had both managed to get some footage playing in local matches, and we then sent this over in anticipation of getting an offer from a college. After several conversations and a few months had passed, we were both accepted onto the same scholarship programme. I was now around 25 years of age, and although I had been arrested and convicted countless times, I had not been convicted of an offence for over four years. I also did not have any previous drug convictions, which was a big no with American visas, so I believed I had a chance of going to America.

After applying, my visa was eventually rejected, and I was told that I was not even allowed to enter America on holiday, but I thought if I could speak to someone directly, then I still may have an opportunity to go at some point. David had got his visa first time, and he had now set off to America to start his new life that summer.

Instead of giving up, I went through a more stringent process by appealing, and after my appeal was considered, I went back to the Embassy in London. After waiting in the visa lounge, I was eventually called into a cubicle. I remember as I entered the room, I sat down and used my charm, which I had inherited from my dad, to persuade the female advisor who was interviewing me. I had been partially honest with her regarding my past convictions and explained further. "Yes, I have been in trouble in the past with the police, but I am now a reformed character." I explained that it was now coming up to my fifth year of no convictions, which was true, and everything that had transpired in my past was due to the circumstances in my life that I was unable to deal with at the time which again was true. I was speaking to her as if I was finally healed and all my problems were now firmly behind me—I deluded not only her but myself as well. After a lengthy interrogation, I was eventually granted a 12-month conditional visa to the United States of America, but only because the college had vouched to be responsible for me. I then remember the feeling of utter disbelief as I received this news, and I could not believe I was now going to be moving to America to play soccer.

As I got ready to leave England, it dawned on me that I had not given much thought into how big of a step this was that I was taking. I had not planned anything, and I had also not done any research into where I was even going. After arriving at the airport, I began to feel agitated about being stopped by security. I had packed thousands of US dollars into my suitcase, thousands of English pounds and thousands more of counterfeit English twenty-pound notes, but luckily, I was not stopped. Again, I was still living

117

my life on the edge, and I was always one disaster away from being right back to square one again.

Although brief, the experience in Texas was something I will never forget. When I arrived, I enjoyed our first non-official training session. After I had finished, though, I knew deep down that this was not going to last long. What I didn't realise was that this decision would be taken out of my hands, on a night out.

One night, a girl from the college drove David and me to some bars, and I treated this night like any I would in England: I got smashed by drinking as much alcohol as I possibly could. At the end of the night, we had all decided to head back to the car to drive back to the college. I remember that David was complaining about needing to go to the toilet, but there was nowhere to go, and as we were now outside and had a long drive back, David decided to urinate by the side of a parked truck that had blacked-out windows and was in an unlit area. Although I could see David, he had run in front, so I was a fair distance behind him and oblivious to what began to occur at first, but eventually, I saw five people get out of this parked truck while David was urinating, and they had then started to throw punches towards him. After seeing this, I ran over to protect David and tried to calm the situation down, but as I approached, David managed to escape and run away, which then caused these people's attention to focus on me, and I was left surrounded by various people who began to attack me. After being punched from all angles, I was knocked to the floor. I remember that once I had fallen, my head had ended up positioned underneath their vehicle, and as I looked up, all I could see was the exhaust pipe and back tyres, but I physically could not move. Every time I tried to move, I was repeatedly kicked and punched, which resulted in me becoming stuck. As this happened, I managed to move my head further under the truck to protect my face, so only the bottom part of my body was now being beaten. I am not sure how long this carried on for, but at the time, it felt like forever and the longer this continued, I realised that these people were not going to stop unless something miraculous happened.

By a stroke of luck, a bouncer from a bar across the road had seen what was happening, and he then risked his own safety and ran over, grabbed me from underneath the truck, and then pulled me to safety. To this day, I still do not know how this bouncer even saw me because this truck was parked on the other side of the road in an unlit area. Eventually, after being dragged from under the truck and taken back towards the bar where he worked, I was picked up by David and the girl who had been driving us. At the time, I felt okay as my adrenalin had kicked in, and I was still very drunk. As we drove back to the college, we all spoke about what had happened, and deep down, I was disappointed that David had left me after I had tried to help him. When we eventually got back to the college, I retreated to my dorm, and again I still did not feel much pain, but I do though remember clearly how I felt the following morning after I woke up.

When the morning arrived, I got out of bed and knew straight away that I was in trouble; I was very stiff and could not move my head properly. After I had managed to look at my face in the mirror, I saw that it had started to swell, and I could also see that my body was covered in bruises. I then made up my mind in an instant that I would return back to England.

After cleaning myself up, I went down to the college reception and spoke to a woman at the front desk. She was horrified to see and hear what had happened to me. I then told her that I needed to leave and I wanted to return to England on the next available flight.

When I finally arrived back in England, I found out that I had sprained my ankle and broken the little finger on my left hand. I had deep

119

gashes on the left-hand side of my hand and thumb, and I have some pretty hideous scars there now. I had dizzy spells and concussion for a few weeks afterwards as well as bruises all over my body where I had been punched and kicked. My front four teeth were also cracked and in pieces, and I had broken my nose in two places which later resulted in an operation. This incident only reinforced that people could not be trusted and the world was not a place which consisted of love. David had left me to potentially get killed, but looking back, I can see that it was not personal, and he had gone into flight mode and fled out of fear.

When we are attuned to our internal feelings, we know when we feel safe or when we feel something is threatening us. We might not always know what that threat is, but we get a feeling that we cannot quite explain. Gut feelings help us to evaluate what is going on by warning us about certain situations and people. Constantly drinking alcohol, self-medicating and not connecting with my emotions enabled a situation like this to nearly take my life because I could not connect with any sense of danger. If you have a heightened or even comfortable connection with your inner sensations and trust them, then they can give you accurate information, and you will feel in charge of your body and your feelings. The problem with traumatised people such as myself, though, is that when you feel chronically unsafe inside of your body, the past is always there and alive in the present in the form of constant interior discomfort, and visceral warning signs consistently bombarding your body. In an attempt to control these processes, I became an expert in ignoring my gut feelings and numbing my awareness, in this instance by drinking alcohol, but by doing this, I would keep putting myself into dangerous situations time and time again.

After arriving back in England, I had no idea what I would do with my life. I did not have a concrete plan moving forward because I did not think I would live into my mid-twenties if I were being brutally honest with myself. I was just living from one episode to the next without really considering my future. Although my mood was seriously low, I carried on moving forward without taking time out to reflect. I needed to create some healthy solitude in my life, and without doing so, I would end up always failing in whatever I tried to do.

Although this incident was not directly my fault, looking back, it was indirectly. I had taken my careless nature to America, and drinking alcohol had put me in an all-too-familiar position. I thought at the time that I was just in the wrong place at the wrong time, but only over time and through reflection have I realised that I was in exactly the right place at the right time. This experience was meant to happen for me to go back to England and face my problems head-on. Ultimately, I would go on to learn that no matter how much I tried to run from my problems, they eventually caught up with me one way or another.

At this time in my life, I did not know that I was carrying such damaging beliefs despite the reoccurring theme of patterns that were now building up one after the other. The situations I kept finding myself in were a manifestation of my programming which stemmed from my early childhood. I was not a bad person, although I thought I was due to the bad things that kept happening. All I was doing was simply living out what I had been taught and learned as a child. My deep-rooted perceptions were ingrained in me, and by disconnecting when I was a child, I was able to survive my circumstances, but my defensive habits, which once kept me alive, were now trying to take my life.

Only once I began to love myself and acquire a deeper level of awareness could I accurately perceive what I was projecting out into the universe, and only then could I begin to change. Paying attention to my

121

mental and emotional state, as well as not self-medicating and connecting to my inner self in the future, would enable me to learn and start to transform. Suppressing my inner cries for help did not stop my stress hormones from mobilising my body. Although I had learned to ignore my relationship problems and block out my physical distress signals, they showed up in symptoms that demanded my attention in one way or another.

"Unexpressed emotions will never die. They are buried alive and will come forth later in uglier ways."
—Sigmund Freud

Chapter 7 – Obsession

(The state of being obsessed with someone or something)

Through the course of my life, I had already been through many setbacks, but I was still determined not to give up. Once I had fully recovered from my injuries, I decided to book a holiday to Tenerife with a friend, and we ended up having a great time.

After returning from this holiday, I wanted nothing more than to make the correct decisions, so I decided to enrol on a course studying Biomedical Science and Medicine at Lambeth College in London. After being invited to an assessment day, I met with one of the college tutors. I remember this tutor was extremely concerned about whether I would be able to fulfil the course requirements as I did not have the relevant qualifications, but luckily, I managed to use my charm to persuade her to give me an opportunity.

I decided to study this subject because I wanted to investigate dentistry, and this was the route I needed to take before I could eventually enrol at a university. My interest in this sector formed when I had recently gotten my teeth fixed at a dental practice in London Colney due to the injuries I had sustained in Texas. I remember becoming intrigued by the process that went into creating my veneers as the dentist explained each step of the way. As well as getting my teeth fixed, I then worked voluntarily in the dentist's surgery to gain some valuable experience, and I used this as bridge to get accepted onto the college course.

After I was enrolled, the course started well, but eventually, I began to crash. Trying to maintain my mental health became just as exhausting as trying to study a foreign subject.

The brain's reward system is responsible for motivation. This system produces chemicals that make a person feel good when they achieve a certain goal, but it never lasted long for me because whenever something went wrong, which it will in everyone's life at some point, I had developed a victim mentality and I would blame the whole world for all of my failures, and this would then quickly put me back into a negative state of mind. I was spending my life unconsciously seeking out rejection and failure as this was part of my inherent belief system, and when I found my evidence, it was familiar and confirmation of what I inherently believed. To me, all the problems in my life were outside of myself, and I thought that I did not have any control over them, so adjusting my behaviour was never going to achieve anything because my behaviour was not the issue in my mind.

This type of behaviour is what psychologists refer to as external locus, which is the perception that a person's behaviour will not result in control of their own environment. Only later in life could I change and alter my perception to internal locus, which is the belief that a person's behaviour can directly influence their environment. Having external locus made it easy for me to resort back to my substance abuse, which would take me further away from where love was. Feeling like I had no control over my own life when it was spiralling out of control felt like drowning without being able to gasp for air.

As well as viewing my life through an external locus perception, I was also suffering from comorbidity. This is a word used to describe the simultaneous presence of two or more diseases or medical conditions in a person, an example of which would be having depression alongside a substance addiction. When a person such as myself suffers from comorbidity, both conditions eventually begin to feed off each other and worsen over time as they become best of friends.

Suffering with comorbidity further heightened my triggers which were happening very frequently. The right-hand side of my brain would react and confirm that a traumatic event was occurring in the present, and it could also happen anywhere at any given moment. Sometimes it could just be the way I was spoken to, which I would perceive as threatening because someone had a harsher tone, for instance. This then could be enough to trigger me, and with the left-hand side of my brain not working coherently, I was not consciously aware that I was being triggered because my triggers had been removed from the thinking part of my brain, so no planning or thought needed to occur to set me off.

After my emotional response passed, the pressure inside of myself would increase, and I would then look outwardly to blame other people. This was my only way of rationalising what I kept experiencing. Constantly reacting to these triggers further devastated my life, and I ended up in destructive relationships with people, I lost close friends and alienated myself further from my family.

Although I did not manage to pass my course, I gave it my best under the circumstances I was in. Studying obsessively without managing my mental state was a recipe for disaster, and I eventually burnt out. Although I had left school with no grades in science, I did, however, halfway through the course, manage to achieve the highest grade in my class for a module in microbiology, as I was the only person who got a distinction which was the highest grade you could get. This was despite me not sleeping properly, having disabled brain functions, and still constantly abusing any substance I could get hold of. When the tutor read out everyone's grades in the science lab, I received a massive round of applause from all the pupils. Looking back, I think this was probably the first time in my life that I felt proud of what I had achieved. By achieving what I had with two hands tied behind my back and being blindfolded, I had finally confirmed to myself that I was not stupid like I had been led to believe, and I was in fact, capable of achieving something substantial with my life. However, it was not going to be in this field.

Achieving what I had in a short amount of time meant that studying became an obsession. Reading textbooks late into the night each evening was my way of convincing myself that this was what I needed to do to succeed. Looking back, I can now see that I was setting unrealistic targets and demands of high pressure, and by doing this, I was stopping myself from ever becoming still, so I would never have to face up to the true nature of my reality. Every time I failed at something, I would beat myself up, and this only caused more negativity to build up inside of me.

An extreme low very quickly followed the high I received from getting the best grade in my class. Although the biology side of the subject came naturally to me, I was failing chemistry miserably. I struggled massively with the number aspect of this subject, and as the subjects were all combined, I had to pass chemistry to succeed in the course. No matter how hard I tried, I was not going to be able to pass as the information would not sync with my brain.

The brain is a powerful and incredible tool, but it can only really focus its attention on one thing at a time, and due to this, the brain decides what the most important thing we give our attention to. The processing of attention becomes seriously disturbed when the brain is configured to seek out the huge reward stimulation, which in my instance, was provided by the substances I was regularly taking. This meant that no matter how hard I tried

126

to focus or concentrate, at times, I would get an overwhelming hungering and draw towards taking more substances. This draw for me felt like a constant need for air, food, or water, so when it was prominently tapping me on the shoulder saying, "*Hey, don't forget about me, your best friend who takes away all of your pain,*" it felt almost impossible for me to say no. However, when I was taking substances, I would still carry-on studying, and on many occasions, I found they actually helped me. This may sound strange, but as soon as I got my fix, I was able to calm myself down enough to draw my attention back towards absorbing the information from the textbooks. With my mind in a more relaxed state, it would calm the unconscious emotional turmoil that was swirling around inside me, so it helped to reduce my stress levels and concentrate better.

As well as failing chemistry, I also began to find the travel into college exhausting and painful. I had to get three separate trains just to get there, and this took me around four hours a day in total. Just to heighten everything that little bit more, before I had travelled to America, I had been involved in a serious road accident that affected my back, and this caused me shooting pain whenever sitting still for long periods at a time. This accident resulted in me going to the hospital and having physiotherapy, and I was left with ongoing issues that only seemed to get worse over time. However, despite the pain, I was still determined to finish the course, and I refused to quit at this point. As soon as I knew it was near on impossible for me to pass chemistry, I got a doctor's note which signed me off from college, but instead of quitting, I asked my tutor if I could email my work to the college instead, which the tutor then agreed to.

Not having to attend college allowed me to move out to Tenerife, and looking back, I was definitely trying to find an escape. When I arrived back in Tenerife, I met up with a few friends, then I started working in a bar, and in my free time, I would go to various coffee shops and work on trying to finish the course.

Although I was struggling, I had not given up all hope of passing just yet, and I had still applied to as many universities as possible. After all my replies came back in, I found that I was only left with one real option: to attend an interview day at Southend University. As soon as my interview date arrived, I travelled back to England, and then I got a train to Southend to complete an assessment day at the university. I did the best I could, but I found it incredibly hard. The assessment lasted for the full day, and there were lots of mini assignments, as well as interviews with different members of staff.

After a few weeks of staying back at my nan's, I received a letter stating that I had been declined a place at Southend University, but I was on a provisional shortlist. This meant that if anyone who got offered a place did not accept, then I would be next in line to be enrolled. Knowing I could not pass chemistry left me with no real alternative but to finally quit, and again, the feelings of not being good enough quickly surfaced. I had tried my best, but ultimately the outcome was still the same, failure. What I could not see at the time was that I had set unrealistic demands on myself, and because I was not prepared to face my trauma, it meant that I was not going to be able to succeed in anything until I did.

I remember feeling so disappointed at the time, but I had set myself up to fail. I then started to question my own judgement and began to have serious self-doubt in the decisions that I was making. With me now deciding to quit my course, I packed my bags again and booked a one-way ticket back out to Tenerife.

By believing I was a failure, I had created an environment in Tenerife that mainly consisted of drinking alcohol, taking drugs and having sex with lots of different females. Alcohol especially became a constant daily habit, and I did not need any further excuse to drink. Still, with it being one of the most used addictive substances on the planet due to its availability, cheap nature, and the fact it is legal and considered socially acceptable, I had my ammunition ready just in case I ever thought what I was doing was wrong. Each time I drank, I was slowing down my brain functions further, but I found the relaxing effects helped to calm down my anxiety, and this also contributed towards an increase in my sociability as I felt less in danger when intoxicated due to my stress response system calming down to a manageable level. The problem is that when you were drinking as much as I was back then, the brain becomes impaired in terms of its higher brain function capabilities, so my ability to think, use my judgement and connect with my intuition became compromised further.

Although viewed in society as safe, alcohol is actually one of the most dangerous drugs to withdraw from after chronic abuse, and in worst-case scenarios, seizures can occur, which could potentially lead to death. Any food I could eat, which was a real minimum at this point, resulted in me vomiting it back out, with my stomach and liver becoming inflamed. Thiamine is an essential vitamin we get from our food supply as the body is unable to create it internally, and a lack of this vitamin begins to interfere with the distribution of the correct nutrition that the brain needs.

As well as drinking alcohol and taking drugs, I also began to have a lot of casual sex with various different females who were travelling over on holiday. This was by no means new to me but being in Tenerife just allowed me to do this even more than I had previously done back in England. By being in the company of various females, I could occupy my mind once again, and the destructive nature of putting myself at constant risk with females I did not know or even have any real connection with, would prove

129

to have serious consequences in my future as you will go on to see. At the time, I could rationalise sleeping with different girls because I thought it was normal; all I had to do was look around in my environment, and I would see various people doing exactly the same as me. By having casual sex, I was able to get a dopamine fix, which meant that I could get some of my needs met without having to form intimacy or trust with another person.

When I had gone on dates in the past, I had found them extremely uncomfortable, and when the conversation eventually came around to, "So what did you do growing up?" I would lie on many occasions because my story was too painful for me to discuss with people. On the rare occasions when I had opened up, certain individuals had not been accepting of my past—and if I could not face it myself, how could I expect others to? The pain I still felt, especially towards females, meant that ultimately until I dealt with my underlying trauma correctly, I could never have a loving girlfriend or a family of my own.

The sexual abuse I had experienced in my childhood meant that I was looking for what I thought was love (sex) in all the wrong places. This is what my environment had taught me, so my reality became a distorted one, far away from where the real truth lay. Correct childhood attachments provide the basis for love and romantic relationships in adulthood. If you have experienced affectionate, compassionate, loving bonds in infancy, you are more likely to report having affectionate, compassionate, and loving bonds in adulthood. Due to my distant, erratic, and untrustworthy relationships in my childhood, I sought out the same type of bond unconsciously in my adult life, time and time again.

My childhood wounds were clearly dictating the pattern of my life, and I followed my external and not internal guidance system. Because I did not have a secure relationship with myself and consistently denied my own needs, I did not know what my needs were, let alone how to communicate them clearly. I also had no emotional resilience, so when shit hit the fan, I was unable to rebound in a positive or healthy way. If something went wrong and I felt a certain emotion that I did not understand, I buried it. Emotional maturity is what allows a person to accept all of their emotions, and the most important aspect is the ability to be aware of and regulate our own emotions in order to allow others to express themselves, or the ability to tolerate all of our emotions without feeling like we are losing control. The narcissism I had clearly formed was a front for me to protect myself from further feeling in a vulnerable state again. Getting to a place of security and safety in my life would enable me to navigate the world around me correctly; I could then make mistakes and respond in a way that would be constructive instead of destructive.

As much as I wanted to forget my past and what had happened to me, it was impossible because the emotions, fragmented memories, and sensations would project into my conscious mind, and I would become trapped inside an invisible prison cell. Unable to understand what was happening, I kept on pushing forward, but it was now getting to a point where I started to realise that something may indeed be seriously wrong with me. Still, though, I carried on fighting the only way I knew how to, which was by using the only tools I had at my disposal, such as my escapism behaviour and willpower.

For the last three months of my time in Tenerife, I felt lost, disillusioned, and unfulfilled with the lifestyle I had created. I had now decided to stop drinking alcohol as well as taking drugs, and although this just heightened my unhappiness, I had gotten to a point where I just did not want to carry on doing it anymore because it was having such an adverse effect on me. I have always been sensitive, and I knew this deep down, but I craved to be like the people in my environment so I could fit in somewhere, so continuing to numb myself throughout my life helped me to deal with the curse I had of being born sensitive. It was only later in life that I would find out that my sensitivity was not a curse but a gift instead.

I now thought that by stopping my addictions, my problems would disappear once and for all. My drug taking and drinking alcohol were the constant themes throughout my life, so to me, this had to be the dominating factor in what had been contributing towards my severe mental health issues. The root cause of my problems, however, wasn't my addictions; they were just the symptoms, but I still could not figure this out just yet.

There were some amazing people in Tenerife, but it seemed to me that the majority of the ones I met seemed lost, just as I was at the time. Tenerife seemed to be a stopgap for a lot of people who had issues at home and were running away from various problems, again, just as I was. Everyone I spoke to seemed to be struggling, and Tenerife was a fantasy environment for anyone who wanted to rid themselves of the fragility of their feelings by indulging in drugs, alcohol, and casual sex. It was no coincidence that I found myself in a place surrounded by people who were all suffering in some way, again just as I was, and I would continue to find myself in places and situations which reflected how I inherently thought of myself and the world around me.

When Tenerife fizzled out, it was time for me to seek a new direction; I then decided to return to England after a couple of years of toing and froing. I now had no money to my name as I had spent everything I had made and saved up; however, despite being skint again, I did not consider going back to criminality as I was still determined to try and succeed in something legal. I also felt that my mindset was different as I was no longer participating in my addictions, and I thought that I just needed a break and that everything would be fine once I got that. Again, I was severely deluding myself.

When I returned back to England, my friend Cheffique who worked in recruitment, managed to get me an interview at the place where he worked. I had decided to go and stay back with my nan with no other options available to me, and she had also lent me the money to buy a car. Once again, people were bending over backwards to accommodate me in every way possible.

After attending an interview, I thought it went really well, but I did not receive a phone call to say I had gotten the job. Two weeks then passed when I had just about given up hope of getting any good news, then the owner of the recruitment company rang and offered me the job with an immediate start. After this call, I felt really optimistic, and I was sure that this was going to be the turning point in my life, so I threw everything I had into this job.

Within my first week, the person training me was sacked in front of all the staff in the office. I remember it clearly because as it was happening, Cheffique and I were just staring at each other from across the room, thinking, *what is going on?* Six weeks or so then passed, and although I did not like the boss, I had adapted and focused as I knew I needed to take this opportunity. Although I had settled at work, my internal suffering was still manifesting in various forms and sometimes, out of nowhere, I would start hyperventilating and gasping for air, and this felt like I was being drowned or strangled. This would appear at any moment without warning, and I began to find it extremely scary, especially as I was no longer masking my pain through addiction. Trying to juggle my job and mental health just became like trying to perform a circus act without training for me, and because I was so consumed by trying to control what was going on internally, I was unable

133

to spot my instinctive reactions to my triggers. I was most definitely spending my life in the monkey mind as the buddha first described it. I never stopped thinking, and my thoughts would tangle together. There was never any space to breathe or even begin to examine them. I was trapped in a state of reactivity, which meant that I could never gain any clarity because I was so far away from being connected to my internal state to perceive things correctly.

Deep down, I have always been a free spirit if you haven't guessed that already, so one time, while at work, I sent my friend Cheffique a picture of a gravestone to his work email. This was to symbolise the environment we were working in because the office was so dead and quiet. The owner then saw the email I had sent as he monitored everything. He then called me into his office and sacked me there and then on the spot. Once again, not for the first time in my life, I was left jobless.

As soon as I left the building, I was so angry, but that anger soon turned into tears and disappointment. I remember feeling hurt because I actually thought I would remain in this job a lot longer. I felt my mindset was different now, I was no longer self-medicating, and although I was suffering, I was sure that I was on the right path.

When you have had such a damning subconscious programming as mine, it becomes the norm to further seek out jobs that you fail at or remain in jobs you hate, and if you inherently think you do not deserve a better life, then guess what? that's exactly what life will give you back in return. As long as I continued to lie to myself by shutting away my deep-rooted feelings, I could never move forward and progress. I was expending such huge amounts of energy on trying to control internal scenarios, that this only prevented me from directing my energy into reaching any purposeful goals.

Not too long after I was sacked, a meeting was held in the office, and Cheffique relayed back to me what the owner had said to everyone. He spoke about my flaws and said that I dressed like a tramp. As I had no money, I had to borrow clothes to go to work because I did not have any office attire. My uncle on my mum's side of the family had kindly lent me shirts, blazers, and some trousers. I found that embarrassing enough, going to work knowing I had to borrow clothes because I could not even afford to buy my own ones, but I had no alternative; I had created this situation by the life choices I had so far made.

I now began to sink into a state of depression, and this began to affect my poor nan as I was staying with her. She became worried because I was just so low and upset. I would often break down crying in my room on my own, and I remember feeling ashamed of myself. "Boys are not supposed to cry," my dad used to say to me, so when I did, I felt disgusting, and these words would repeat in my head over and over again. Crying triggered me to think about my dad, which then just intensified things even more. Due to the pain I had suppressed, I could not create any consistency in my life, and once again, I began not eating, I was not sleeping properly, and I became painfully thin. Without the correct nutrients my body needed and by not getting enough rest, I was damaging myself so severely that I was being sucked further into a very dark place. I was now so low that even the thought of taking drugs or drinking alcohol would not grab my attention; I just felt tired and helpless because I could not formulate any plans for my future.

Getting sacked from my job allowed my past to channel through into my present-day life and cause mayhem. These singular incidents were just vehicles for unresolved traumas to express themselves, and they were ultimately directing me towards healing myself. I desperately needed a sense

135

of purpose in my life, but everywhere I turned, I was just unable to either feel capable or happy in what I was doing, and my behaviour ultimately always ended up letting me down. When you fail at so many things in life, self-doubt begins to set in, and I started to question myself. The positive to this was that I was now beginning to understand that something needed to change; I was still not quite there in terms of finding the answers, even though they had been right in front of me for the entirety of my existence.

Each person's mind acts based on perception, and perception is there for us all to eventually discover the true nature of our own reality. No matter how much I tried, I could not influence the outside world before I began to change myself inwardly. Studies all over the world emphasise that we have been culturally programmed to believe that if we reach our goals, we lose 25 pounds, we get that new car, or we land that high-paying job, we will be happy through external means. I can tell you this formula for happiness is inverted, as I would go on to find out the hard way: happiness is what fuels success and not the other way around. Simply stated, success won't bring you happiness; happiness is what creates your success.

So here I was in an all-too-familiar situation, and again, without listening to what the universe was trying to communicate to me, I had decided that I needed to keep moving forward, regardless of how I felt. *I have no time to feel upset. I need to find something—and fast,* I thought.

Running away from your problems solves nothing.
The answer is staring straight at you.
Look again closer... Stop running.
—Jamie Gregory

136

Chapter 8 – View

(The opinion or way of thinking about something)

Surrendering and coming to terms with my life was something I had not managed to accomplish yet. I could no longer stay at my nan's due to losing my job, but one of my friends, Michael, who I had lived with in Tenerife, had moved back to his hometown of Leeds, and we had remained in regular contact. In a passing conversation, I had mentioned to Michael that I was feeling lost, and he had asked me if I wanted to visit Leeds and stay with him for a weekend. After deciding to go, I had a really good time and could envisage myself starting fresh and living there, so with nothing going right for me, I decided to turn left and view my situation differently by moving to Leeds. Again, I was running, and I did not have the awareness to recognise that wherever I ran too, my problems would continuously follow me around like a dark shadow.

After returning to my nans from my trip to Leeds, I packed all my belongings into my car and left to start another chapter in my life. I had no plan in terms of where I was going to stay long-term, but I believed I would sort something out. As I could not find a place to rent in such a short space of time, I spent the first two weeks in a bedsit just outside of Leeds city centre. I then used my time during the day to go and view various apartments, but I was really struggling to find anywhere due to not having a job or even much money. Falling asleep in a bedsit made me feel incredibly alone and distanced from where love was, and I remember crying myself to sleep as I thought about how I would fix the devastation in my life.

137

Two weeks had now passed, and I was literally on the verge of giving up, but then I got a phone call back regarding a room I had expressed an interest in. At the time, I only had enough money to pay a month's rent and then the equivalent of another month's rent as a deposit. After finally moving in, I had no money to my name, and I could not even afford to eat. I have never been a big eater, so going without food was not a problem for me, and I had been in much worse situations before.

With the room being in the city centre, I no longer required a car, so I decided to sell mine to get some much-needed cash. With my rent now paid for the next four weeks and money to now buy food, but, more importantly, cigarettes, I started to search for a job. I had previous experience in recruitment, and although it had been minimal, I thought that this would be the best area to concentrate my efforts on. After looking online, I found that there were many recruitment jobs being advertised, so I was confident that I would find something quickly. After printing out my CV, I either emailed or dropped it off to all the companies that were advertising, as well as ones that were not. Over the next six weeks, I attended an estimated 10 to 12 interviews, and some I thought went well and others not so well. I then became increasingly disheartened when each and every one rejected me. I remember an interview I attended, and the person who had interviewed me said, "You just look tired, mate." It was as if he thought I needed a break! If only he knew my predicament! I did not need a break; I needed a job—and fast.

Despite the continuous rejections, I was determined not to give up. One interview I attended was going well—or at least I thought it was until they asked me to come back and give a presentation. After returning, I presented a motivational video I had been watching regularly to try and raise my spirits. It was a video about rising up, through struggles and hardships, to make

138

something of yourself. After watching the video, the interviewer then paused as soon as it had finished and said, "Have you suffered from depression before, Jamie?" My presentation had gone down like a lead fucking balloon.

This time in my life became extremely difficult because I was lonely in a new city, abstaining from alcohol and drugs, and trying my absolute best, but it was just not good enough. Getting out of bed each day became harder, which then contributed towards me not eating again, and the more I was rejected from these jobs, the more I distanced myself away from love. Whenever I became unhappy, I would lose my appetite, and I could go for days without eating. Rejection in any form has always been extremely difficult for me, and this stems from the deep-routed pain I experienced in my childhood. Each rejection would trigger me, I would then experience negative emotions such as shame, apathy and guilt, which would contribute to the already low opinion I had formed of myself.

A month had now passed, and it had reached the last day I had paid my rent up until, so I decided that it was time to pack my bags and leave. Clearly, Leeds had not worked out. Maybe I would go back to my nan's—I was not too sure. After walking out the front door of my apartment, I received a phone call. After answering, I found that it was from a person who had interviewed me about a week ago and he had rung to offer me a job! Granted, it was not the job I had interviewed for, but instead, it was a trainee role on minimum wage, with no fixed contract. Despite the evidential downgrade, I was grateful for this opportunity and determined to take it. Once again, I thought that this was the break I finally needed.

Eager to impress, I threw everything into work, but after only six weeks, I crashed again. *I am just not capable of working for anyone,* I thought. I could never even attend school consistently, let alone live by the rules of an office! I would try my best, but my mental state was ultimately

139

holding me back. Some days my head would be in a complete mess which felt like for no apparent reason. Nothing had fundamentally changed, and if anything, my problems were now becoming more severe.

Crashing again was confirmation that I needed to seek some form of outside help. By not reaching out, I was the one who was responsible for my continual decline. Sometimes, a person needs some guidance to get out of a lifetime of bad habitual thinking and destructive behaviour patterns, and they need some support which will enable them to see and do things differently. I was beginning to understand this, and I could not carry on down the road I was going as it was completely soul-destroying. When I look back, I can see that the big problem I had, was that by admitting to myself that I needed to accept some form of help, meant in my mind that I was, in fact, fucked up and that I was not a good person, and this again ultimately felt like a form of rejection. Although I had accepted that I needed help at this point, I was not going to accept it willingly, and it was going to take an extreme situation to force me to do so, as you will go on to see.

After eventually being sacked, I decided to isolate myself for a time. While working at this job, I did, however, meet a person called Simon, and although we were very different, we used to get on.

After staying in touch with Simon, he told me that I had a flair for sales and that I was good at the job. Simon had previously set up his own recruitment business, but due to stress and finding himself in a difficult financial situation, he had decided that the security of a paid job and normal working hours were the best things for him and his family. A few weeks had passed of me isolating myself when Simon explained to me that I should set up a recruitment business, and if everything went well, he would eventually join me. I got the impression that I was being used as a guinea pig at first, and although I was very cautious, I did not mind being a guinea pig because it felt better than being rejected. With no other options available to me, I decided to give it a go.

Over the coming month, Simon spent the evenings guiding me through all the necessary steps that were needed to set up a legitimate business. I remember there was so much work involved, with no guarantee of success, but I genuinely believed I could make it work. I remember finding the logistical side of the business very hard as I was building a website and setting up accounts, stuff I had no experience in. I tried my hardest to do as much as possible myself because I did not have a lot of money, so I had no choice. In total I paid out around £1,000 for external help and although it was not a huge amount, it once again left me on the brink with no money to my name.

After I had set the company up, Simon gave me a telephone number for a client he knew that was looking for staff. Simon had told me to ring them as he had found out that another company had let them down. After calling this company, I remember speaking to a person called Shane, who immediately told me that he had indeed been let down. Shane then went on to say that he needed 30 merchandisers for a two-week period, starting in three weeks' time, and he then asked me if I could supply him with the staff. My reply was, "Yes, of course, Shane." He then asked me to send over some business terms.

After this phone call, I called Simon straight away and said, "Simon, Shane wants 30 merchandisers—which I agreed to, but what's a merchandiser?" Simon then burst out laughing and said, "This is why you are going to be good at the job!"

After Simon gave me a briefing about the job role of a merchandiser, I put adverts out to recruit the staff I needed. After working day and night, I kept my promise and delivered. Luckily, I managed to find

141

most of the required staff; if I remember correctly, only two out of the original group of 30 did not turn up.

All in all, I thought it went well, considering—although admittedly, that client never used me again. The job was eventually completed with some minor hiccups due to the lack of experience on my part, and I was shocked to notice that the profit I had made in those two weeks was just over £7,000 in total.

After receiving my money, I went from struggling to afford to buy food to feeling that I could live quite comfortably for a time, and this then gave me massive motivation to pursue this avenue further. Things would eventually turn sour with Simon, as I will go on to explain later, but I will be forever grateful for the knowledge and opportunity he gave me to start this business.

After the work with Shane had ended, I was left shattered. I had worked 14 continuous days signing in all the candidates, making sure all the paperwork was in place each night the staff worked, communicating with the store directly, and remaining by the phone in case there were any on-site problems.

At this time in my life, I knew I needed help, but having money again enabled my problems to ease, and I would then fall back into the same trap I had done previously, assuming that everything was now under control again. Money was always some type of proof that I was back on the right track because it was one of my core beliefs that I had held so dear to me. Instead of trying to heal by facing my past head-on, I was using money to create a barrier that enabled me to bury my issues deep inside whenever my fragility would appear.

Starting up a new business and working for myself meant that I no longer feared being sacked, and this helped to settle my anxiety because it

142

reduced my stress levels. I could now work on my own terms, so when my symptoms intensified, I was working in isolation, which meant I did not have to worry about how other people would react to me. In essence, all I did was take my problems in-house. I was shutting the curtains, so my problems were no longer visible to the scary outside world.

Being homeless in my past created a certain pressure because the fear of living back on the streets was always consciously evident. This fear that was driving me will become apparent later in my story as it would continue to dictate the pattern of my life, even at the point in my future when I had created a certain degree of financial security. Regardless of the money I would go on to earn, all it took was one bad day at work for me to be triggered and projected back into my past, and those fears of being homeless again would become very evident and present.

After the work had ended with Shane, I decided to ring Simon again and asked if he knew of any other similar businesses that could potentially give me work. Simon said there were many companies that did merchandising, and he then proceeded to give me a couple of numbers to call. After making several calls, I was then invited to a meeting by one of these companies. Simon knew this company well as he had worked with them before, so he called in sick at work that day and decided to join me. Although Simon was helping me, which I was very grateful for, he was still unwilling to leave his job or commit to this venture due to his circumstances which I understood. I would pay Simon for his help, but what I really wanted was commitment to this venture as I felt that I did not have the relevant experience to run this company. After the meeting had ended with this client, I was taken out to the back of their building into a warehouse and given a box of staff uniforms—they were ready to onboard my company straight away!

The scale of work was slow at first, but within a couple of months, I consistently had between 20-30 merchandisers out working for the next five months. My profit in that time period ranged from between £3,000 to £3,500 each week, and I was now living comfortably but also legally, which brought a certain amount of pride to what I had achieved.

The money, however, did not come easily, and although it happened extremely fast, there was a lot of drama, which eventually affected the trust this new client had placed on my shoulders. The hard part was not getting the work as it was there in abundance, but instead, it was finding competent, reliable people who would turn up and want to work. As the positions I was offering were only temporary, I would end up with all types of people, and although I would do my due diligence, I still had people who stole, people got caught with drugs and alcohol on site, and one person even got caught with a knife. Various people would lie on their CVs, which was no different from how I had previously lied on mine. At the time, I felt like all the karma from my past was now coming back to finally haunt me.

With the drama unfolding daily, I remember ringing Simon and saying, "What am I doing wrong, mate?" to which he replied, "Jamie, why do you think I don't do this anymore?"

I would then go on to find out that none of this was personal, and it happened to everyone. I was fishing in a pool of people who had no job and were available to work for minimum wage at the drop of a hat. With the job only being temporary, it did not offer them any security either. I had dreamed of earning the sort of money I was now making legally, and I actually thought Simon was weak when he first told me that he could not put up with the stress when he was working in this sector. To me, the stress was a small price to pay for what I was earning, but yet again, I was so wrong. No matter what consequences came with the money, the most important thing to me was money, and not my well-being. Now under severe pressure and shouldering all the responsibility, I began to feel trapped and unhappy again.

A few months into starting this business, I had decided to join a gym in Leeds and met some people while training there. I used to always talk with a guy called Bodi, who was from Essex, and another person called J. Eventually, we all became friends, and having not really experienced Leeds properly, I started to go out to bars with these people—especially Bodi.

Making friends with Bodi especially was a game-changer for me. Attention is what controls then directs a person's consciousness, and certain elements of my world would jump out, such as the places and people I could associate with my self-medicating; everything else would then fall back into the background and become insignificant. With Bodi now on the scene, my consciousness was directed towards environments where I could distract my mind from having to face the true nature of my reality, come to terms with any pain I felt and deal with the accumulating stress in my everyday life. My substance and alcohol abuse had stopped towards the end of Tenerife, but now going out with Bodi, I started to think I could drink and take drugs again in a social environment. At the start, I had convinced myself this was for social reasons, but as work became further stressful, I found myself going out more and more, and this then became an unhealthy escape for me. Alcohol and drugs were not the answers to my problems, but I can tell you that they most certainly helped me to forget the questions most of the time.

Due to the development of my brain in my childhood, my ingrained perceptions of people were flawed, and I would find myself around familiar people to whom I would attach myself to. These were not bad people, far from it in some cases, as Bodi and J, for instance, were two of the nicest guys I have ever met, but they were not the people I needed at this stage in my life to start my journey of healing.

145

Although going out relieved me of stress, sometimes just the smell of alcohol made me physically sick, and it could cause me anxiety. The odours from alcohol are registered by receptor cells in the nasal cavity, which sends electrical impulses to the olfactory bulb (this is part of the brain's limbic system), where emotions and behavioural responses are involved. The olfactory bulb is also close to the hippocampus, which is associated with a person's memory and when I encountered the smell of alcohol, it became connected to the emotions I associated with that smell when I was in a bad place in my life. This process is called the Madeleine effect, and it is named after the French writer Marcel Proust (1871-1922). It is what we call an involuntary memory recall.

Socialising did not come naturally to me because being in social environments always brought a certain amount of difficulty due to my upbringing, and without alcohol or drugs, I felt anxious and fragile, which meant I could be very socially awkward. I was always on high alert and trying to protect myself from people and this could cause me to come across as arrogant, stuck up, and rude when in reality, I was just deeply insecure and scared.

My love for cocaine around this time began overstimulating my body by hyper-charging my autonomic nervous system. After a heavy session, I began experiencing severe irritability, I struggled to sleep yet again, I became very jittery and unstable, and my anxiety only increased. Rather than continuously using substances, I was now abstaining for a period and then binging on them severely, which only made the crash worse each time for me.

Due to the pressure I was putting on myself with work, going out getting fucked, and my general lack of self-care, I started to decline further, and I began to feel like I was in a bucket being lowered into a well. I was so far down that well that when I looked up, I could no longer see the light at the top, and I was just waiting for the bucket to hit the base of the floor so I could finally see where rock bottom was; at this point in my life, I was almost there. People must "reach their bottom", as it says in the 12-step programme, before they can beat addiction, and mine was fast approaching. Luckily for me, my bottom was the start of my rising up, but for others, that bottom is, unfortunately, six feet under in a grave when it is too late.

To know myself, I had to connect with my body, which is done through interpreting physical sensations. By understanding what I was experiencing, I could then navigate a path through life, but by numbing myself, a disconnect had formed, and although I was able to survive, I lacked a true sense of awareness of what was actually transpiring inside of myself. Being traumatised and lacking any sense of what was happening inside my body meant that I could never get to the root cause of my issues because I thought they were always outside of me. Life, in general, lacked meaning, and pleasurable experiences did not exist, despite now socialising frequently, earning a comfortable amount of money, and owning my own business. My biggest issue was that I was stuck in the past and not fully alive in the present.

Although my brain was severely dysfunctional, it was doing exactly what it was expected to do, considering what I had experienced so far in life. What was adaptive and kept me alive in my childhood became maladaptive and began killing me as I grew into an adult. Without alcohol or drugs for sustained periods of time, I went into a constant state of fear, which meant that I behaved, felt, and learned very differently from a person who inherently felt safe, for instance. When fear is present, there is no way of accessing the smart part of the brain (cortex), so instead, the lower systems of my brain (reptilian) began to dominate my functioning, and my higher brain capabilities became disabled. I did, however, use my cortex to build

147

my business, but once it was up and running and the stresses increased, I turned to my default mode, which were my unhealthy coping strategies.

Unfortunately, my willpower was not going to be enough to get me out of the hole I was digging, and I can tell you through experience that willpower is not enough when working with addiction and trauma. The human mind is capable of great things, but once you have been exposed to addiction, the brain has made changes to facilitate the need to fulfil each addiction further. Thinking your way out of addiction does not work. Trust me, I tried countless times. The brain has specific networks that participate in the ability to exert self-control, but these networks are disrupted through substance abuse, for example, and the brain's circuits which enable a person to learn from past experience, have been negatively affected. Relying on my willpower only meant that I would have a further excuse to prevent myself from trusting people. My view was that I had achieved monetary goals with my willpower, so why could I not make myself better in exactly the same way?

I had now rationalised my addictions through the environment I had created, and this consisted of socialising with people who were doing the same as me. "Let's go to a club tonight" became a cue for my learned responses. Also, my definition of an addict was someone who sniffs a line or drinks an alcoholic beverage as soon as they wake up in the morning, which I was not doing, so to me, my addiction was not a problem because I did not see it as an addiction.

Social learning plays a prominent role in this as well, and to thrive in the new environment I had created meant that I felt a need to get people to like me. To do this, I thought I had to change as a person to be accepted, as I did not want to be outcasted, abandoned and rejected just like I had throughout my childhood. I then portrayed the image of a carefree party

148

person who had tons of money to burn. Addicts crave some form of acceptance, and associating with people who were involved in the same behaviour as I was, helped me to feel better about myself because it reduced cognitive dissonance. *What I'm doing can't be that bad, can it?* I thought. *Look, everyone else is doing it as well!*

Being in this new social environment and being accepted opened my eyes to a new world, which swiftly brings me on to social media. I had now learned what Instagram was and how to portray myself on there to be further accepted. After opening an Instagram account, I began copying what everyone else was doing in my environment, which would only damage me further.

I was spending so much of my time on social media, motivated by the ability to obtain likes, followers, and friends, that I ended up constructing a cyber alter ego that craved social acceptance and esteem. For this reason, social media became an unhealthy environment for me, and many studies have shown its detrimental effects on health, including an increase in depression as well as low self-esteem.

Social media is definitely a double-edged sword. On the one hand, it offers the opportunity to discover and forge new friendships as well as share information, but on the other, there is self-criticism, alienation, and a thriving acceptance of narcissistic behaviour, which contributes towards mental health issues. Unfortunately, there is no such thing as perfect technology because we imperfect humans use it.

Social media made me question myself further: *What's wrong with me? Why don't people like me?* It made me buy things I could not afford, and it made me feel like I was lazy in comparison to other people, unattractive, poor, lonely, unpopular, and excluded. Perfect in this world is based on an amazing smile, blemish-free skin, happy relationships, Gucci,

Fendi, Prada, a perfect home, a well-maintained body, and a successful career that pays a shit ton of money.

Perfection is a state of being or becoming perfect, the process of refining something until it is flawless. In the age of social media, the action of perfection is something we have quickly learned to master through deluding not only others but, more worryingly, ourselves. Each and every fault can now be photoshopped, retouched or tweaked and replaced with the best digital fake version of yourself, and why not? That's what people want to see, right?

As social media has become more prevalent, the space devoted to real-life problems and collective empathy around life's challenges has diminished drastically. Scroll on your feed on Instagram, and you will find that lifestyles are a procession of idyllic holidays, career promotions, material consumption and happy family moments, all captured in the most aesthetically pleasing pictures possible. Ill health, failure, loss, sadness, struggles, hard work, setbacks and indeed anything that is not positive has been erased from this world because it does not fit the model of the image-focused world of Instagram. The standard social media has set on self-promotion means that no one dares to look foolish in front of others.

One of the reasons we keep coming back to social media is that we believe there will be a chance it will make us feel better, but in reality, when you're in a big fucking hole, just as I was, it makes you feel worse and traps you in a vicious cycle. I cannot believe how much the world has changed since the advent of social media, or should I say how much social media has now changed our world.

Social media's standard of flawlessness and comparison has depleted millions of people's self-belief every second of every day. People are working so hard to live up to this benchmark that they burn themselves

150

out, get into debt, lose touch with reality, and become sick. Social media is a constructed fake reality, so I would suggest that if people are struggling as I was, they should stop comparing themselves to the people on these platforms because they will never reach happiness by doing so. There is nothing wrong with a picture that is artistic, fun, and fashionable. There is nothing wrong with taking positives from social media through creation and interaction, but the dangers are very real if you do not set yourself boundaries.

After beginning to socialise with some of the blue tick community, I can tell you through experience that these people with millions of followers on Instagram are no different to me and you; they struggle with self-doubt and feel under pressure to be perceived a certain way by their audience. Though they may be projecting a lifestyle that you think you would want, the reality is, a lot of them are addicted to their phones, deeply insecure, and highly anxious about their social media profile.

This then leads me to some research which I have done that I will now share with you.

It has been conclusively proven that the longer your screen time is during the day, the worse you sleep at night. As well as having a profoundly negative impact on life, sleep deprivation has been associated with everything from weight gain to high blood pressure and lower life expectancy. Social media can also erode our ability to be, well, social. Sherry Turkle, a leading professor on technology's impact on society, has warned of an "empathy gap" in which young people are unable to develop the social skill of empathy due to their need for constant stimulus and their increasingly distracted family interaction. "These days, we find ways around conversation," she explains in *Reclaiming Conversation: The Power of Talk in a Digital Age.*

"We hide from each other even as we're constantly connected to each other."

Tech insiders have revealed how programmers have exploited our brain's natural reward system to hook us to our feeds, which some call brain hacking. Our compulsive need to stay engaged has penetrated our lives so much that billions of us around the world are suffering from nomophobia—a dread of being separated from our phones and accounts. Consequently, our lives have changed so dramatically with far-reaching implications in how we build relationships, value ourselves, and map out our life expectations.

Terri Smith, CEO of the Australian perinatal depression helpline PANDA, has spoken about the damage caused by "social media representations of ideal families." Even when we have reached a level of maturity to know that these images can't be entirely reflective of real life, they can still get to us and undermine our happiness.

Social psychologist Leon Festinger's classic 1954 social comparison theory suggests that individuals evaluate their own abilities and success by gauging their position in the social pecking order. His argument is that we can only really rate our own position in life by comparing it to those of others in our community, which means the boundaries of those communities really matter. When all we see is the very best side of people in our communities online, curated especially to exclusively highlight their best attributes, is it any wonder that most of us feel that we are on the back foot in relation to pretty much everyone we know? Upward social comparison has a massive knock-on impact on body image, self-esteem, expectations, and life satisfaction.

Dr Pippa Hugo, a leading eating disorder consultant at Priory Hospital Roehampton, says that as many as nine out of ten teenage girls now

152

digitally enhance social media images of themselves. This creates unrealistic memories of your own face and body.

In 2015, we uploaded approximately 24 billion selfies to Google's servers. According to recent research, on average, teenage girls in the UK spend 84 minutes preparing for selfies every week, and it is estimated that the average millennial will turn their phone camera on themselves over 25,000 times over their lifetime. The impact of consuming these millions of images needs to be fully addressed by academics and medical professionals because we are sitting on a huge sociological and psychological time bomb that is altering our relationship with our own bodies.

According to a report released by research firm Dscout in 2016, the typical mobile phone user touches his or her phone 2,167 times a day. For the top 10 per cent of users in the study, that increase to 5,427 touches a day. Data confirmed by Apple themselves indicates that the average user with Touch ID unlocks their phone every 11 minutes and 15 seconds. Most of us will spend a staggering seven years of our lives on our phones.

A 2016 study from UCLA (University of California, Los Angeles) used MRI scanning to examine the brains of teenagers aged 13 to 18 while they used social media. The results showed that viewing likes underneath a picture they had posted activated the same brain signals as eating chocolate or winning money. Another interesting finding was that teens were much more likely to click the like button on images that had already received lots of likes from their peers. Showing that endorsement from others made them more likely to offer validation. The validation or instant gratification can feel like a rush or a sense of something which clearly matters to people on a biological level. This is only natural as we are social creatures at heart, and we are hardwired to feel this way about approval from others. If everyone else thinks it's cool, why don't we? Like button clicked.

153

Today we jump from laptops to tablets to smartphones, seamlessly switching from games to social media platforms and smartphone apps to web pages. A 2016 GlobalWebIndex survey of more than 50,000 global internet users found that the average person has eight social media accounts and spends one hour and 58 minutes a day on them. Drawing from his work on social media and smartphone addiction, Dr Roberts explains: "Generally, people are reluctant to think of behaviours as addictions. We're programmed to believe that we could be addicted to alcohol or drugs, but when it comes to behaviour, we're certainly resistant to accepting that addiction could apply. With social media and smartphone use, what we see in many cases certainly fits the definition of behavioural addiction—engaging in behaviour which you know will have negative consequences for both you and the people around you. It does not make logical sense for people to do things that harm them—unless they are addicted."

A 2017 *Harvard Business Review* report surveyed the academic literature to argue that social media may "detract from face-to-face relationships, reduce investment in meaningful activities, increase sedentary behaviour and erode self-esteem."

A 2017 survey by Accel and Qualtics revealed that 79 per cent of millennials keep their phones by or in their bed, and over half check their phone in the middle of the night. Elsewhere 55 per cent of British respondents in a 2015 Deloitte report said they looked at their phone within 15 minutes of waking up, and 28 per cent checked within five minutes of going to sleep every night.

Sean Parker, one of Facebook's earliest inventors, told news and information website Axios in an interview in 2017 that a social media site is a "social psychology". He explained that he and other early social media pioneers built their platforms to "consume as much of your time and

154

conscious attention as possible" with the "like" button devised to give users "a little dopamine hit", which in turn would fuel a desire to upload more content.

A *New Statesman* 2017 survey showed that 89 per cent of social media users feel happy when they get a high level of likes, but it also revealed that for 40 per cent of those people, the happiness only lasts as long as the likes keep coming in. So, conversely, a perceived lack of engagement can create a huge dent in our self-esteem.

Worryingly it was suggested in a 2018 article by the Canadian Globe & Mail that social media platforms are capitalising on our hunger for validation by holding back likes to keep us checking our accounts. You have to remember that this is a business at its core, and the more we connect, the more these people profit. It is in the interests of social media platforms to make us feel this way, as the more we use them, the more they earn. Escapism is an entirely understandable drive, and social media can offer a platform to express and explore fantasy identities. However, we've failed to develop a collective understanding that many of the images and captions that make up the many profiles are, at best, misinterpretations of the truth, and at worst, they are outright lies that have a massive influence on our perceptions of the world and ourselves, and through our addiction, we have lost the ability to recognise that.

UK charity Girlguiding found that 35 per cent of girls aged 11–21 said that their biggest worry online was comparing themselves and their lives with others. But it's not just girls or kids; in a recent study by UK disability charity Scope, 60 per cent of adult Twitter and Facebook users reported feelings of jealousy when comparing themselves to other users. Our careers, children, wardrobes, and lives are no longer good enough.

You will find that some people's content is now basically the same. What people do is research which images have generated the most likes in the past, and they use and recreate a duplicate shot for their own feed. Some people don't care anymore about the experience of travelling; they just want the picture to show everyone where they have been. Instead of diversity and originality, what the majority of people on social media appear to want is more of the same. Conformity is regarded by both the community and the system, and what we like drives algorithms which, in turn, feed us more indistinguishable content which we are happy to consume. Social media has become an echo chamber of mainstream predictable content through a process that has been described as the memeification of human experience. This can have an obvious impact on identity formation: expectations, benchmarks, and important signifiers of individual identity are being channelled through a very narrow lens.

If you thought Instagram and Facebook were programmed to serve you, think again. No matter your age, how much money you have or where you come from, you or someone close to you has experienced the detrimental effects of health issues. It's the fabric of all of our lives, and social media has contributed massively to this epidemic.

Happiness is not a medal to be showcased, nothing beautiful demands attention, but social media can obscure this by creating a wildly misleading and dangerous yardstick for those seeking to discover who they are. A human being is a vulnerable person, and it can be a dangerous place to be psychologically.

While posting a picture of your cleavage or abs may seem like the height of vanity, I can tell you it's more of a reflection of low self-esteem. What may look like straight narcissism can often be insecurity and a craving for reassurance.

156

People are eager for validation, so what happens when no one engages and when you don't get enough likes? In today's digital age, validation is the cornerstone behind creation because each clearly indicates how much we are liked. Instead of looking inwardly to develop ourselves and our confidence, we are caving in to try and obtain this from external means, which does not work because it is an inversion of where the real truth lies.

Life consists of duality, so I cannot only speak about social media's negative effects when there are some amazing benefits too. Some people use their platforms for positive means, which is to spread important information that can help people, raise awareness, and connect with friends and family. Social media has embedded itself into our civilisation, so all of its implications need to be understood. You can't smoke, have sex, or drive until you reach a lawful age simply because these activities are potentially harmful, and that should also be the case with social media. More legislation, safeguarding and education should also apply to the digital world, especially with how it impacts the real world.

Having come from the struggles of having no money at points in my life, having money really started to affect my behaviour, although it was not something I was consciously aware of at the time. I was not grounded, so I spent the money I earned on unnecessary things such as jewellery, designer clothes, tattoos, and tables on nights out. If I could project an image of success to the outside world, then maybe the outside world would believe I'm healed, and if I could gain this acceptance from others, I could also convince myself; again, my thinking was totally delusional. I got so caught up in my ego and how the outside world perceived me, I lost myself further.

I was now at a stage where I was feeling bad every time I drank alcohol or took drugs, and I used to beat myself up internally for it after the night was over. My disapproval was not coming from family or even friends, it was coming from a place inside of myself, knowing that what I was doing was wrong, and this just added to the negative self-evaluation I had formed of myself. My negative psychology was filled with anger, guilt, and shame; despite all the years that had passed since my childhood, nothing had changed, and I still felt like a victim of the world.

As long as my energy was consumed by superficial experiences, the concerns and desires of my ego would never afford me the ability to change. I was too busy worrying about socially conditioned desires instead of focusing my attention on processing the information from my environment. I needed to listen to what my mind and body had been crying out for all my life. Trying to heal and get help at this point became a distant memory, and every like I got on Instagram, every positive comment on how I looked and every bit of female attention I received just confirmed that I was now part of a thriving crowd. I needed this outside validation because my self-esteem was so low.

Being so caught up in this type of lifestyle meant that there was only ever going to be another crisis around the corner. The people in my environment were not the people I needed, as I struggled to relate to them. Over a period of time, I started to get into internal conflict in terms of who I truly was, in contrast with what I was doing and who I was associating with, and this type of life was never going to satisfy or fulfil my deep desires and needs. All everyone was talking about was celebrities, *Love Island*, and followers on Instagram. I was now feeling lost again as I felt I could not interact on a deeper level with the people who had accepted me, especially in such a superficial environment.

Everyone in my circle was taking drugs, getting drunk, and having casual sex; I had done all of that in Tenerife, but I found myself doing exactly the same again, and I just thought that this is what everyone in the world must be like because no matter where I went, I ended up in very similar circles. Looking back, I can now see that I was recreating similar circumstances, and the universe was giving me back exactly what I believed of the world. It was the universe's way of communicating to me, The Talking Universe.

Deep down, I was searching for real connections, but I was looking in the only places I had become accustomed to, which were bars, nightclubs, and now social media.

I knew this was a phase in my life that had lasted too long, but I wondered how I would move away from it. Then, suddenly, it happened— and it happened in the most distressing way possible.

The clearest sign of a healthy relationship is if there is no sign of it on social media.

–Jamie Gregory

Chapter 9 – Elsewhere

(In or to another place)

Could I leave the life I had now created in Leeds? The answer was no, so I needed a gentle nudge. One night I had decided to go out with Bodi to a bar. After arriving, Bodi had introduced himself to a girl who was nearby, and the conversation began to flow. After they had spoken, this girl began speaking to me, and she said that she was from Winchester. This caught my attention immediately, as Winchester was where my sister had attended college. It then turned out that this girl had not only gone to the same college as my sister but also knew exactly who she was! The conversation flowed, and after a few more drinks, we decided to go back to mine. At this time in my life, it was not uncommon for me to meet a girl in a bar and then go home with them afterwards.

As we walked to mine, we chatted, joked, and laughed. When we arrived, it was not long before we had consensual sex. Afterwards, while in my room, this girl's phone rang, and she decided to answer it in the living room whilst closing the door behind her, so I was unable to hear the conversation. Within what could have only been a couple of minutes, this girl returned to my room and told me that she had to leave.

A couple of days then passed when I received a phone call from my sister. I remember answering the phone and saying, "Hi Alex, what's up?" It was uncommon for my sister to ring me as she would usually text if she wanted to speak. Alex then asked me straight away, "Did you sleep with this girl?" To which I answered, "Yes, why?" My heart then sank when Alex told me that this girl had gone to the police and accused me of rape.

160

After this phone call, I felt myself getting into a state of panic. With nothing to hide, I drove to the local police station in Leeds. I would estimate that it took me about 30 minutes from the time my sister called me until I reached the police station. When I arrived, I went inside and headed towards the front desk. I then explained that I had received a phone call from my sister about an allegation of rape, and I wanted to speak to an officer, to which I was told to wait in the reception area. After what could have only been ten minutes or so, two officers came out, asked my name then arrested me on suspicion of rape.

At the time, I just could not believe what was happening. After being locked in a police cell for a few hours, I was then taken into a nurse's room. I knew the procedure within a police station better than most people, but this was different from anything I had experienced previously.

In the nurse's room, I was told to remove my underwear, and I had swabs taken from my genital area. This was all done while a police officer stood over me watching, and I remember feeling so humiliated and embarrassed. Afterwards, I was then interviewed on tape, and I told the police exactly what had happened by giving them the factual story, from start to finish.

After the interview, I was released on bail, and both the policemen who were dealing with the case tried to make me feel at ease as they could clearly see that I was distraught. In the waiting area downstairs, I sat with them after I was released, and they said—off the record, as they put it—that they believed this girl was lying because parts of her story were not adding up. The police, however, had decided to confiscate my phone to search for further evidence. Due to shock, I had totally forgotten about the 30 staff I was supposed to have out working in several Asda stores that night, and I forgot to communicate the relevant times and locations to them. That night,

161

none of my staff turned up to work, and the trust from the only client I had built my business on was now left in tatters. I had been spending my adult life looking for love in all the wrong areas, so it was now time to suffer the consequences of doing so.

I can remember feeling so disappointed in myself. I had put all of my eggs into one basket with this client, and instead of focusing on developing my business further, I had taken my eye off the ball to go out partying as much as I possibly could. The resulting factor of this situation meant that I lost my business that day, as that client never gave me another opportunity. Not for the first time in my life, I had found myself in an all too familiar situation that was distanced very far from love, but losing my business was only the start of the nightmare about to unfold.

The next four weeks for me were not filled with love. Instead, I was being embraced by the devil at the gates of hell again. Being accused of such a disgusting crime further destroyed me internally. I remember I would sit in the bath crying to myself, and at this point in my life, I was the most distanced I had ever been from love, and I no longer wanted to continue living out this pointless existence of severe pain and torture. When I used to sit in the bath, I would submerge my head under the water until I lost touch with reality, I wanted to end it right there, but each time before I fully drowned, a part of me would fight back and not want to give up.

The feelings that I was experiencing came in waves of emotions that I could not understand or even begin to work through on my own. I wanted to feel love, but instead, I felt worthless, dirty, insecure, sad, upset, low, traumatised, scared, weak, anxious, depressed, secluded, vulnerable, trapped, and lonely. Each emotion that surfaced would come attached with a belief which originated from every place that I had been running from since the start of my childhood. If I felt scared, for instance, then the image

162

that would project into my conscious mind would be in the form of an episode from my childhood when I felt scared due to some action my dad had taken towards me. No matter what I was scared of at that moment in time, the deep-rooted pain I was experiencing was coming from my childhood, and my current circumstances were just a vehicle to express what I had buried deep inside of me for many years.

The rape allegation I had been accused of had now triggered everything from my past to surface all at once, and I could no longer contain or bury this. My nights would consist of me spending time in isolation, and I was now trying to understand how the world could be such a cruel place with love not present. The images that appeared in my head would play over and over again like I was stuck in front of a revolving film. A way to describe how I felt would be to say that I was trapped inside a small cage which I could not escape from, and although I was still alive, it felt easier to just be dead. Finally, I had hit a point where I could no longer function, and I went into a meltdown. I believed that all my opportunities in life had passed me by, and with no purpose, there was no point in carrying on, in my mind. I just had not formulated a strategy at this point in how I could take my own life without my conscious mind interrupting the process by fighting back.

At the time, I had not realised that such extreme experiences give a person an opportunity to grow. There was a challenge right in front of me that if I could accept and overcome, I would be able to rise above my suffering and gain inner strength.

The Dutch philosopher Baruch Spinoza said, "Emotion, which is suffering, ceases to be suffering as soon as we form a clear and precise picture of it." But with no other point of awareness, suffering just meant pointless suffering to me at the time, and what I could not see was that I was being pushed towards finally healing. Only now can I look back and understand the meaning of Baruch Spinoza's words.

Due to my early conditioning and the current position I found myself in, I felt that females were a species I could never trust. I was unable to understand that because I had inherently thought this, it meant that I had manifested my belief into existence. Although I would have sex with various females, I would never trust them, and the rape allegation was just more evidence to believe that this inherent belief was indeed true. Every time I had sex with females that I had no connection with, I was putting myself in a position of danger and vulnerability, and this meant that a situation like this was inevitable for me at some point in my life.

Your beliefs become your thoughts.

Your thoughts become your words.

Your words become your behaviours.

Your behaviours become your habits.

Your habits become your routine.

Your routine defines your destiny by becoming your future.

The severe pain I felt coincided with me not eating again—surprise, surprise!! I would then chain-smoke cigarette after cigarette, with each one tasting worse than the last. Only after I could make myself physically sick would I stop smoking. It was not uncommon for me to go through 10 to 15 cigarettes one after the other, and this way of self-harming was me outwardly expressing my internal feelings. A person views the world through their dominant emotions in the here and now, so if we are happy, the world is a wonderful place, and if we are upset, the world is a sad place, and these are the energies we then attract into our lives. Many parts of my book have made me cry as I have written away, and this chapter is definitely one of those times because looking back, I can see how much pain I was in.

As time progressed, my horrific nightmares got worse, and I would wake up in cold sweats and burst into tears. Every time I heard a noise, I would get a dreadful feeling that something terrible was going to happen. Looking back, I was traumatised and suffering from PTSD. We have briefly touched on the effects of PTSD in a previous chapter, but I will now go on to highlight and explain this further.

Within the limbic system, two related areas are central to memory storage: the hippocampus and the amygdala. There is research that indicates that these two parts of the brain are involved in recording, storing, and remembering traumatic events. The amygdala is known to assist in the processing of highly charged emotional memories, such as fear and terror, and these become highly active both during and while remembering a traumatic incident. On the other hand, the hippocampus gives time, space, and context to an event by putting memories into their correct perspective and place in a person's life timeline. The hippocampal processing gives these events a beginning, a middle and an end. This is vital when discussing PTSD, as one of its features is feeling that the trauma has not, in fact, ended. Studies have shown that the hippocampus often becomes suppressed while experiencing a traumatic event, so its usual assistance in processing and storing an event becomes void. When this happens, the traumatic event is prevented from occupying its correct position in the individual's life history and continues to destroy their present. This is why the perception of past events being finished, or me having survived were never present. The flashback episodes that I endured were incidents of reliving past trauma through my mind and body in the present moment. I pray that my worst enemy never has to go through the problems I have encountered in my life because, up until this point, my existence had been truly inhumane. What I went through in regard to the rape allegation is no small thing—it would seriously impact most, if not all, individuals—but the flashbacks I had to contend with and the feelings I was experiencing were related to the trauma I had suppressed in my childhood.

My PTSD resulted from dissociating in my childhood when I was subjected to traumatic abuse; I needed to dissociate to survive, but like everything in life, there are consequences to all of our actions, and in this instance, PTSD in my future was the high price that I had to pay in return for protecting myself as a helpless child.

The constant flashbacks and reminders, which appeared out of nowhere, made it impossible for me to be consistent in whatever I was trying to do in my present-day life. My fear was not only based on the instant panic at that moment, but also on how I could react in those situations because everything in my environment, once triggered, immediately became a threat or danger. The brain doesn't have a Rolex, it cannot tell the time, and instead, it will activate the stress response when triggered, and then a full-blown activation could occur, and I would feel as if I was under intense

166

threat. My brain did not have the capability to say, "Jamie, what are you doing? You are reacting to a trigger from your childhood." PTSD affected me so drastically that it began to further change my thinking and behaviour even more negatively than where it had already been.

In many instances, people are able to experience traumatic events, and they are able to process then resolve them without having to dissociate. When this is done, there is no suffering such as the long-term consequences of PTSD. When PTSD is not present, it enables a person to recollect and recite the events that occurred to them, which means they can make sense of what happened. The emotions that have been experienced are suitable to their memories, and the incident remains where it should be, which is in the past. Because my issues were so severe and I dissociated to such a degree in my childhood, I was unable to remember many of my traumatic experiences until I had hypnotherapy in my future. Because of this, I was unable to make sense of events, emotions, and bodily sensations whenever I became triggered. Many cues become associated with the initial trauma during a traumatic event, and those same cues can elicit a similar response. The reaction to these triggers can then become very distressing and overwhelming, and until a person is able to make an association, they will end up travelling through life like they are walking on a minefield, not knowing where they can put their foot down, in fear of it being blown the fuck off. The severe problem with PTSD for me was that my traumatic memories became so dominant that I was never living in the here and now. I was living my life in all the places from my past when I was a zombie to this world. Dealing with my PTSD became the least of my fucking problems; making it through the day intact was what took all of my energy.

When a person suffers from PTSD, flashbacks occur. The term *flashback* is a narrative tool from the early 1900s, but it was popularised in

167

the 1960s to describe a disturbing sensory experience reported by individuals who had used the drug LSD. After the use of this drug, some people experienced aspects of their most frightening hallucinogenic trips days, weeks, and sometimes even years later. Traumatic flashbacks are comprised of sensory experiences of terrible events which become replayed with such intensity that they are impossible to distinguish from the in-the-moment reality. Now, if you imagine that when in these panic or danger states, there is no longer access to the cortex, we can see that the more traumatised I became, the less able I was to make sense of what was transpiring as my stress levels were directing my focus to the lower brain functions (the reptilian part of the brain).

On top of my mounting issues, which, when stacked up, made mount Everest look like a bungalow in comparison, the stress hormone cortisol causes detrimental effects on a person's mental and physical health when the body continually releases it, and I was releasing it as frequently as I was breathing air. Cortisol impairs the immune system, making people like me more likely to get sick and stay fucking sick. Epinephrine, which is also released in chronic stress situations, results in elevated blood pressure and a rapid heart rate. Both can damage the heart and blood vessels of a person, statistically increasing the risk of a heart attack or stroke. This then contributes to sleep deprivation, memory and concentration become compromised, and without these key components in check, I was less able to handle the stress I was experiencing.

My suffering got to the point where I decided to reach out to my mum, and I remember crying down the phone to her. Although she was always a sceptical mother, and she had every right to be with the way I had behaved, she never doubted my innocence once, the same as my sister and my stepdad. They knew I had stolen in the past, gotten myself into fights,

168

and that I drank alcohol and took drugs, but they also knew I was incapable of this. Having my family believe in me at this moment really enabled me to push through and eventually get myself out of the dark hole I had been digging and nesting in. The positive to this situation was that I was left with no alternative but to surrender and seek the help of my mum, so this incident built a small amount of trust between us. This was no easy feat, though, because although I spoke to my mum occasionally, the trauma I had suppressed and the infrequent patterns of females in my childhood contributed to my inability to form or maintain a healthy, consistent relationship with her.

Four weeks had now passed, and I was told that the charges had been dropped, but to me, the damage had already been done, and my pain had not subsided. I then decided to pursue a counterclaim against this girl because of the pain I had experienced and the business I had lost. All my questions were continuously left unanswered, and this just heightened the negativity swirling inside of me. Although this girl's story had completely contradicted the actual events in every way possible, I was told that she had been under the influence of alcohol when she went to give a statement, so there was nothing I could do to press charges against her. She had told the police so many lies that if she were to continue to give a statement and she was found to be lying, she would be the one facing charges, the police said to me. Although the charges had now been dropped, which was positive, I was left shattered with my business in ruins, and I had to rebuild my life once again. On reflection, I can look back and be thankful for what this situation taught me as it redirected me onto the correct path I was supposed to be on.

For a time following this period, I turned into a nasty person, and I carried severe hatred towards this girl. I found out later on that she had a boyfriend, and she had cheated on him with me, and maybe accusing me of rape was her way of justifying her actions. Because I was too scared to share what had happened to me with my friends, I isolated myself and got into petty arguments, so I did not have to see them. After I fell out with most of them one by one, I became very cold, and I was now suspicious of the whole world; any small part of me that had been willing to trust had now been obliterated.

Several months had now passed, and although I still felt fragile, I decided to push myself. I mean, I had to because things were just not improving, so I tried working through how I felt with the only tools I had been accustomed to, which was my self-medication, such as drinking alcohol and taking drugs. I wanted to try and feel normal again—and normal for me was blocking out any form of pain.

Going back outside again felt very strange; I would describe it as being surrounded by an invisible protective bubble. Everything now appeared different, and I tried to avoid all close contact with people. I would then struggle to get into any lengthy conversations, and I was fully on guard because I wanted to protect myself from what I now perceived as dangerous threats everywhere. When I left my apartment, I would have to push myself so much due to my anxiety, that I would drink straight vodka to help me be able to take one step outside my front door. On most occasions, I would vomit from the anxiety I would feel. Again, I concealed this, and only Bodi knew some of what was going on, but he did not know the full extent of the issues I was struggling to come to terms with. I am sure people will read my book who knew me around this time in my life and will now understand why I behaved in the way I did, because to a lot of people, the dark change in me did not make sense.

After trying to get back to normality, I eventually began seeing another girl, but we did not have sex for several months, even after sharing a bed many times. This girl had found it strange, but what she did not understand was that I did not feel comfortable because sex felt dirty to me after what I had been accused of. I now needed to be 100 per cent sure that I was not putting myself at unnecessary risk again. This relationship did not last long, and eventually, we stopped seeing each other. This girl used to go out partying a lot as she was young and at university. She was at that stage of her life when she should be enjoying herself. She would invite me to join her, but on most occasions—including my birthday—I just could not force myself to go out, no matter how hard I tried. Of course, I wanted to go out, I wanted to see and spend time with her—but I was just so destroyed emotionally and mentally. The very few times when I did decide to go out, I was on high alert and felt vulnerable in a social environment, even when I was drinking or taking drugs. For me, neither now masked my pain.

When this girl and I stopped seeing each other, I decided that my time in Leeds was finally done, and I was now intent on packing my bags and leaving. This girl had rung me up around Christmas time and told me on the phone that she wanted to end things. She no longer wanted to keep seeing me and said that I was always down, complaining, and negative. Looking back, I would not have wanted to be with me either. My perception of reality had become further distorted, and all I saw was negativity, sadness, and pain in life.

Not too long after we had decided to stop seeing each other, I met another girl, Cori, which, again, looking back, was not the best idea at the time. I had found myself in a lonely situation, so it was nice to have the distraction of another female. I never saw anything serious with her, as I knew I would not be staying in Leeds for long, but I did become attached to her. I was suffering from some serious trauma, but because I was able to speak to her without any judgement on her part, I kept seeing her for longer

171

than I should have. Again, I eventually found myself getting into arguments with Cori, most of which were based on her going out. For me, nights out represented danger because of what I had experienced, and I wanted to detach myself from that reality as much as I possibly could.

I had now shrivelled into a tiny shell, and I had stopped leaving my apartment. Instead, I would stay at home as I tried to rebuild my business. I decided to throw myself into work, and I gave it my all for a good couple of months, but I got nowhere. I worked seven days a week, fell asleep with the laptop on my lap after completing 16-hour days, and was no joy to be around. It became further mentally exhausting, and I felt myself becoming disillusioned with life even more. I now had no social life, hardly any money, a destroyed business, and I was barely eating. I had also isolated myself from all of my friends apart from Cori; I had stopped showering, cutting my hair and generally cleaning myself. Although I expected nothing from life, life was still expecting something from me.

The German philosopher Friedrich Nietzsche once said, "That which does not kill me makes me stronger," and that's exactly what was about to happen.

One night, when I was at Cori's house, I remembered I had gone to bed. I had completely hit rock bottom, and I could not see a way out of my predicament. Everything throughout my life had finally become too much for me to bury. I then began grieving and struggling to come to terms with my past because I had never faced it, and without the drugs or alcohol, everything was coming to the surface to now be released. Before I fell asleep that night, I broke down crying and told Cori I no longer wanted to be here anymore, and if I did not wake up, I would finally be happy and at peace. The following morning, I did wake up, which I felt was unfortunate at the time.

172

It is no surprise to me that traumatised individuals who cannot tolerate remembering due to the intense pain resort then to self-mutilation, drugs, or alcohol to block out the unbearable pain that they are imprisoned with. The healing process, though, depends on acknowledging the true reality of your body, no matter how painful that may be. The more isolated and unprotected a person feels, the more death will feel appealing and the only escape, especially when it is critical to connect to friends and family to feel safe.

As time progressed and I carried on seeing Cori, she asked me if I wanted to go to a festival in Leeds. She had asked more out of being polite as she knew I would say no, but on this occasion, although I said no, for some reason, I changed my mind a few days before. I had decided that I could not carry on living as I was, and I needed to try and take my mind off what I was experiencing. I then decided to get a haircut—something I had not done in months—and tidied myself up. On the day of the festival, I was very nervous around so many people I did not know, so I had a few drinks and a lot of recreational drugs. In the end, I felt very relaxed by reducing my stress levels, and I ended up having a great time.

The following morning, I remember waking up, and something very bizarre occurred. To this day, I have tried to make sense of what happened to me, and the only way I can describe it is to say that I was not the same person anymore. Initially, I put this down to all the trauma I had suffered in my life and the drugs I had taken the previous night. I had concluded that I had finally snapped and lost the plot as that was the only way I could describe or rationalise what I saw and now felt, but on further reflection, and after reading of similar experiences from other people, I now know I had what is called a spiritual awakening.

173

There are certain points in life when something happens that changes everything for good, and this was one of those points. Poets and mystics always seem to have their transcendental awakening somewhere divine—on a mountaintop or near a waterfall or a sunset, for instance. Mine happened in a run-down council house which looked like a fucking caravan site because the bins had not been collected in months. I can tell you that awakenings are not mystical experiences reserved only for monks, mystics, and poets. They are for each and every one of us who need divine intervention. With my awareness all of a sudden now awakened, anything was going to be possible in my life, and the death I had just experienced created space for my rebirth. It was now finally time to start healing myself although this was not a linear process.

There will come a time in life when you think you are finally finished. You feel as if you cannot move another step forward, and all you can see and feel around you is darkness. I can tell you through experience that this is the point when you have finally reached the start of your journey.

–Jamie Gregory

Chapter 10 – Power

(The ability to do something or act in a particular way)

I became very strange at this point in my life. Many people had a certain image of me, but no one got the full picture. I certainly didn't. My world had now changed, and after researching my experience on the internet, I came across various pieces of information that described very similar experiences that other people had also been through. I then went on to discover that there were certain individuals who actually went in search of a spiritual awakening, and to have one was apparently a blessing. Although, at the time, it felt anything but that. When I now looked at myself in the mirror, I saw my reflection staring back at me, but I no longer felt as if I was the same person anymore.

My awakening had caused my world to become more vibrant and colourful. It felt like I was living on a different planet or in an altered plane of existence. With everything changing, I begun to walk around without shoes on, and I found myself being unconsciously led towards parks, waterfalls, and natural environments. After a couple of months, I felt the need to wear shoes again; however, I wanted to know why I had the desire to go to places that involved nature. After further research, it made perfect sense: surrounding myself in nature would help to facilitate my healing process, and by not wearing any shoes, I was able to connect directly to the earth through my bare feet. The healing properties left me feeling rejuvenated, refreshed and energised.

"Once the soul awakens, the search begins, and you can never go back. From then on, you are inflamed with a special longing that will never again let you linger in the lowlands of complacency and partial fulfilment. The eternal makes you urgent. You are loath to let compromise, or threat of danger hold you back from striving toward the summit of fulfilment."
—John O' Donohue

My life-force energy exploded as I burst into life, and it was far too much for me to handle at the time. The symptoms I experienced are listed below.

1. My sight, hearing, taste, touch, and smell became highly sensitised.

2. I got a yearning to eat natural foods.

3. It became near on impossible to sleep due to my heightened senses. When I did sleep, my dreams were vivid, and I began to have premonitions.

4. I began suffering from severe headaches, which left me crouched on the floor for hours, crying in pain due to the information overload I had to contend with.

5. My sex drive became non-existent.

6. I experienced strange tingling sensations and spontaneous feelings of vibration emanating throughout my body.

My awakening was very intense, and I went through a stage referred to as a spiritual emergency.

My process had accelerated to such a degree that my mind and body became very disorientated. In life, we must encounter various difficulties before we reach bliss, and the spiritual awakening process is no different. This is a sacred process, and in order to allow the new in, space must be created by removing the old.

Why do spiritual emergencies happen? There is no one definitive reason, but I discovered four:

1. Destiny is a very prominent reason. An accelerated process enables a person to learn profound lessons and begin to work through karmic debt. These are patterns in a person's life that are being repeated, typically bad or unresolved issues. Examples include struggling with money, sabotaging relationships, or avoiding responsibilities.

2. A person may experience a particularly strong conditioning throughout childhood, through society and/or caregivers, such as beliefs and ideas which form habits and patterns. A spiritual awakening will break through these conditioning forms and remove barriers holding a person back. These awakenings can be extremely intense because it feels like everything that person has been holding on to throughout their life shatters around them.

3. Shamans or healers can go through an awakening process which involves a connection to the spirit realm.

177

4. An existential crisis is when there is no meaning or purpose in life, and it can consist of a lifetime of not listening to your inner child.

Unfortunately, due to the lack of knowledge regarding spiritual emergencies, many people are often committed to mental health wards and given high doses of medication to suppress their transformation. Spiritual emergencies can cause people to be rejected by their families, society can deem these people as crazy, and the system can proceed to label them with various mental illnesses. Luckily, I had already created a certain amount of space in my life, so my process was allowed to take its natural course.

My spiritual awakening consisted of 12 stages, which are known as the Hero's Journey. This was popularised by Joseph Campbell, who found out that for thousands of years, people all over the world communicated with stories having similar patterns and basic elements. He structured these patterns and elements into 12 phases.

1. **The Ordinary World:** This was my everyday life before my awakening (Chapters 1 to 9).
2. **Call to Adventure:** This began after receiving a call to action through my spiritual awakening.
3. **Refusal of the Call:** Doubts surfaced, momentarily holding me back from following the call.
4. **Meeting the Mentor:** This was in the form of a therapist who would assist me on my journey.
5. **Crossing the Threshold:** I crossed from my familiar everyday life to one that was not.

6. **Tests, Allies, Enemies:** Struggles and difficult challenges appeared in a variety of ways, which caused obstacles that temporarily thwarted my progress.

7. **Approaching the Innermost Cave:** This was reaching the central crisis of my journey.

8. **The Ordeal:** Undergoing the plunge into darkness, the great death and subsequent rebirth.

9. **Reward:** When I emerged triumphant with new inner gifts and strengths.

10. **The Road Back:** My journey back to the normal world.

11. **Resurrection:** Meeting the final test and the most dangerous encounter with death.

12. **Return with the Elixir:** This was when I returned to the ordinary world a changed man. I had grown and learned so much. I had faced numerous dangers and difficulties which I had overcome, and it was now time to start a new life.

My story shows you three key elements: proof of my journey, change, and success. However, I was unaware of the Hero's Journey until the latter stages of writing my book, which enabled me to put the final pieces of my story together.

Stage 1, The Ordinary World, is what you have already read between Chapters 1 to 9. My awakening experience had propelled me into Stage 2, or the call to adventure. The remaining ten stages are described simultaneously alongside the rest of my story.

Stage 3: Refusal of the Call. *Doubts surfaced, which momentarily held me back from following the call.*

After what I can only describe as going through hell with my awakening, I felt like I was starting to lose touch with reality. For example, I began to hear words in the music I was listening to. Knowing what I know now, I can see that my unconscious mind was sending me signs and a path to follow, which was directing me towards healing.

My awakening had made the process of leaving Leeds much easier because I had burned most, if not all, my bridges with the people I knew there. Letting certain people go was the right decision, and I soon realised that I had stepped in puddles deeper than most of the people's personalities I had been associating with. After leaving Leeds, I decided to move to a place called Batley, where I knew no one, and this helped because I did not have to worry about other people's perceptions of me.

After moving, I tried to get back into some form of normality by going back to work. I had hoped that this would push me into my old self, but after continuously trying for around a month, I gave up. I remember many days when I just sat staring at my laptop as the thought of making a sales call just filled me with intense dread. I was 29 years old and had absolutely nothing to my name. I was emotionally and mentally unstable, and now I thought I had also lost my sanity. At the time, I did not understand the purpose of my awakening, and as I felt frightened, I tried to ignore it as much as I could. The problem was, though, it became the dominating factor in my life, no matter how much I tried to forget it.

Stage 4: Meeting the mentor. *This was in the form of a therapist who would assist me on my journey.*

After a few months passed, my symptoms eventually settled down. I then decided to ring my mum to explain my experience to her. I remember at the time, it was coming up to my birthday, and my mum had asked me what I wanted. After thinking long and hard, I decided that it was finally time to accept the urgent help I had always needed. It had now been 12 years since I had refused to go back and have any form of therapy, but I had now reached a point where I had tried everything and failed. I knew without outside help, nothing would get better, and in actual fact, it was only continuing to get progressively worse. Understanding this meant that the thought of speaking to someone did not seem as frightening as it once did, and in actuality, I was looking forward to attending because my awakening had left me in such a vulnerable state.

After searching online, I found a therapist, and I decided to give him a call. At first, I did not know where to start. Most people go to therapy for a particular reason, but I had a multitude of issues.

During the next few months, I attended ten sessions, and I spoke about my life in detail, which consisted of the issues I had buried and how I ended up in the situation I was now in. At first, it was far from easy, but I began to feel more comfortable as trust was gradually built. The therapist did not judge me, and this made me feel safe. I can tell you through experience that safety is the most important aspect of any therapy one wishes to have. The more the sessions progressed, the more I began to feel like a human being, especially when I was told that my abnormal reactions to my abnormal life experiences were indeed normal behaviour.

"The first rule of any trauma therapy is safety."
—Herman 1992

Finally, my mentor had appeared. Looking back, I can see that this was the first time in my life that I was able to open up, confide in someone, and discuss most of what I had been through in my life. I say 'most' because there was still another layer of therapy to go through in my future due to certain memories which I could not recall yet because I had dissociated in my childhood.

Therapy was hugely beneficial as it became an important steppingstone on my healing journey. Although admittedly, I had mistakenly thought that I would be healed after ten sessions. In fact, the consequence of this delusion will become more apparent the deeper we delve into my story.

The first topic we discussed revolved around my problems with trusting people. I discovered that if I were in control of situations and outcomes, I would never have to feel the pain I felt when I was a helpless child. I began to understand how this deep-rooted pain was affecting my decision-making abilities, which, in turn, destroyed many of my relationships. I was always anticipating untrustworthy individuals based on my familiar childhood experiences, so I kept manifesting these similar, repetitive, and destructive encounters. I wanted to trust, but I had formed various unconscious defensive mechanisms to protect myself from ever getting hurt again.

An integral part of learning to trust required me to connect to my internal state, and this would enable me to understand how I felt around myself, people and certain situations. As you can imagine, that was very hard for me to do because, inherently, I did not trust myself due to the many destructive past decisions I had made so far. The reason I struggled to connect with my internal state was due to the abuse I had suffered as a child, and with my pain being so severe, I had unconsciously created a disconnect to protect myself from harm. Not understanding myself meant that when my emotions would surface, they would always come through very powerful and highly charged, and this frightened me because I was unable to understand them. Not connecting fully with my emotions was also entwined with my trust issues, which affected my decision-making abilities. If I never understood my feelings, then how could I understand myself and then communicate to other people how I felt. The resulting factor was the story of my life so far, absolute fucking chaos.

After the topic of trust was discussed in depth, we moved on to my dad. It was crucial that I understood his situation. Due to my dad's upbringing, which he had not healed from, he could not give me the protection and love I required. To a child, affection is based on action, and while a parent may truly love their child, if that child is wide awake in the other room, hungry and crying, then that child does not feel any love. A child needs warmth from the skin, the scent of a parent, sounds and visuals, which are followed up by attention and a response. This is what becomes love through loving interactions. After discussing my dad, I no longer saw an evil man; instead, I realised he was a sick man who needed help. When we are confronting people who have addictions, we are dealing with the

183

symptoms of that addiction, not the vulnerable person underneath who is clearly in pain and displaying negative behaviour.

My childhood was a common subject of discussion, but I had never really considered up until this point the impact my dysfunctional upbringing was still having on my everyday life. Another important discovery was made when we broached the subject of boundaries. Growing up with so much freedom and around characters who were involved in crime meant that as I grew into an adult, I made reckless decisions based on my dysfunctional upbringing. My world was always a dangerous place, but that was my familiarity, so in my adult life, when things became extreme, there was no reference point for me to go back to and correct myself. Setting boundaries, creating discipline and self-care was what I needed to incorporate into my life, and these processes would contribute towards my self-care instead of my self-destruction.

When you have such a damning childhood as mine, it is no wonder that a person will go on to make such crucial fundamental mistakes in their adult life. This then leads me to the discussion we had about my addiction to crack cocaine, the world of crime I was involved in, and my father's death. A pattern had started to emerge, and once again, my childhood came up. Yes, my father should have protected and shielded me away from the world I was exposed to, such as crime and drugs, but instead, due to how distorted his life became, he involved me to the point where his reality became mine through his influence. I am not absolving myself from the things I have done, but constantly beating myself up got me nowhere, and it was not beneficial for me to carry on doing so. I felt ashamed and disgusting, and for me, or any person for that matter, to truly begin to heal, acceptance with compassion for the self is crucial. It was time to acknowledge that what had happened was now in the past and that I was not disgusting. Instead, I was

184

strong and had enough courage to eventually remove myself away from a situation that was so devastating. Inherently feeling ashamed only increased the blame I attached to myself for my dad's death, and holding myself accountable for many years only destroyed me and the people around me. My dad had made his own decisions in life, and he was killed when I was 17 years old. No amount of intervention on my part would have saved him and understanding that I was not responsible took a massive weight off my shoulders that I had been carrying around with me.

Next on the list was my school years. We spoke in depth about me not fitting in anywhere, being labelled with dyslexia, and struggling academically. Being constantly afraid and on alert never allowed me a consistent amount of time to access the thinking part of my brain, the cortex. Instead, I was always dominated by my lower brain functions, which severely impacted my learning capabilities. If my energy was primarily focused on trying to stay alive, is it any wonder that trying to learn fucking maths at school or make long-lasting friendships, for instance, did not go according to plan? The impact of not fitting in anywhere became a crucial component in my life because I eventually found a place in Leeds where I was accepted. This caused a belonging and an attachment for me, but that was with a crowd that was not conducive to what I needed to learn, grow, and excel.

Anxiety and my relationship with food came up directly after we spoke about my school years. Whenever I was unhappy, I did not eat, and even when I was happy, I was very particular with food. Being unhappy would project out into my external environment, and by not eating, I aligned my inner and outer worlds together. Anxiety is something I had suffered with for quite some time, and a huge contributing factor was that I never had any real stability or a true forward-thinking plan. I now needed to create a foundation point to move forward from, and this would need to consist of balance and consistency in all areas of my life.

An important topic which came up was my arrest and accusation of rape. At first, it was not easy to discuss because my anger surfaced and dictated my perception, but in time I saw that I was the one who was prepared to put myself in such a vulnerable situation by having casual, emotionless sex with various females who I did not love or have any true connection with. I inherently did not trust females, so I then unconsciously manifested my beliefs into existence. I was incapable of having a loving relationship with anyone until I began to change my inherent beliefs and first love myself. Sex in its base form is sacred energy exchange between two people; when we each have sex, we are intimately exchanging our energy. Having sex based on the lowest vibration possible (lust) where the highest vibration (love) was not present meant that I was creating dangerous situations for myself each and every time I rolled that dice.

At first, I had put off speaking about my mum, but eventually, we got around to discussing what I felt was her abandonment of me from a young age. Growing up, my dad conditioned me into believing that my mum did not love me. This became an ingrained belief of mine which warped my mind and created an illusion far away from where the truth really lay. My mum has always loved me, but due to the situation that my dad created, she had no choice but to sacrifice me. My dad would not have taken my sisters. Alex was a new-born baby, and Chrissy was disabled. I was the only boy, and we had formed a bond that he did not have with my sisters, so I believe this is why he gravitated towards me. My belief system revolved around all females and not only my mum. This was because of the consistent damage my brain was subjected to again when I was a child. I had not formed consistent patterns at a crucial stage of my brain development around my mum, my sisters, Tracy, or any other female for that matter. To me, females all said the same thing and left, so my brain had developed to not trust, and when I did or had tried to, it left me feeling vulnerable and terribly upset each time someone disappeared from my life.

The more we spoke about my mum, the more I saw that by viewing the situation from a selfish perspective, focusing only on the impact it had on me, I was unable to see and understand my mum's perspective. When a person is in danger, the main focus is directed towards protecting the self. We can then become narrow-minded and unable to widen our perspective past the self, and this is what happened in my instance. I had spent a large proportion of my life hating my mum, but after therapy, I was able to have empathy and compassion towards her situation, recognising how hard it must have been for my mum. Yes, she has made mistakes, and she is a wise woman who does not need me to tell her that; the thing is, we all make mistakes. No one is immune to making mistakes, and I have made more than most people. I know these mistakes have haunted her, but as I have said to her many times, I have forgiven everyone for what transpired in my childhood. Who am I to sit and judge my mum for what she had to go through herself? And who is anyone else to judge my mum because she has received a lot of criticism in her life for the way she has handled the situation with me? Who is to say I would have dealt with the situation any better if we had traded places? The same goes for me. Who is anyone else to judge me or tell me how to tie my own laces when they have not walked a day in my shoes? My mum did her best at that given moment in time, and offering forgiveness and understanding of the situation was the only way for me to eventually cultivate a new set of circumstances. This is the same for anyone else who holds on to anger and resentment towards other people. As you will see from my story, only when we can accept our own flaws and forgive

187

can we truly move forward in life. One thing I have learned is that many people expect forgiveness, yet they are unwilling to forgive.

After discussing my mum, the topic of being homeless came up, and this was a big issue because it left me feeling constantly insecure. As I spoke to the therapist about my experiences on the streets, I decided that I was going to focus all of my energy on working as hard as I could so this situation would never happen again. The devastating effects of trying to acquire as much money as possible became another addiction of mine, and this will become prevalent later on as it took over from any form of healing I required. No matter how much money I made, all it took was for one bad day at work, and I would be triggered and sent straight back into the same mindset of being cold, lonely and in danger again.

The last topic we discussed, and by no means the least significant, was my deep-rooted anger, which was sabotaging my life. Anger is one of the most misunderstood emotions, which can become an effective tool that can be used to your advantage when you begin to harness it as fuel. When I began utilising it in this way, it became a creative outlet that I used to give me extra motivation towards achieving my goals. At this point in my life, every bad thing that happened to me was bottled up and used as fuel to prove people wrong. This managed to get me to a certain place in life, but it was not a healthy position to remain in. When I had no one left to be angry at, I had no desire at times to move forward, so to push myself, I would create delusions in my head and I turned the whole world against me because in its essence, it gave me extra fuel and motivation to succeed.

My therapy sessions had now finished, and I was able to discuss the uncomfortable nature of the subjects in a relatively calm and composed manner. Being in a state of calm allowed me access to the cortex part of my brain, so I was able to process and understand these delicate topics with both more depth and clarity than I had ever had before.

Despite having therapy, I felt very low and depressed, and it dawned on me one evening that I may need to consider taking anti-depressants. The therapist I was currently seeing, previous doctors and also my mum had all said at various times in my life I would benefit from taking anti-depressants. On each occasion, it was explained that this would assist me in healing from the devastation which had occurred in my life. Despite everyone's continuous recommendations, I always decided to decline any anti-depressants that were on offer, and I then went on a journey to discover more about medication. The more research I did, the more my decision to not take any felt like the right thing to do.

After dissecting my situation and considering the implications of anti-depressants, I came to this conclusion. I had hit rock bottom in my life, and I have known other people who had gone in search of some type of magic pill from their wizard doctor to solve their problems. They then realised that this either did not work, or they became dependent on the medication for survival and ended up back where they had started months or years later. After looking into the actual effects of anti-depressants and what they could potentially do for me, I saw that I would get an increase in serotonin, norepinephrine, and dopamine levels within my brain to bring me up to a manageable level. *Okay, but how is this going to help me heal?* I thought. *How is burying everything and creating more unconscious pressure going to help me? It could potentially stabilise me for a time to give me a point of reference to work from, but what if I became addicted?* I mean, there was a high chance with my already addictive personality. The more I read, the more I found how highly addictive these anti-depressants were.

Many prescription medications have the potential to be highly addictive, and because people take them for medical reasons, it does not mean they are insulated from becoming addicted. There can be a very subtle transition period from taking medication for a medical purpose to a person going on to use it improperly. Medication, such as codeine or oxycodone, can be used for recreational purposes due to their euphoric effects, and this can cause people to rationalise their consumption of these medications. Prescription opioids are a route towards addiction and potentially harder drug use as well. This is big business, and data from the 2018 NSDUH shows that street/drug dealers confirmed that prescription opioids play a huge part in their business. More than half of them stated that they acquire their opioid supply from clinics with lenient prescribing habits by what is known as 'doctor shopping'. A serious problem with any drug is that they are very easy to overdose on, and this, in its worst-case scenario, can cause fatalities. Taking opioids suppresses the brain's functioning capability to breathe. Opioids suppress the brain's reaction to inadequate oxygen intake, and when taken in unsafe doses, people are put to sleep, and their brain forgets to keep breathing. If you consider the withdrawal effects and typical symptoms when opioids are stopped, you can see how dangerous this can be.

1. Watery eyes and runny nose

2. Intense sweating

3. Skin bumps

4. Nausea and vomiting

5. Diarrhoea

6. Loss of appetite

7. Dilation of pupils and sensitivity to light

8.	Muscle tightness and cramps

9.	Fever and chills

10.	Rapid heart rate and breathing

11.	High blood pressure

12.	Fatigue

13.	Anxiety

14.	Depressed moods

15.	Insomnia

16.	Intense drug cravings

I was now confident that my issues stemmed from the deep-rooted pain that I had suppressed from my childhood, and after research, I was not prepared to go down the route of a temporary fix by taking medication to increase the neurotransmitters in my brain. I made the decision not to alter my emotions and numb myself to my environment. Instead, I wanted to feel, and even when my feelings became utter pain and gut-wrenching sorrow, at least I could work through my pain in the correct way by understanding the true nature of my reality.

This was a slow process, but like anything long-lasting in life, it takes time to see life-changing results.

This then leads me on to the subject of pain, and I can tell you that although we are genetically wired to avoid pain, and while no one wants to feel it, there are huge advantages to understanding and feeling pain naturally. I have listed 12 benefits which I have personally experienced.

191

1. Pain is an internal warning system which informs you that change is required.

2. Pain provides an opportunity to improve, learn and grow.

3. Pain keeps you safe from danger.

4. Pain brings clarity to a situation.

5. Pain is understood when looking back, which in turn provides wisdom.

6. Pain brings each person together because it is part of everyone's story.

7. Pain puts into perspective the appreciation of a positive relationship.

8. Pain provides us with strength so we can go on to comfort others.
9. Pain gives balance and reminds us of what is really important.

10. Pain builds a resilience each time we overcome an obstacle.

11. Only through pain can we begin to break ourselves down and build back up again in a better position from where we were.

12. Lastly, pain informs us that we have been wounded, but do you know what the best aspect of pain is? It tells you that despite what may have happened, you are not dead yet, and you are in fact still alive.

Days then weeks passed as I sat and contemplated what I had been through, and I felt extremely proud of myself that I had managed to speak to someone. Therapy had shown me that the disastrous situations I had experienced were not actually personal, and each time something happened, it was a sign from The Talking Universe. I was always being pushed towards seeking help and healing, and when I could not heed the signs, the universe spoke louder and louder until I eventually listened. Communication from the universe is universal and not only based on my life, although my awakening had started the process of making the signs consciously available to me.

Therapy had given me the insight to see who I had become, and this scared me as I did not identify with that person. I was not a bad person, far from it, I was just a natural consequence of what I had experienced so far in my life. With this new insight, I realised why I had tried to bury everything instead of facing it, and this was because I did not have the capability to reach out and ask for help because that meant I had to trust someone.

I now spent less time blaming or torturing myself for where I was in my life. I say less time because therapy is not an instantaneous switch where everything miraculously improves. Patience, persistence and pain are necessary to see any long-term benefits of therapy, so please do not go under the same illusion as I did, which was to think that everything would be a quick fix.

This now leads me on to the importance of time. When looking to embark on a journey of healing and change, time should be of no relevance to you. By specifying a certain timeframe, you will only ever increase the pressure on yourself by creating shortcuts. Anything long-lasting has to come from a solid foundation point, and without this, everything will eventually crumble before your eyes with nothing to fall back on. I based my unrealistic

193

expectations and trajectory on other people's lives. I believed I had to rush to catch up with people who were already married, had kids, owned homes, and had financial security. What also contributed to me rushing my process was the fear of ending up back on the streets again and not being in a position to support myself. I did not want natural growth because I was ready to change now, and I wanted to see these changes reflected in my life immediately.

I was finally waking up from what felt like a long bad dream, and although I knew the road ahead was not going to be easy, I had taken the hardest step yet. I now had a feeling that I was going to be okay, and this came from my internal guidance or higher self, which I had rejected for the entirety of my life. I had no idea at this point how I was going to accomplish anything, but I had set a conscious intention, and I can tell you through experience that we do not always need to know the path. The universe will respond as soon as we surrender and accept that we are vulnerable and need help.

True intelligence cannot be taught; it can only be learned, and my life experiences up until this point had given me the most remarkable opportunity to succeed and excel in my future. Although I was on the right path, there was still a long way to go. My mindset at this point in my life was that I would rather shoot for the moon and miss than aim for the fucking gutter and make it.

"*Those have most power to hurt us, that we love.*"
—Francis Beaumont

Chapter 11 - Efficient

(A change that results when something is done or happens)

Eventually, change was inevitable, and after moving to Batley, I created solitude, and this helped to remove any unnecessary distractions from my life. It was time to become efficient and focus on creating a foundation point from which I could start moving forward from. Although I was again running, this time, I was not running away.

I had now achieved a target I had set for myself by attending therapy, and although on paper, it seemed small, the first step is always the biggest.

After taking a leap of faith into the unknown, I was unsure what to expect. The recent therapy sessions I had attended had left me feeling vulnerable, exposed, and emotional. Despite feeling low, I was starting to understand that my feelings were due to what had happened to me and not what I previously thought: *My feelings are who I am.* I was no longer continuing to mask my pain, and this caused life to become very uncomfortable. I can tell you through experience that if a person wants to truly begin healing, they must get comfortable being uncomfortable. As we each grow older, we fall under the influence of external influences, and we tend to become disconnected from our intuition as it becomes less prominent. It's not lost, it's just buried, and mine had always been there, but this was the first time I had allowed it to surface.

Although I began working through my pain in the correct way, I had once again run out of money, and I remember thinking to myself, *how much harder are things going to get?* Having no money always intensified my situation, and the feelings of being homeless again would surface relentlessly. While I had made the right decision in seeking help, I desperately needed a sign from The Talking Universe to signify that I was indeed on the correct path.

I now had no alternative but to ring my stepdad Ian to borrow some money from him to pay my rent. My wallet at this point was like an onion; every time I opened it, it made me cry. I have always trusted Ian's judgement, although I have not always been able to incorporate it into my life. Asking for money made me feel horrible, embarrassed, and a failure yet again. After Ian agreed, I got off the phone and started crying; Ian's act of kindness and support left me feeling ashamed, and I was so angry that I had found myself in an all too familiar position.

Negative thoughts were now consuming my body, but, on this occasion, they were becoming consciously apparent to me—whereas before, I had not been aware of them. In order to change my life, I knew that I first needed to change myself inwardly, and that started with my thought processes. We are all products of our own thoughts, and thoughts are what create reality, so if my thoughts had always stemmed from a negative perspective and they consisted of pain, suffering, and survival—then that was all I was ever going to project out into my future. Understanding this was one step, but changing a lifetime of negative thoughts entirely was another step. Logically, it seems simple—*Think happy thoughts, and you will become happy!* The problem was, each time I got out of bed in the morning, my thoughts would be of a negative nature because that was what my natural state had always been, and I had spent the entirety of my life unconsciously gathering evidence to further support this claim.

196

Stage 5: Crossing the Threshold: I crossed from my familiar everyday life to one that was not.

"Whoever is delighted in solitude," goes the saying from Francis Bacon, "is either a wild beast or a god."

When a person knows they have hit rock bottom, it can concentrate the mind to work in two particular ways. The first way is to create a barrier, which then stops a person from achieving a certain target as they continue down the same familiar path. A lot of the time, a barrier is created due to fear of onslaught or failure. What happened to me was the opposite, and I was provided with a clearer new direction to overcome my challenges. The ability to absorb, learn, and then evolve from misfortune in life is a very rare gift; indeed, it requires a certain genius, as the odds are heavily stacked against people like myself. Those who can move past huge obstacles are survivors who show courage and have extreme amounts of resilience no matter what the circumstances. Everywhere in life, people are confronted with their own fate and the chance of achieving something long-lasting and worthwhile through their own suffering.

I had now decided that I would do whatever it took to succeed, but there would prove to be constant daily challenges which would take me over six years to navigate my way through. One of my first tasks was working through the anxiety and paranoia which I was suffering from, as they had both become so severe that I hardly left my apartment for a year. Outside represented danger, and every time I seemed to open the door, something bad used to happen, so I thought, *If I keep my door closed and lock myself away, then nothing bad can happen.* Although I had created a barrier, it was a temporary one that I needed at this stage of my life. My subconscious mind was taking steps to force me to face my problems head-on without any further distractions.

The more time I spent in solitude and allowed my intuition to surface, the more my perception began to change. The experience of opening my eyes to a whole new world was very painful, and I can tell you that being conscious in an unconscious world is just about as uncomfortable as it gets. Carl Jung sums this up perfectly.

"There is no coming to consciousness without pain. People will do anything, no matter how absurd, in order to avoid facing their own soul. One does not become enlightened by imagining figures of light, but by making the darkness conscious."
—Carl Gustav Jung

Everything eventually settled down for me, as I managed to get myself into a consistent routine. At first, my subconscious mind was threatened by change, and this is because its main focus was to keep me safe. Each person will experience a pull towards their familiar in the different discomforts which can be felt when change begins to occur. When we try to push ourselves out of autopilot mode, resistance is met from both the mind and body. This response has a name: the homeostatic impulse.

The homeostatic impulse regulates a person's physiological functions, from breathing to body temperature, and this all happens unconsciously as they are automatic. The purpose of the homeostatic impulse is to create balance in the body and the mind, and where there is dysregulation, the imbalances can be problematic and even self-betraying.

198

The unconscious mind prefers to exist in its comfort zone, and the safest place, it turns out, is one it's been to before because the mind can predict a familiar outcome. Habits, or behaviours that we repeatedly return to, become the unconscious mind's default mode. The brain prefers to spend most of its time coasting on autopilot as its best able to conserve its energy by knowing what to expect; this is why our habits and routines feel so comforting, and it's also why it's so unsettling when our old routines are disrupted. The practice of making consistent, daily choices through these push-and-pull resistances helps to empower a person to eventually maintain a change.

Although my existence was uncomfortable, I knew that my short-term pain would be worth it in the end. As I began forming a new daily routine, I started to get an urge from my inner voice to read, and I was gravitating towards certain books of which I had no prior knowledge. I then began reading every day, which enabled me to expand my mind to the many possibilities and opportunities available. The main genre of books I began reading were spiritual and self-development books, and at this point, with my addictive personality, I could easily read a standard 300-page book in one day.

"The man who does not read books has no advantage over the man that cannot read them."

–Mark Twain

Some of the books I read during this period of my life are listed below:

Flow (Mihaly Csikszentmihalyi)

The Road Less Travelled (M. Scott Peck)

The Power of Now (Eckhart Tolle)

The Chimp Paradox (Steve Peters)

Human Race, Get Off Your Knees (David Icke)

7 Habits of Highly Effective People (Stephen Convey)

Journey of the Souls (Michael Newton)

Destiny of the Souls (Michael Newton)

Think and Grow Rich (Napoleon Hill)

The Monk Who Sold His Ferrari (Robin Sharma)

With reading taking a prominent role in my new life, I began learning at an incredible rate. I had started the process to change with a conscious intention, which in turn altered the way I began to think, and over time this then transformed the way I behaved. I was now motivated every day, whereas in the past, I had been accustomed to feeling demotivated, anxious, and depressed. Creating an environment conducive to my needs enabled me consistent access to my cortex, so I was then able to start formulating well-thought-out plans for my future.

Through reading, I started to focus my attention on my diet. I knew I needed to build a relationship with food if I wanted to give myself the best possible chance to succeed, so out went the majority of processed foods I was eating, and in came as many natural foods as possible. These included the fruit and vegetables I once hated that my mum used to feed me. Although reading about the importance of diet had given me new insights, the more I became attuned to my higher self, the more I noticed the drastic effect processed foods would have on me as they knocked me out of alignment every time I ate them.

Stress affects our food choices and the makeup of the gut microbiome, which constantly communicates with the brain. When a person is feeling stressed, the body will automatically send out cortisol, which is known as the stress hormone. Cortisol can make a person crave salty, fatty and sugary foods because the brain thinks it needs fuel to fight whatever threat is causing the stress. When stress is present, the body is denied essential nutrients—either because it is not breaking down food fast enough or it's discharging the food before it processes it. Without a well-functioning digestive system, sickness becomes prevalent in all areas of the body.

Processed foods have a lot of chemical additives, such as monosodium glutamate, which is used to enhance the flavour. This has been associated with various forms of toxicity and has been linked to obesity, metabolic disorders, and damaging effects on the reproductive organs, to name a few. Also, with processed foods, you will find sugar substitutes such as saccharin and aspartame. Saccharin is used to sweeten low-calorie candies, jellies, jams, and cookies; it can also be used to sprinkle onto food such as cereal or fruit. Saccharin is a compound that can cause allergic reactions in people who cannot tolerate sulpha drugs. Common allergic reactions can include headaches, breathing difficulties and skin irritations. Aspartame is no angel either, as it can increase the risk of metabolic diseases, including type 2 diabetes; some research reports state an increase in risk or disease acceleration for cancer, seizures, weight gain and birth defects.

Consuming a lot of processed foods has also been associated with a higher risk of depression, and I did not need another reason to get depressed. I had always been addicted to high-sugar foods from a young age, and I found that this was contributing towards my neurotransmitter dysregulation, which was putting me out of balance every time I consumed them. Although I would get bouts of a high-energy increase from sugary foods, the energy was fleeting at best, and a sharp drop then followed in my blood sugar levels. This is what we refer to as a "crash".

Next on my list to research was fluoride and this comes from fluorine, which is a common, natural, and abundant element on Earth. Fluoride is found naturally in water, foods, and soil, but it can also be produced synthetically for use in toothpaste, drinking water and chemical products. Excessive exposure to fluoride has been linked to many health issues, such as the bone disease known as skeletal fluorosis, and thyroid problems such as damage to the parathyroid gland, which can result in hyperparathyroidism, the symptoms of which include uncontrolled secretion of parathyroid hormones. This can then result in lower calcium concentration in bones, making them more vulnerable to joint pain and fractures.

After forming a basic understanding of my body's requirements, I started to then focus my energy on failure. Previously I was very narrow-minded and viewed each mistake as a disaster; in turn, this would have an emotion attached to it, and that emotion was always projected from a belief that originated in the past: *you're not good enough, and you're still a bad child*, the voice in my head would say. Understanding failure without the negative emotions attached was crucial. Failure is the most important component to achieving success, and if your perception is only focused on the negative aspects of failure, then it becomes very hard to keep getting back up and trying again. Failure, I learned, was only temporary if I was not prepared to give in, and the tools I had been looking for were right in front of me all along, in terms of the lessons The Talking Universe had been trying to communicate to me; I had just not been consciously aware of them.

Despite my evidential progress, I still was failing, but I would now try again in a different way, and even when that way failed, and it became a repetitive failure, I would again try a new strategy. Because I was not prepared to give up, eventually, I found myself stumbling across success, even if it was not deliberately manufactured. The constant throughout was my determination to keep going, as well as the intelligence I had now acquired to try different approaches. Albert Einstein sums this up perfectly.

"The definition of insanity is doing the same thing over and over again and expecting different results."
—Albert Einstein

My goals were very small at the start, but the more I progressed, the bigger they became. A whole host of people have been through severe degrees of trauma and gone on to succeed, so why couldn't I be one of those people? The one constant I took out of all the books I read was that in order to achieve any goal, there will be many setbacks. The people who achieve what they set out to complete very rarely accomplish it the first time. The one constant I picked up was that no matter how many failures one encounters, getting back up and trying again was the most important ingredient one should have. I knew it would not come immediately, or easily, for that matter, but if I had the determination to not give in, then I would achieve whatever I chose in this life of mine.

My pain had now been reduced significantly due to the therapy I had immersed myself in, and a path which I could follow began to emerge. I was now up early each day, focusing on myself, and it did not take long before I began to stop missing the alcohol, drugs, and nights out because I could see the detrimental effects they had been having on me trying to achieve anything substantial with my life.

I was now monitoring myself obsessively and I became very mindful of my behaviour, habits and routine, which I would adjust accordingly. Success is not something that magically happens to you by chance, it's something that happens because of all the small, consistent actions you are willing to participate in daily. The more I began to raise my expectations, the further I retreated from the society I used to be part of. Expanding my limiting beliefs changed my consciousness, which then began to alter my reality.

I was now investing in myself by eating healthier, exercising at home, and expanding my knowledge through each book I read. It was no coincidence that my skin became clearer, I began to sleep better, and my energy was no longer so fluctuating. I had started the process of raising my vibrational state, which contributed towards my well-being. Each person's vibrational state is reflected in accordance with how well they interact with

204

the natural laws of life. Previously I had been trapped in a low vibrational state which consisted of trying to shy away from my darkness, drinking poison (alcohol), taking drugs, and eating processed food that was not aligned with what my body needed to function in an optimal way. I have made a list of low vibrational attributes, which will create distortions and disharmony in your auric field that will eventually manifest into physical disease.

Low vibrational:

1. Limiting beliefs.
2. Suppressing trauma and not expressing your emotions freely.
3. Processed or junk food.
4. Anxiety or stress.
5. Living in the past or future tripping.
6. Consistent exposure to electronic devices such as your phone or computer.
7. Negative self-talk or negative thinking patterns, including judging or criticising.
8. Energy vampires.
9. Spending a lot of time in places that are not natural.

When you are not living in the natural laws of life you become disconnected from your higher self and a bad copy of reality manipulates your perception, and you have created this through your own actions. When a person becomes distanced from a healthy environment— through either suppressing their emotions or losing access to clean air, fresh water or healthy food a separation begins to form, and this is where you will find disease. If we take a plant as an example and we look at the total system a plant requires to grow, flourish, and then reach its potential, we will see that it needs the correct temperature, sunlight, moisture and nutrients. when a plant does not receive what it needs, the whole plant will not reach its maximum potential; a human being is no different to this basic system. The understanding of self comes from understanding the animals, plants, and planet; once you are able to grasp that, you can then begin to understand how we can all use the natural resources that have been put here on Earth to help us go on to thrive. The polar opposite of not living in accordance with our higher self is called soul loss. Jeff Brown describes it brilliantly.

" Consider the following as possible symptoms of your spiritual homelessness: chronic illness; listlessness: unconscious consumerism; self-distractive behaviour; egocentricity and narcissism; nightmares; images of gloom and doom during waking hours; dullness of eyes; perpetual dissatisfaction; addictive behaviours; heartlessness; hopelessness; chronic rigidity; inexplicable agitation, rage, or grief."

–Jeff Brown

When soul loss is experienced, a part of our psyche hides or shuts away, and this hinders us from experiencing and then expressing our true potential as human beings; often, entire aspects of our psyches are completely blocked out or repressed. When people think of soul loss, it's easy to believe that parts of our soul become lost mistakenly, like how we lose a set of keys that we have put down somewhere, but this is not the case. Rather, soul loss literally means "losing connection with the soul". Each soul is completely whole, undivided, and can never be destroyed. Instead, it is our psyches or psychological egos that become fragmented, so when a part of our conscious self goes into hiding, it creates a blockage in the subconscious mind, and we refer to this as soul loss because we lose connection to our souls. In other words, it can be a psychological trauma that prevents us from fully opening ourselves to the soul and its sacred source of power, strength, and love. Unfortunately, these days soul loss is the rule rather than the exception. As individuals, we lose our soulful energy every time we identify with our ego, and we seek to feel whole again through various addictions and external validation. Self-love is a direct path of communion with the soul, and solitude is a direct pathway to your own inner world. Solitude, if used correctly, can give insight, perspective and reinstate harmony in your life. The result of not practising self-love is depression, bitterness, and resentment.

By living according to the natural laws of life, a person can connect to their purest state of being, consisting of innocence, light and purity. Everything has a vibration, and in order to attract what I wanted into my life, I had to match that vibration through my thoughts, but what I consciously wanted was only a small piece of the larger puzzle to yet unfold. In order to become high vibrational, which would facilitate my healing process, I needed to focus on as many high vibrational attributes as possible. I have listed the ones I know.

High vibrational:

1. Become conscious of your thoughts; everything you think or feel can become your reality.

2. Find something beautiful and love it (love is the highest form of energy that there is)

3. Surround yourself in nature as much as possible and let your bare skin touch these environments (nature has healing properties which we can connect to)

4. Invest in some crystals, but only choose ones that you feel aligned with. A lot of the healing I required could be facilitated by rose quartz.

5. Be conscious of the foods you consume and eat natural foods whenever possible. Try to include different coloured fruits and vegetables as digested food is consumed and then altered into colour light impulses; this creates a level of vibrational energy our blood cells absorb (nothing is physical, everything is energy, even food).

6. Drink lots of natural water. Filtered water is advised to reduce any unnatural chemical consumption.

7. Meditate consistently, create silence, and allow your inner voice to surface. All the answers you require will come from within (I was not meditating yet, but I will move on to this later in the book.)

8. Be grateful and appreciate your blessings. Sometimes we take for granted the small things in life, such as clean water and a roof over our heads.

9. Practise acts of kindness, give where possible and help others where you can.

10. Get your blood pumping through physical exercise.

11. Express all of your emotions

All of these are vital and essential for our existence and all of the barriers we face, can be traced to energy blockages in the human energy system, and it is one of the reasons why preserving nature is urgent; it is the most important place where we gather energy from for healing ourselves. You won't find such a high quality of energy in a nightclub or while driving down the motorway; this beautiful energy comes from nature alone.

Energy is neither created nor destroyed, but the form and qualities of energy can be changed. Through our thoughts, our intentions, and the choices we make, the energy that we put back into our world can reach a more vibrant level than it did when we first took it in. This happens when we have a pure conscious intention for it to occur. By doing this, everything around us will benefit from this change, and that's how we then start to change the world, by each of us taking small actions inwardly to change ourselves.

Okay, let's now discuss the energetic field. We all live in an energetic field or an energetic ocean, as some call it, but what does this mean? It's the total of all energy in all forms of existence. Our awareness only includes a microscopic percentage of this; however, we can be affected by every single thing that is in the energetic ocean, both positive and negative. Through the field, we are interconnected with our environment through emotions, nature, time, colours, food, objects, and sound; we experience the effects when any one of these comes into our range of influence. Addiction, abuse, and suppressed trauma produce negative vibrations, which cause imbalances and imprints on a person's auric field. This becomes detrimental to not only our own well-being but everyone else we come into contact with as we go on to contaminate everything in our surroundings.

So, does this energy field really exist? Scientists can actually measure the electromagnetic field close to our skin. Throughout the ages, people have been fully aware of the human energy field, whether it be from ancient Egypt, Greece, or China to name a few. In Hindu tradition, it was called Prana, in China, it's called Ch'i, while Pythagoras in ancient Greece wrote of "vital energy" as in the luminous body. Many researchers now agree that the human energy field exists before the physical body, and this is an electromagnetic field which is our aura or what some call our light body. This field constantly interacts with our physical body through concentrated energy which we call our life force energy, and it is imperative that you keep this topped up correctly with all the right ingredients; you have a duty to yourself to do this, as no one will do it for you.

In the 1940s, Russian scientist Semyon Kirlian discovered a type of photographic image that was later named Kirlian photography after him.

This provides us with evidence that living objects display an electrical discharge, known as corona discharge, close to the skin. An advancement later came called electrography, a technique that enables images of the whole body and internal organs to be seen.

The more I began to learn about energy I saw how our healing process is hindered by Western medicine and the idea that the mind and body are both separate entities. Clinicians treat the mind (psychology or psychiatry) or the body (every other branch of medicine) and rarely, if ever, incorporate treatment for both at the same time. This arbitrary separation of mind and body holds humanity back from its potential for healing, and sometimes in the process, we become sicker. Indigenous and eastern cultures, on the other hand, have fully recognised and honoured the connections between the mind, body, and soul/spirit—the sense of something higher than ourselves—for thousands of years. Mainstream Western medicine has long deemed this connection unscientific, so it decides to ignore it in many instances. In the 17th century, the concept of "mind-body dualism", a literal disconnection between mind and body, was birthed by the French philosopher Rene Descartes; this dichotomy persists hundreds of years later, and yet we still treat the mind as distinct from the body.

As technology advanced in the 19th century, the world learned more about human biology and the ways in which things in our environment can harm us; medicine then became a field of intervention. When symptoms emerge, a physician manages them by eradicating or treating them with prescription medicines that come with known and unknown side effects. Instead of listening to the body—after all, symptoms are its way of communicating to us—we instead seek to silence it, and in the process of suppressing symptoms, we often suffer various new harms. The idea of a

211

whole-person approach to care has been cast aside in favour of the symptom management approach, which does not treat the root cause of the issue, and this has created a vicious cycle of dependence where we focus on treating individual symptoms as they arise instead of looking for the underlying cause. The Western medical philosophy is no different from how we handle our societal problems: we treat the symptoms and not the root causes. Healing is a daily event. You don't go somewhere to be healed. Instead, you must understand yourself and how you interact with your environment. Your body always vibrates at a certain frequency, and if you let your energy get too low, you begin to suffer from harm.

By engaging all parts of the brain simultaneously, we are each able to make changes in our minds and, therefore, our bodies at very deep levels. Each person's reality reflects what they think, so if we are not living within the natural laws of life and healing ourselves, and instead if we are suppressing trauma and being victims to our subconscious programming, then negativity is what projects out into our existence through ourselves unconsciously. What we need is a well-balanced integration of all parts of the brain and a method for dealing with the subconscious mind and its inherent belief system. I will discuss the one I used further throughout my story. Beliefs carried by the subconscious mind can wreak havoc on people's ability to create the life and health their conscious mind desires. A huge part of manifestation is related to the subconscious mind and today's science estimates that it controls around 95 per cent of our brain's activity. This relates to the majority of the decisions we make, our everyday actions, and our emotions and behaviours, all of which lie beyond our conscious awareness. Now when a person manifests, only a very small percentage is attributed to their conscious desires, and that's why so many people are living a life that they cannot relate to. So, in my case, I would go to manifest my conscious desires alongside a huge amount of my ingrained beliefs from my childhood which were stored in my subconscious mind. Part of healing is about changing our beliefs and, therefore, our perceptions of reality; in fact, how we experience all of our emotions, whether anger, hatred, or fear, is greatly affected by the beliefs we hold on to. Beliefs are essential to our survival, so the whole manifestation process heavily involves understanding the subconscious mind.

At the turn of the 20th century, a new breed of physicists evolved whose mission was to probe the relationship between energy and the structure of matter. Physicists then began to abandon their beliefs in a Newtonian material universe because they had come to realise that the concept of matter is an illusion, for they now recognised that everything in the universe is made out of energy. Quantum physicists discovered that physical atoms are made out of vortices of energy that are constantly spinning and vibrating. Each atom is like a wobbly spinning top that radiates energy. Because each atom has its own specific energy signature (wobble), assemblies of atoms (molecules) collectively radiate their own identifying energy patterns. So, every material structure in the universe, including you, me, and your pet dog, radiates a unique energy signature. The fact that energy and matter are one and the same is precisely what Einstein recognised when he concluded that $E = mc2$. Einstein revealed that we do not live in a universe with discrete, physical objects separated by dead space. The universe is one indivisible, dynamic whole in which energy and matter are so closely entangled it is impossible to consider them as separate elements. Although the awareness that different mechanics control the structure and behaviour of matter should have offered biomedicine new insights and understanding into health and disease, people are still trained to view the body only as a physical machine that operates according to Newtonian principles. Because of the Newtonian, materialistic bias, conventional researchers have completely ignored the role that energy vibrations play in health and disease.

For thousands of years, long before Western scientists discovered the laws of quantum physics, Asians have honoured energy as the principal factor contributing to health and well-being. In eastern medicine, the body is defined by an elaborate array of energy pathways called meridians. In Chinese physiological charts of the human body, these energy networks resemble electronic wiring diagrams. Using aids like acupuncture needles, Chinese physicians test their patients' energy circuits in exactly the same manner that electrical engineers "troubleshoot" a printed circuit board, searching for electrical pathologies. Understanding the above meant that in the future, acupuncture would be the course of action I would need to take. As a society, we need to step back and incorporate the discoveries of quantum physics into biomedicine so that we can create a new, safer system of medicine that is attuned to the laws of the natural world.

The reality of the quantum universe and the mind (energy) arises from the physical body; however, our new understanding of the universe's mechanics shows us how the physical body can be affected by the immaterial mind. Thoughts, the mind's energy, directly influence how the physical brain controls the body's physiology. Thought (energy) can activate or inhibit a cell's function of producing proteins via the mechanics of constructive and destructive interference. When I started to change my life, I actively monitored where I was expending my brain's energy. I had to examine the consequences of the energy I invested into my thoughts as closely as I examined the expenditure of energy I used to power my physical body. A big problem I had was dispelling huge amounts of energy in the wrong direction without being consciously aware. This is a huge problem I see in society today because the majority of people are just not conscious.

So, with my newly adopted philosophy, I began to put into practice what I had learned. So, you would think the first thing I would manifest before anything else would be to heal myself, right? *No, no, no, I had ten therapy sessions, I am already healed,* I thought. Being healed in my mind meant that I wanted superficial things above anything else, and the spiritual path was now a gateway for me to achieve exactly that. I was still holding on to anger and resentment at this time in my life, and I wanted to prove every single person wrong who had disregarded or doubted me, all the people who said I would be dead or in jail by the time I was 21, and what's the best way to do that coming from the world I was once part of? It was to show that I had acquired a substantial amount of material wealth! All of my manifestations were coming from a deep routed place of negativity which consisted of resentment, rejection, and pain; it was no surprise then that I would eventually manifest material wealth alongside people who became resentful of me, people who rejected me, and people who caused me serious pain. My childhood issues had still not been resolved, and until they were, I would never be able to find what my soul longed for:

TRUTH LOVE PEACE

As time progressed, work began to improve, and my nightmares were now few and far between. Instead, they were replaced with vivid dreams and imaginations. After eight months of solitude, I had gone from earning £45 a week with my new business to £3,000 a week. The dark days still arrived, but they were definitely fewer, and my moods had gradually improved. I had not taken any medication, and this was the proof I needed to realise that I could, indeed, work through my pain in the correct way. I was not a powerless biochemical machine, popping a pill every time I was mentally or physically out of tune, as I knew this was not the answer. Drugs and surgery are powerful tools, but the notion of simple drug fixes is fundamentally flawed. Every time a drug is introduced into the body to correct function 1, it inevitably throws off functions 2, 3, or 4. Our beliefs are what control our bodies and minds, which in turn direct our lives, and my story will show you living proof of that.

"It is not the strongest of the species that survives, nor the most intelligent, but the one most responsive to change."
—Charles Darwin

As work gathered pace, Simon eventually took the plunge and came to join me full-time. I felt apprehensive at first as I had taken all the risks, but I was grateful to him for opening the door, which enabled me to run a business in the first place, so I felt I owed him. I had now diversified and gone in search of multiple clients across two sectors, and I had learned from my past by not having all my eggs in one basket. After getting several smaller clients to trust and give me work, I managed to get a client on board who, following a successful loan period, wanted to take three of my men on full-time. The candidates I had were joiners, and they were working on a project at the University of Leeds. The client was extremely impressed with them, so they called and then proceeded to offer me £9,000 (£3,000 for each joiner). The money was extremely tempting at the time, and my initial instinct was to take it, but by doing this, I was only thinking short-term. Instead, I thought about what options I had available to me, and I listened to my inner voice by allowing it to surface, and after sleeping on it, I decided to go back to them with an alternative offer. I thought about what would benefit me long term, and the answer was to have consistent business from this client, which I knew could be available due to the projects they were working on at that time. I then said to the client, "You can keep the £9,000 and take the guys for £1,000 each — so, £3,000 in total." It was a huge discount for them. I said, "In order for you to have them at this price instead, I want the sole right to supply any staff required into your company."

I was not sure if they would accept my counteroffer, but I had been working with them for around six months by this point, and I had supplied them with candidates not only in Leeds but also in London and Bournemouth. I had always delivered on each occasion this company had asked anything of me. After a couple of further conversations and having been slightly reluctant at first, the client agreed to my proposition. The main issue they had was that they did not want to get tied into something if I could not deliver, so I put a clause into the contract which stated that if I could not source the labour for them within 48 hours, they could use alternative companies. This turned out to be a great business decision as I consistently had up to 15 men out working with this client for the next year.

I had now realised the impact of having money and how it had made me feel, which was secure, but what was equally as important at the time was having my stepdad Ian and my new clients believe in me. I spent a large proportion of my life thinking my mum and Ian were against me and that they thought I would not amount to anything. By thinking these thoughts, I closed the door so tightly that they could never open it to get

217

inside and help me. As soon as I was prepared to trust and open that door, I saw that they loved and believed in me. All along, it was my destructive thinking patterns that were causing the cycles of devastation I kept finding myself trapped in.

I was now ready to start living my life with clarity, imagination, and, most importantly, honesty. I had begun the process of change, and I liked the new person I was now becoming. Before, when I looked in the mirror, I saw an old, washed-up 30-year-old with no future, but I was now a 31-year-old, vibrant young man with the world at his feet, and everything was attainable and within reach.

By making and keeping small promises to myself, I developed my daily routine and habits. Discipline is an important part of the healing process, and cultivating it helps a person to show up for themselves. By creating new habits and proving to ourselves that we are worth showing up for, we build a sense of inner reliability, resilience, and courage that instils a deep sense of confidence that touches all aspects of a person's life. The key is to do something every day and do it consistently.

My greatest asset would be found in my ability to learn from experience, for even though I had made many mistakes, my newly acquired knowledge and determination were my salvation. Whenever my depression or despair was at its peak, I could self-reflect and start rebuilding myself again.

"Absorb what is useful,
Discard what is not,
Add what is uniquely your own."
—Bruce Lee

Chapter 12 – Actor

(A person who acts)

Change was now apparent, but it had taken extreme courage and many disappointments. A year had now passed, and I felt ready to integrate myself back into the world, so I left Batley and moved to Manchester city centre. Settling into Manchester was easy-going, and although the dark days would still arrive, they were definitely less frequent than they had been before, and I was now well equipped to deal with them. Waking up each day with my newly acquired mindset helped my brain to naturally produce dopamine, serotonin, oxytocin, and endorphins; this then transformed my previous destructive thinking patterns into creative ones.

At this point in my life, money was still the biggest factor in what I deemed 'success'. From the outside, people could view me as a very money-orientated person, which was correct to some degree. There was a deeper meaning behind this though, money enabled me to feel safe and when I had struggled in the past, I found myself triggered and the feelings of being homeless again would come to the surface very quickly.

The more I practiced self-care the more my environment changed. As I felt myself changing the thought of running a recruitment company long-term was something I no longer felt aligned to. Although I was earning a reasonable amount of money, I found it unfulfilling, and I knew that this was not my purpose in life. I had now consciously started to think about other opportunities and at this stage, it was just my thoughts. I have previously spoken about the power of intention and as I began putting thoughts out into the universe for a desire to change my circumstances, guess what happened? The Talking Universe responded and gave me what I thought I wanted.

*Stage 6: **Tests, Allies, Enemies.** Struggles appear, and difficult challenges happen in various ways, causing obstacles that thwart my progress.*

      With Simon and I no longer working together in the same place, I began to feel distant towards him and my intuition began warning me something was wrong, so I started looking for evidence. After deciding to log into Simon's work emails, I found information that I was not happy with, and looking back, I can see that this gave me the excuse I needed to end my relationship with him. After searching, I found emails that Simon had purposely kept from me. One of the emails was from a manager of a client I had built a relationship with to supply them with traffic management staff. The email stated that Simon had sent nine candidates down to an interview in which they had not been briefed about the job role. After continuing my search, I found more disturbing emails, so I decided to ring two of my clients. One of these clients told me on the phone that if Simon continued to manage the account, they would stop giving me further work. The second client—the client I had previously struck a deal with by supplying them with three permanent joiners—said they wanted to deal directly with me, as they did not like Simon's approach. Simon was taking advantage of me, but I inherently felt that I owed him for helping me start this line of work in the first place.

      After a discussion with Simon, I was left feeling let down, and I decided that it was the right time for us to part ways. Simon was far from happy with my decision, but as the company was in my name and I had taken all of the risk initially, and every single client was brought on by myself, he had no choice but to accept my decision, and this resulted in a falling out between us. I was angry at the time, so I reacted in an angry way instead of rationally discussing everything with him. I had made my mind up within an instant, and nothing was going to change it. When I look back, I can see that we were both heading in different directions in our lives and although I made the right decision, I could have definitely managed the situation in a better way. After Simon left, I started to lose interest in the business and was now doing the bare minimum.

At the same time as losing interest in my business, I had begun to make some new friends, and I started to enjoy getting my social life back again. I was now spending my time going to the gym, out to restaurants for food, and mainly just socialising. The first time I went out for drinks in Manchester was with a girl I knew who lived in my apartment block. I had decided to have a drink after not touching alcohol for over a year, and I recall feeling tipsy when it came around to me ordering the second round of drinks. I had debated internally about not drinking, but I knew I would never return to the same life I had before.

On this night out, I was approached by a person called Ben, who was with a few of his friends. Ben had walked over to me and started making random conversation, and after a chat, he asked me if I fancied a shot at the bar. At the bar, I got talking to two of his friends, Jason and Ben, again. These people all seemed very friendly, and they decided to join us at the table. After chatting for a while, I decided that I was going to head back home, but Jason had brought up the idea of going to a nightclub, and the girl I was with knew a promoter who could get us a table. After deciding to stay out, I ended up having a really good time, and I did not get anxious or feel

221

panicky. Throughout the night, I struck up a good relationship with Jason, and by the end, he had taken my number and said that he would drop me a text the next time he was going out.

A couple of weeks passed, and I had exchanged a few text messages with Jason, and he had asked to meet on two separate occasions for a catch-up drink. On both occasions, I declined because although I had enjoyed myself that night, I was also wary of slipping back into old habits. One afternoon, however, Jason texted me for a third time, asking if I was free to meet up for a chat in a bar. He wanted to speak to me about something business related as I had told him that I owned a recruitment company. With the bar being only a short walk away from my apartment, I decided to pop down and meet him as I was interested in what he had to say.

Jason had turned up with his laptop, and as I sat down, he explained his current job role to me. He said that he worked as a transformation manager for OYO, which was the second-largest hotel chain in the world. I was surprised at how big this company was, mainly because I had never heard of them before. Jason then explained that he was in charge of the northern region, and he got to choose what contractors he used to redevelop these hotels. If I was interested, "I can throw some work your way," he said. With me already looking for a new opportunity, I thought, *why not?* Jason had also explained about the money that we could earn; I say 'we' because he wanted a cut, of course, but to be honest, I took his figures with a pinch of salt as they sounded very extravagant.

After our chat, I began redeveloping hotels with Jason within four weeks. The workload became manic very quickly so Jason's friend Ben, whom I had met during the night out with Jason, came to work with us as well. Ben was looking for a new opportunity, so I gave him some training and got him to run my recruitment company, but after several months of Ben trying to kickstart the business, it eventually closed itself.

As I began working in the hotel industry, the figures Jason spoke about then became a reality, and I earned in excess of £50,000 some months. The money was nothing like what I had experienced before, and I felt so thankful for the opportunity that Jason had given me. At the time, it did not even cross my mind that this opening was too good to be true, and I had assumed everything was happening because of all the changes I had made in my life; life was now finally rewarding me, I thought. As I based money above everything else, I manifested this current set of circumstances I had now found myself in.

The more money I would go on to earn, the less I focused on my self-care routine as it became not important for me to maintain once I was earning money. I had always dreamed of being in a position such as this, but eventually, I started to decline, although I would never end up back where I once was.

My situation was essentially this:

Me: Finally, I have everything I wished for.

The universe's response: Wait a sec, I'm not done with you just yet, boy.

At the start, Jason was great: he was charming, intelligent, and we became good friends. With everything going well, work became entwined with us going for food and nights out on the weekend. What had started to happen, though, was I began slipping back into a routine of socially drinking and taking drugs on the weekends again. Although I went out and enjoyed myself, I knew that I had to be careful because I had been down this road many times before. I could have easily lost myself around Jason because he was reckless and a free spirit at the best of times.

Because I was so inexperienced in this new sector I was working in, I started spending a lot of time with Jason. I was trying my hardest to absorb as much information as I possibly could, as I did not want to ruin this opportunity. I would go with Jason to hotel meetings, I went to the main office in Manchester, where I met other transformation managers, and I even went with him to sign hotels on occasions. Some of the hotels we worked on were operational at the time, so Jason had to coordinate which rooms would be blocked out on the days we worked. Often problems occurred, and deadlines felt impossible to achieve, which would then cause severe disruptions. The work we did was very varied, and we supplied people to do jobs such as fitting fire alarms, doing fire safety checks, installing emergency lighting, fixing anything from the roof to a boiler, building false walls, painting and decorating, fitting new bathrooms, and laying flooring.

For the next six months, I gave it everything I had. Because I had come from such struggles and had been looking for an opportunity like this all my life, I could not see that if I carried on as I was doing, I would eventually burn out. The deadlines and stress only increased the pressure for both of us as time passed. With not enough time to think or formulate any plans, I became consumed by the nature of the job, which then raised my stress levels to an unmanageable level. The pressure I put on myself to attain as much money as possible, coupled with having no infrastructure or permanent staff I could rely on, meant that a disaster was always around the corner, and eventually, it just became too much for me. I was never going to walk away from the amount of money I was earning, but I needed to figure out how I could carry on without the job, causing me so much stress.

I had now decided to take a much-needed break to the Dominican Republic to clear my head. Instead of relaxing, though, I kept worrying about work as I knew I would have to return back to the same situation. I had started to gravitate away from Jason in the weeks leading up to my holiday. On one occasion, he was supposed to go on holiday to Ibiza for three days, but instead, he returned nine days later without telling or keeping me informed. At that time, he did not answer his phone, and I was left to make decisions with which I had no experience to do so, and I was put into so many difficult situations with people demanding answers. I had always accepted that there would be some consequence for earning the amount of money I was because money had always come with consequences in my childhood, and it was another belief of mine. I was where I always dreamed of being in life, which was earning crazy amounts of money, but I began to feel so unhappy again. I had based all my desires on achieving monetary success, so I believed that once I had achieved this target, I would be relieved of the pain I still inherently felt, but this just wasn't the case.

Anyway, back to the holiday. In the Dominican Republic, I remember being in a bar in the hotel complex watching Manchester United vs Liverpool (I never missed a United game). While watching the match, I got talking to a guy at the bar who was also on holiday from Manchester. On my way home, I saw the same person again on the plane, and we said hello and had a brief chat on the aisle of the aeroplane. Then, after returning back home, three weeks or so had passed, and I was training at a local gym and guess who randomly walks into the gym! The same person who I had met at the bar over in the Dominican Republic and had seen on the plane. We were both in total shock to see each other, so this time, we decided to exchange phone numbers. Over the coming weeks, we went to the gym together, and I found out that this person had just left his job and he was actively seeking a new opportunity. It then turned out that the role he had left was working as a project manager for the hotel chain Premier Inn. *What a coincidence,* I thought. *Maybe he could do my job!*

So, what is synchronicity? Synchronicities are moments of meaningful coincidence where our inner and outer worlds align. Often synchronicity is an excellent way to tell that you are on the right soul path because everything feels right and as though life is unfolding without your conscious effort. Science, as we have discussed, attests to the fact that everything is energy and thus connected, so synchronicity is when the vibration of our thoughts matches the vibration of our personal destinies. These signs confirmed to me that my manifestations were working, and although my conscious mind had manifested this situation, my inherent beliefs were about to dictate and control the bigger picture.

I then decided to introduce this person to Jason, and we all met up for a coffee and spoke about him taking over my role, and I could then move into the background overseeing everything. Jason liked him straight away and was happy, so I decided to give him an opportunity, and he began working.

I realised that I was burning out, and I had changed the dynamics of the situation to relieve my stress levels. I had made a change and thought I had made a responsible decision; this decision was proof that I was learning to listen to my body, and I was indeed progressing.

Stage 7: Approaching the Innermost Cave. Reaching the central crisis of the journey.

Having money and more time available allowed me to go out and spoil myself, so I moved into a bigger penthouse, I bought a Bentley Continental, and I spent some of my hard-earned money on further material items to validate myself. Was I showing off? Of course, I fucking was—I wanted to prove to everyone that I had overcome what I had lived through. By behaving in this way, not being grounded, and being more concerned with my external environment, I was letting my anger and low self-esteem dictate the direction of my life, and I made myself an easy target. The way I was behaving was not contributing to my healing process, and in my mind, I was already healed, so it meant that my healing process was a thing of the past.

Despite therapy, my opinions and beliefs had not inherently changed. The decisions I would then make and how I would assert myself were conflicted as I still did not trust myself. I believed inherently that I did not matter and was not good enough, which created internal feelings of shame, guilt and that all-too-familiar depression. I never believed I deserved happiness because inherently, I still thought I was a "bad child".

With me now showing off, Jason became jealous of me. I was told this by another contractor who worked for me at the time, and I was sent certain conversations that he had recorded. The conversations consisted of what car I was driving and how much money I had, and they revolved around the way I looked. Jason denied all of this and played the role of an actor despite me having physical evidence. Despite this, I had not helped myself in the slightest with how I was behaving, and yet again, my childhood was continuing to dictate the pattern of my life.

Once my project manager became involved, as well as other contractors like the one who was supplying me with information in regard to what Jason was saying behind my back, things started to turn very messy. The relationship between Jason and me had started to decline massively, and Jason was now socialising with my project manager and spending time with him just like he did with me at the start. Things were now about to change significantly. A big argument had transpired when Jason took my project manager out for what he called "a champagne lunch". They had both run up a £300 bill on my card! The money did not bother me, but what did was the fact that I was only told the following day when I received a text message stating, "Thanks for the champagne lunch yesterday. Jason LOL". *What a fucking tool,* I thought as I looked at my phone. Light travels faster than sound, and this is why people like Jason appear bright until they open their fucking mouths.

The final straw came when I received a phone call one afternoon from the same contractor who had recorded and sent me several pieces of information in the past. At the time, I thought this contractor was being loyal to me, but what I found out eventually was that he was trying to get the work for himself from the hotel chain, so he was playing me off against Jason and our project manager. I am sure that a contributing factor in how Jason behaved was also due to this contractor feeding Jason lies. Things got so bad that this contractor refused to work with our project manager, and he had made threats on the phone to me that he was going to attack him, so there were dramas happening everywhere at this point. This contractor had warned me that Jason and my project manager were going to set up a rival company to cut me out! At first, I did not believe him, but I felt my heart sink when I took a moment to piece everything together. This contractor then said to me, "I am going to send you proof again." I then remember putting the phone down, and feeling anxious, unsettled and sick! All were apparent signs to inform me that a disaster was about to happen.

Later that afternoon, as promised, the contractor sent me a voice recording. This recording confirmed that my project manager had set up a bank account, and he and Jason were just waiting for the right time to get rid of me. After hearing the voice recording, I completely lost myself, and those dark emotional feelings I had felt from my childhood came rushing to the surface quicker than a hit of crack cocaine; I had now been triggered massively.

I was not totally oblivious to what had been going on, and I knew prior to this voice recording that Jason's behaviour could result in me getting burned at some point. I had thrown all my eggs into one basket before, and I was never going to make that same mistake again, so I had set up a contingency plan. A month or so prior to this happening, I had contacted other transformation managers. Jason's character had started to raise red flags with me—with his excessive drug taking, drinking, and missing time off work. I knew that he was not going to be in this company long term, and I had to protect myself. All the meetings I had attended went very well, and I told Jason about this as I had nothing to hide. Jason did warn me against this, though, and he said he could not protect me if I messed up without him there. Although his statement was true, I could sense an ulterior motive once again.

Stage 8: The Ordeal. *Undergoing the plunge into darkness, the great death and rebirth.*

Each person has their own journey in life, and just as my mum could not save me, I could not save Jason. He needed to be the one to help himself. I mean, I couldn't even help myself despite therapy, and I was still using external validation to cover up my rock-bottom self of esteem. At the time, I could not see that in an attempt to heal my own vulnerability, I viewed others as helpless, incapable, and needing of my help.

Jason became an opponent, and this upset me. My ego then went into hyperdrive in an attempt to figure out why and to keep myself safe by insisting that I would never do something so terrible. Our egos do this when a person does a bad thing: we reason that since we are good ourselves, we would never behave in the way they have. This is why judging others becomes so addictive; it relieves us from the ego's internal struggle with dealing with shame. When we identify the fault of others, we can ignore our own issues and even convince ourselves that we are superior.

Our physiology communicates the level of safety through the process of co-regulation. Our internal state is often mirrored by those around us, making our inner worlds contagious; when we feel safe, others feel safe too. The trouble is that the reverse is also true. This is the key reason why I found it impossible to connect with people because I was still living with a dysregulated nervous system, and inherently, I still felt unsafe. Despite going through therapy, I never felt safe enough to fully connect with others because I had not accessed or worked on my subconscious programming.

After I had processed everything, I realised that what was coming was inevitable. I then began to doubt myself and even thought, *Have I changed as a person? Is Jason doing this to me because I am just a bad person, deep down?* All those feelings from my past resurfaced again; however, this was a clear sign that there was an underlying issue that was causing the situation I had found myself in, but again, with no other point of awareness, I put everything down to Jason being an untrustworthy person. Why? Because I believed inherently that people were untrustworthy. Jason was untrustworthy, as you will go on to eventually see, but I had manifested his energy into my life due to my belief system.

After confronting Jason, I tried to approach the situation rationally, but as soon as I spoke to him on the phone, I lost it—something I am not proud of. The old Jamie came out, and I threatened to drive to his house, and I got as far as my car before I called my mum out of desperation. I remember my stepdad Ian came onto the phone, and he knew straight away that I was in trouble and not thinking rationally. At this point, I was not accessing my cortex, and all my lower brain functions had taken over. Ian had told me to calm down and not to do anything stupid. He had said that I was better than that, and I could not go back to being the person I once was. Getting good advice from Ian and my mum over a sustained period of time built up trust, which gradually changed my perception of them. Now when they spoke to me, I viewed it as positive reinforcement instead of what I used to, which was a negative reinforcement.

After coming off the phone, I realised I did not want to be an angry person anymore, and by reacting how I did, I had shown that I still had a long way to go in my self-development. My first port of call was to act on my negative emotions. Luckily, though, this time, I had recognised it before it was too late, and out of desperation, I had turned to my mum and Ian. The conversation with Ian saved me from serious harm that day, and I felt like he was a guardian angel who had been sent to me just at the right time. What had actually transpired, though, was that because I was changing as a person and had allowed positive influences to come into my life, in a moment of crisis, I had a support network around me whom I could fall back on, so I took the advice of Ian which was coming from a place of love and protection towards me. When you do not have people around you who can help rationalise your own thoughts within times of extreme emotions, things can get out of hand and escalate very quickly.

After getting angry, I eventually calmed down and broke down crying; I did not want to be this angry person in an angry body anymore. You can read a thousand books and listen to as many podcasts as you want, but the information will only sink into a certain level. As they say, the proof in the pudding is in your actions during any testing experiences that follow. Only at that point will a person truly know what they have absorbed and then learned.

A few days had now passed when I was driving to see my friend. When I pulled into the car park, I received a 10-minute, 36-second voice recording from Jason. He was crying in this recording, saying how bad he felt for betraying me and that he was sorry. He was begging me to forgive him and said that he had made a huge mistake. Jason explained that he had spoken to his mum and that he needed to make things right between us. I then sent this voice recording to Cori, the girl who I had been seeing in Leeds previously, as we were now friends, and I then asked for her opinion as she was one of the few people I trusted. Cori said under no circumstances should I have any contact with him ever again. She had listened to the voice recording and said, "He has acknowledged that you have tried to help him, but he still went and stabbed you in the back. Remove him immediately."

232

Despite Cori's advice, I decided to give Jason another chance, and I employed a new project manager, my friend Leon, but things were never the same. The work had now started to decrease, and although I tried to trust Jason again, Leon told me certain things that Jason was again saying behind my back. Eventually I messaged Jason and said, "Stay out of my life." I then transferred him £10,000 and said, "This money is for what you have done for me."

In Batley, I had created a healthy, balanced life, but that went out of the window as soon as I had achieved my primary objective of earning money. I had not grasped that in order to continue my healing process, I had to live by the daily routine I had created in solitude, and it was not a destination to get to and then bin off. Being in a negative environment which revolved around money, distrust, and anger, coupled with no self-care, had created a negative life for me once again.

An enormous obstacle on a person's journey to inner work and spiritual wholeness is our tendency to become enamoured by the promise of peace and love. In the process, a person can shy away from experiencing the more challenging and darker elements of self-exploration. Love and light have a place on each of our journeys, but if these brighter, more appealing qualities are empathised to the degree that involves repression of the darkness, and resistance to the harder aspects of inner exploration, then we are creating an imbalance within ourselves, and that's exactly what happened with me. I buried my darkness further because money was my main target as it gave me validation, and the negative experiences just became acceptable as long as they came with a financial reward.

After all the commotion, I decided to finally shut the business down. I had decided that it was time to ring my accountant and tell him what had happened. Jason had initially put me in touch with this accountant,

Haroon. After I briefly explained the situation on the phone to him, Haroon paused, then after a few seconds, he told me that he needed to tell me something and he would ring me back after he had finished work. I remember putting the phone down and wondering what Haroon might say when he called me back.

When Haroon rang me back, he proceeded to talk "off the record", as he put it. He explained to me that Jason had done a very dishonest thing years back to a friend of his, Jangir. Jangir and Jason had opened up a company together, and Jason had run up £50k worth of debt, then left the company, dissolving his name. Jangir was then left with the liability to pay back all of the money on his own. I was shocked at first, but when I thought about it, I was not surprised.

Haroon then gave me Jangir's number after I asked for it. At the time, Jangir was in Saudi Arabia on holiday. When we spoke, we arranged to meet when he was back a month later.

A month had now passed, and I drove to a service station in Burton-upon-Trent, where I met with both Haroon and Jangir. We all spoke in depth about my situation and what had previously happened with Jangir and Jason. After I left, I felt uplifted. Although what happened to me felt personal at the time, this proof that Jason had done something dishonest to someone else made me think that this had nothing to do with me and that, in fact, it was because Jason was a bad character. In reality, it was just another lesson from The Talking Universe informing me that no amount of money was going to heal me, and I was looking to fill broken parts of myself in all the wrong places. The warnings from the universe were only going to continue to get louder until I fully listened and changed the direction of my life.

A few months then passed, and I found out what I believed would eventually happen. After several warnings, Jason was sacked. I knew he would be sacked at some point due to his erratic behaviour and unstable nature. Looking back, Jason was deceitful, intelligent, manipulative, a drug abuser, and a womaniser. He was no different to my dad and they shared all the same characteristics. Because I had been accustomed to this type of behaviour from my dad growing up, I gravitated towards these types of people because it was familiar to me and familiar feels safer than unfamiliar. Until I was able to consciously recognise this pattern, I could never live the life that my soul truly wanted.

As work came to an end, I realised that I was owed as much as a quarter of a million pound. Jason had always been the bridge for me to get my money, but after we had seized contact, I struggled to get what I was owed. Despite being passed from department to department, I could never seem to get a straight answer. My payment terms were 30 days, and it had now been nine months since I was last paid. Eventually, in 2019, after 12 months and me threatening legal action with the help of Cori who was a lawyer, I received some, if not all, of the money I was owed. I then decided to take a much-needed break and went travelling. My stress levels were all over the place at this point, and as you have already seen a number of times in my life, running was a way of trying to rid myself of my problems.

Stage 9: Reward. Emerging triumphant with new gifts and strengths.

I spent the next six months travelling to various places all over the world. First, I set off to Canada to see one of my old friends who had moved over there. While in Canada, I spent some time in Toronto, I went to Wasaga, which has the largest freshwater beach in the world, and I visited Niagara Falls, which was an amazing experience. After Canada, I travelled with some friends to Edinburgh for a weekend. While in Edinburgh, we all visited the castle, and I could not believe how beautiful the city was in general. After Edinburgh, I went with another friend to Italy and France. We decided to hire a car, and we spent our time driving through the most beautiful places. First, we went to Milan, and then we headed to Turin, then Lake Como. Lake Como was somewhere I had always wanted to visit, and as soon as we arrived, I remember thinking that this was the most beautiful place I had ever been in my life. On our first evening, I remember sitting down by the swimming pool of the hotel which looked out onto the mountains and the lake, and I thought deeply and hard about my life. Although I was going to these magical places, I was in a crisis again, and I felt immensely upset with what had transpired. I also felt scared and did not know what the future held for me once again. I wanted to try and put a plan together, but I just did not know where to even begin. I thought about going back to recruitment, but it only lasted for five minutes; I had left that job because it did not fulfil me, so going back would be no different from the last time.

After Italy, we drove to the South of France. I should have been having the time of my life, but I was running once again from my problems back at home. On the drive to France, my friend turned round and said, "Jamie, what's up? Cheer up." Once we arrived, we visited Cannes, Nice and

Monaco. We went and saw the castle in Monaco, and we booked a private tour around the city.

After returning home from my travels, I got an urge to read again, and I began meditating for the first time in my life. I thought this might help me, but while it helped to quieten my mind, it did not take away any of my triggers or reconstruct my internal belief system. What I was doing is called spiritual bypassing.

The term spiritual bypassing was originally coined by psychologist John Wellwood in 1984, as he explained in an interview:

"Spiritual bypassing is a term I coined to describe a process I saw happening in the Buddhist community I was in, and also in myself. Although most of us were sincerely trying to work on ourselves, I noticed a widespread tendency to use spiritual ideas and practices to sidestep or avoid facing unresolved emotional issues, psychological wounds, and unfinished development tasks."

Spiritual bypassing is largely about avoiding or escaping from difficult life experiences. In other words, to spiritual bypass is to use spirituality to avoid, suppress, or escape from uncomfortable issues in life. The main issue for me was the trauma from my childhood which I had suppressed. For a lot of people, spirituality becomes a sort of crutch used as a way of standing back up again in the face of life's turmoil—and sometimes, this is necessary. We all need support at some time or another in our lives. But the problem comes when spirituality is used as a drug which we become dependent on to bypass the darker elements of our lives.

As psychotherapist P. T Mistlberger also writes:

"Many 'feel good' approaches to personal transformation or diluted new age teachings, in their rushed desire to reach an idealized state of unity with existence, gloss over the need to face and assume responsibility for one's inner shadow element, or darker nature."

Around this time, I really started to consider not so much writing a book but more writing down my experiences. When I began to write, which at first was just jumbles of experiences and feelings, I found that I could express myself which over time, gave me clarity. Although it was painful to read back, I would find it therapeutic as time progressed.

After not seeing Jason for about 6 months, he popped up out of the blue and contacted me. Jason said that he wanted to meet up to clear the air. After deciding to meet him, he kept apologising and then talked about another business venture I should consider. His idea was to set up a maintenance company, but of course he needed my money. Although I was reluctant at first, I had no other means of making money on the horizon. I did not trust Jason, but I decided to give him another chance yet again because there was a financial opportunity available. Being scared of not being able to provide for myself and not fully trusting my higher self and what I had learned would keep putting me back into similar situations, as you will see, but the time was nearly here for me to finally change my life around once and for all.

"Success is not final; failure is not fatal: it is the courage to continue that counts."

—Winston Churchill

Chapter 13 – Challenge

(To test the ability, skill, or strength of someone)

And once again, I was allowing my desire for money to destroy me that little bit more.

After my conversation with Jason, I found myself setting up yet another business in a sector I had no knowledge of, which became a huge challenge for me. Jason's idea was to set up a maintenance company to carry out work for estate agents. Jason and his friend James were going to complete the repairs which needed to be carried out. Both described themselves as multi-skilled tradesmen, but over time, it transpired that they were anything but that. With me being in the office, I needed help, so I asked Ben to help me run the logistical side of the business.

Six weeks had passed, and we managed to get some clients to trust us with work, but it was not long before we had burnt most of our bridges with them. I would receive complaint after complaint, mainly due to the work both Jason and James were producing, which was not competent.

At the same time as the complaints began, we had all decided to go for some food in Alderley Edge as a team. Ben and I had started to become closer due to the amount of time we were spending together, and he had raised concerns regarding both Jason's and James' general attitudes; Ben had told me on several occasions that he did not trust either of them.

After eating, we all made our way over to a bar. I remember I had spotted a girl, and when I looked at her, I felt a shift in my energy. My internal voice then said, *you need to speak to this girl urgently.* After Jason saw me looking over at her, he said, "She is pretty, isn't she?" He then said that he had been on a date with her last week, but it did not go well.

The night had now ended, and I tried to remember the girl's name, but I had totally forgotten it. When I arrived home, Ben came back to mine, and I borrowed his phone to search for her on his Instagram account. Eventually, I found her on the feed page of Piccolinos in Alderley Edge. My motive was to try and find out if Jason had said anything to her when they had been on a date together, and I was looking for evidence to see if he had indeed changed. Jason had spoken badly of me to girls in the past, so this was going to be the confirmation I needed.

After messaging the girl and explaining who I was, I asked if I could ring her, and she then sent me her number. After speaking to her on the phone, I told her briefly about my situation with Jason and asked if she would be prepared to meet me in person. After agreeing, we met the following day over in Alderley Edge. When I met her, we spoke in-depth, and I discovered that Jason had fabricated various stories about me. *Here we go again*, I thought. Jason had not changed! He had told this girl many lies, one of which consisted of me throwing £1,000 worth of pound coins at a contractor to show off. Previously he had told someone else that he owned half my dog and that I could not afford to buy dog food, and he had to pay for it. One minute I can't afford to buy food for my dog, and the next, I have £1,000 to throw away; it was just absurd. This was now the confirmation I needed to finally remove Jason from my life once and for all.

After deciding to call Jason, I said to him, "I know what you have done—AGAIN—and this time, you will get out of my life for good." I was now finished with Jason, but he was not finished with me just yet, as you will go on to see.

Stage 10: The Road Back. Journey back to the normal world.

With Jason and now James gone as they came as a pair; I was left with a business which I had no idea how to run. Despite having no one available to fulfil the work, I was still getting daily requests from some of the few remaining clients I had left. In desperation, I tried to find another engineer fast, and this increased pressure, caused me to rush when doing my due diligence. Luckily, I thought, I did manage to find someone else to start the following, week and with this new person in place, I could envisage salvaging the business.

A few weeks had now passed, and the new engineer was found to be sleeping in his van, smoking weed on the job and not completing the work correctly. Despite giving this person various opportunities time and time again, nothing changed, and he kept causing problems that escalated, and the clients I had, started to lose faith in my company's capabilities. Eventually, I sacked this person, and I spent several months taking on various engineers, but they would either not turn up or last a few days to a week at most. This then began to impact on both mine and Ben's confidence as we kept losing clients due to my inability to recruit competent staff.

I would say I was about two weeks away from closing the business as I just could not get it to work, no matter how many hours I spent trying. Then a person named Paul attended an interview. I was not sold on Paul at first, mainly due to the constant disappointments which had scarred me. Paul, however, turned out to be a good honest man. He was reliable and did the job to a good standard. After Paul started, I began to receive excellent feedback from clients regarding his work and demeanour. I then started to get phone calls requesting Paul back by name to complete other jobs, and this started the process of building the reputation of the company. After Paul, we managed to get a few other engineers in place, but it wasn't long before we began to experience the same difficulties we had with the previous ones. My inexperience shone through as vulnerability, and various people would come into the business, steal, cause problems, and then leave time and time again.

Ben had started to struggle at this point and doubted the business vision I had. Over time nothing changed, and if anything, it progressively got worse, so I decided to bring Ben's friend Mike on board to help share the workload. After no longer than a few months of Mike starting, Ben finally made the decision to quit. Shortly after Ben left, Mike also decided to leave. The reason for Mike leaving was that the world had just gone into a lockdown due to the coronavirus pandemic, and I was unable to offer Mike any security in terms of his job position. Mike had been offered a full-time job working for Amazon as a delivery driver, and with a family to provide for, he had no alternative but to accept this job.

With Ben and Mike leaving the company, I became isolated at home due to the lockdown, and I started to become addicted to my job as a means of escapism. I spent my time in lockdown reviewing the countless mistakes which were being made, and I then began changing and refining the business. I was not going to let my dream of building financial security go down the drain, but in order to get this company to where it needed to be, I convinced myself that I had to work 16-hour days, seven days a week on my own, and it was far too much pressure for any one person to contend with.

The importance of creating a balanced life is paramount for anyone to live healthily, and when there is too much stress, a person will become dysregulated and distanced from love. I was about to learn this the hard way.

Despite using my time in lockdown productively, I had no physical human interaction for months on end, and this really impacted me—although I was not consciously aware of it. My fixation on work only increased after I received a phone call from my mum who said that my grandad had died. A few weeks after this phone call, I received another call to say that my grandma had also passed away. I had convinced myself that I could end up homeless again, so I spent every waking hour focusing on work and could not even begin to acknowledge either of their deaths. Instead, I did what I had done throughout the majority of my life: I disconnected from my emotions by keeping myself insanely busy, so there was never any space for me to allow my emotions to surface.

I was now pushing myself to the limit, and I had fainted several times at home and ended up in hospital. At the hospital, I was told that my issue was the accumulating stress in my life. What I could not see at the time, was that I was driving myself so hard into the ground that no human being could cope with the amount of pressure I was putting on myself. Some days I would not sleep, and I could worry so much that I would end up having a panic attack. My fear of failing and not being able to support myself caused me to carry on this destructive cycle, but I was now close to breaking point. In my distorted version of reality, I was one mistake away from losing everything despite now having hundreds of thousands of pounds in the bank. Although this was the road back to the normal world, this was the normal world I had created.

With lockdown rules slightly easing over time, I began to have engineers out working again. However, with me being totally engrossed in my work, I began to lose sight of reality. I had employed a roofer who had proceeded to steal £12,000 off of me. This roofer had said he had completed various jobs which I had sent him to over a four-week period, but I would find out this was a lie. An estate agent who I worked with had rung me and said that a roof which my roofer had apparently attended to and fixed was still leaking. When I sent another roofer back to check the job, I was told that no work had ever been completed. Over the coming weeks, I got phone call after phone call, as each job that the roofer had said he had completed had not been done. This situation caused me to become suspicious of everyone, and although I carried on working, I found it extremely difficult to trust as there where many people stealing and taking me for granted.

After ringing the police, I was told that this was a civil matter and there was nothing they could do. With me being so consumed by work, I decided not to pursue the matter any further. By not enforcing a boundary, I had created an environment where I had become an easy target for the rest of my watching staff. Everyone knew what had happened, including a new member of staff called Nick. By not taking action against this individual, I had shown weaknesses, and everyone then knew that they, too, could do what they wanted without any consequences.

After the roofer left, the next problem swiftly entered my life, and his name was Neil. I liked Neil, but not long after starting work, he began not turning up with the same excuses I had heard before from other engineers. In the first week of starting, his van had broken down, and in desperate need to fulfil my requirements, I lent Neil some money to rent a rental van. Although I felt uncomfortable about doing this, the detrimental effect of Neil not being able to complete the ever-increasing workload, meant that I could potentially lose some of my clients. I had previously lost many clients due to various engineers' poor quality of work, the roofing incident

244

and also jobs which I could not complete due to staff quitting or me having to sack them.

As things progressively got worse with Neil, I remember I took a call from an estate agent who said, "Hi Jamie, how are you, my love?"

I lied and replied, "Yes, great, thanks."

She then said, "Can you tell me why a member of your staff is taking his dog to work and inside the tenant's houses?" I just did not know what to say, and everything started to become incredibly intense between Neil and me. Neil had also come to an office meeting with cans of beer and started drinking. He had also been abusive towards my new account's woman, Alex, and she felt threatened. Alex had also confirmed there were many discrepancies with Neil's receipts and that he was potentially stealing, but this was never confirmed. Eventually, I had enough, and it was time for Neil to leave the company.

Just when I thought things could not get any worse, they did. I received a phone call in the midst of all this happening from a company I had not done any work for. The woman on the phone then asked if they could check my VAT number. I said, "Yes, sure. Why?"

She then proceeded to say, "We have an invoice for work done at one of our properties, but when we Googled the VAT number on the invoice, your company name came up."

I said, "It must be a mistake. We do not work with your company."

I then asked for the company name on the invoice, and it was the surnames of both Jason and James. I then Googled the company and saw that it was not a VAT-registered business. Jason and James were both using my VAT number to claim money for work that they were completing. This is referred to as VAT fraud. Within the next few months, I received several of these phone calls from various companies stating exactly the same thing.

All these situations in my life contributed further to the decline in my mental health. When I thought about my spiritual awakening, it felt like another lifetime ago, and I questioned if it had even been real. At the time, I could not see that my awakening was not some magic power I had inherited; it was a path that was available to me, but I needed to fully indulge in it to see the benefits appear in my everyday life.

I thought I had healed, so I did not understand why I felt so low and why bad stuff kept happening. This was confirmation that there was something deeper which I needed to investigate, so I then decided to go online, and I paid to have weekly sessions with a therapist. The positive in this instance was that I had reached out and asked for help. Although speaking to a therapist on the phone helped me initially, I decided to stop speaking to him when he advised that I go on some form of medication. I did, however, take what he had said into consideration and wondered if maybe everything I had read in the past was wrong. I mean, I have been wrong many times before, and here I was years later, in exactly the same place as where I had started. I felt down, miserable, and upset. However, after some deliberation, I eventually declined his recommendation, stopped speaking to him and then pushed on and engrossed myself further into work. This was one of the best decisions I ever made, as you will go on to see as its forms one of the most important messages of my story.

Despite my life crumbling, I refused to give in, and no matter what, when the morning arrived, I would be at my computer ready to go again, but I knew something needed to change. After some deliberation, I decided to close my company down. The reputation was tarnished due to Jason's and other engineers' actions, as well as my mistakes but instead of quitting, I was going to start a new company. With the experience I had gained, I believed I could eradicate any of my past mistakes. The biggest problem I had, which I could not see at the time, was that due to my inherent beliefs, I would only continue to create the same situations again, and each time I was unable to learn a lesson, the universe spoke to me louder and louder.

Stage 11: Resurrection. Meeting the final ordeal and test and most dangerous encounter with death.

Nick had been working for me for a couple of months, and despite the early warning signs in terms of his past (having spent time in prison) and warnings from Paul and other staff members regarding his personality, I continued to work with him. Nick began helping me with interviewing candidates, and he had far superior knowledge to me, he always turned up, and the quality of his work was of a good standard. I really thought Nick cared about the business, and I could trust him. With Nick by my side, I could envisage having a successful business because whatever I lacked through experience and knowledge, Nick had in abundance.

Nick had been in the building game all his life, and I looked up to him for advice and protection for the business. This then created a bond between us, but what I could not see at the time was that Nick had an ulterior motive as he was stealing from me, and he had set a company up on Companies House in anticipation of stealing my clients in the future.

I learned very quickly not to go against Nick's words because it would always end up in a volatile argument. Nick began manipulating me, but I could not see it because I was so consumed by the bubble I had created.

247

It was only later, when other people began to recognise his behaviour towards me, that I would start to see what was really transpiring. Nick's past did not bother me, and if anything, I gravitated towards him because, in my childhood, I had spent time around many people like Nick who were criminals. In essence, I was looking for that bond with a male figure which I had missed out on, and I had gravitated towards Nick because he was similar to what I had experienced in my childhood which was familiar and unhealthy. I was looking for someone to give me guidance, and Nick gave me that, despite the flaws in his character. Nick could do no wrong in my eyes because my company became successful after he started, and I believe a big part of this was down to him.

Because I had an unsafe and destructive childhood, I believed that the world was full of dangerous and threatening people. This worldview meant that I projected out to people that I was not safe, and that projection elicited negative experiences in return. People such as Nick preyed on my weaknesses, and this was an opportunity he took with both hands. The eventual result was chaos, conflict, and destruction.

When I was a child, I had to dissociate many times, which became an adaptive capability as I learned to escape into my inner world. A key component of this sensitised ability to dissociate caused me to also become a people pleaser, and in many situations, I did what others, such as Nick, wanted because I did not want any conflict, and I wanted to ensure other people were happy and building towards the common goal, which was to have a successful business that everyone could be a part of. I was finally reaching my financial goals, so I did not want to rock the boat, but the consequence of bending over backwards to accommodate various people became exhausting.

248

Now I do not want to paint a picture of myself as a saint, and once my buttons had been pushed or my trust had been broken, there were times when I could react in a very sharp way and explode. I was stressed and angry with what had transpired with other members of staff, I was not sleeping correctly, and I was generally not looking after myself. All of this caused me to become totally out of balance, and I became disillusioned with life in general. At times my anger would reflect exactly this.

The universe communicates through other people, and when we do not heed a lesson, it will only increase and become more destructive. Simon was the first lesson and I had allowed him to take the piss and use me for far too long. Jason had burned me in the past, but despite this, I continued to work with him because there was a financial opportunity, and although there were many individuals who portrayed the same lesson time and time again, Nick would be the upgrade that would be the catalyst for me to re-evaluate and change my life once and for all.

With the new company in place and Nick by my side, it took 18 months to get to the point where we were completing between 50 to 70 jobs and quotes a day. I had built the company's reputation on Google, and at my peak, I had 300+ Google reviews, with the lowest one being a 4-star review; the reputation of the business was now immaculate, and we were the first port of call for many of the clients that used my company. At peak, I had over 30 different subcontractors working for me, and I went on to work with the majority of the largest agents in the UK.

I finally thought that I was implementing my vision, and with everything progressing and Nick by my side, I decided to focus some energy on finishing my book, but due to my dyslexia, I decided to hire a ghost writer to complete it for me. However, when I received my book back, it was not how I envisaged it to be. This left me facing the daunting prospect of starting from scratch and writing it myself.

Eventually, my company was on target to make me a profit of between £200,000 and £300,000 in the year ending 2021, and that was no small achievement considering what I had gone through in the space of the last 18 months. In my mind, Jason and the other people who stole from me were bad eggs, and Nick had shown me that there were trustworthy people out there.

As time passed and I became more experienced, I started to see that Nick was taking advantage of me. Each engineer had to supply receipts for the materials they bought for the job, which would then be paid back to the engineer each week, but Nick never did this. Nick was someone who saw an opportunity due to the poor structure of my business, my vulnerability and my weakness in setting boundaries. I tried to take the appropriate steps at first and approached him, but Nick's response to this was that he would quit and take all the staff with him if he had to supply receipts. Nick had brought a few of his friends into the business to work, so these new people rarely listened to me, and their loyalty always lay with Nick. By allowing Nick to bring people he knew into my business, I lost power, and I almost felt helpless at times. Feeling threatened by Nick's words, I decided to bury the issue and not face it with my business being threatened. This avoidance on my part led to me repressing my emotions, but they were left bubbling underneath.

I had tried to enforce boundaries with Nick, but I was not strong enough. I was not naïve about what was going on, as I began looking online and googling the materials Nick was charging me for, I saw that he had been overcharging me. This was not the odd £10 here or there either; eventually,

I worked out that over a nine-month period, he had overcharged me in excess of £20,000 in material costs.

What I can now see is that people in your life that are offended or become angry by boundaries you try to set are the people that you most need to set boundaries for. These people, in general, will try and talk or threaten you into bending and changing those boundaries to satisfy their selfish needs. By me folding, I just continually showed Nick that I was an easy target who would accept anything he would do or say. A contributing factor to this was that Nick had seen exactly what happened with the roofer who stole from me, and my reaction was I did nothing. I should not have to explain my boundaries, nor should you; each person has a right to decide their boundaries. By allowing people to talk me out of my boundaries, each time I tried to set a further one in the future, it just became useless.

I then kept bringing up the conversation regarding the receipts time and time again without directly telling Nick that I knew he was stealing. I even got others to communicate the importance of this directly to him, such as my accountant Harry and my new accounts lady Sharron who had just taken over from Alex. I thought they might be able to get him to supply receipts, but again he refused or would make up some lies to stall for time. Sharron would turn around time and time again, stating to me that Nick was an exact replica of her manipulative and narcissistic ex-husband, but despite her words, Nick had been my rock, and I did not feel capable of running this business without him, so I was left with conflicting emotions, just as I had in my childhood with my dad.

At the same time I was having issues regarding the receipts, I had Nick's wife, Lisa, send me a text message. It was late at night when I received a message which stated, "I am not going to be with Nick for long, he is abusive, and he has put cameras in the house to monitor me and a tracking device on my phone." My loyalty lay with Nick, so I messaged back, stating that I did not want to be involved in their personal disputes. I also told Nick the following day as I was scared of his reaction if he ever found out that his partner had messaged me and I had not informed him. After telling Nick, I received another message from Lisa the following day apologising and saying she loved Nick very much and she was drunk when she sent that message. This message from Lisa confirmed that Nick behaved like this with others and not just myself.

The change for me came when I no longer wanted to work anymore, as I knew Nick was continuing to deceive me despite my efforts to stop it from happening. Every time I tried to raise an issue, he threatened to quit, which then turned into threats of violence. On one of these occasions, he had called up Shenade, a new girl in the office, in the first week she had started the job and started threatening all sorts of violence towards me through her.

By the end of 2020, I felt my mental health was declining severely, and I had no control over my company. Like many times in my life when I felt everything closing in around me, I decided to run. I then went on holiday by myself to the Maldives, and I spent Christmas over there on my own. At the time of going away, I had told Nick that I was going to think about my future as I felt seriously unhappy, and I did not know if I wanted to carry on any longer.

Physical boundary violations are a safety issue, and if these are continuously violated, as they were in my case, then they are likely to worsen the more you tolerate them. Emotional boundaries, such as being bullied, criticised, and called names, are also crossed when we feel shamed into doing things we inherently do not want to do. When we base how we internally feel by how others treat us, this begins to affect our emotions and how we view ourselves. We should find happiness in ourselves and not allow people outside of us to confirm whether we are happy or not.

I was stuck in this cycle of emotional addiction, and I was subconsciously seeking that emotional hit time and time again. Although these were stressful emotions of feeling sad and upset, it was familiar as it was exactly what I experienced as a child, and as we know, familiar is more safe than unfamiliar. My body had become so accustomed to the powerful hormonal responses that I continued to seek them further, although I was not consciously aware of this. By doing this in my adulthood, I could repeat the emotional baseline which I had established in my childhood.

In the Maldives, I focused on trying to finish my book, so I had something else to fall back on if I decided to close the business. The name of my book at this time of my life would have been called *How to Become Financially Successful and Extremely Fucking Unhappy.* The more I wrote, the more my book did not make sense to me, and I could not understand certain elements of my story with the clarity I needed, so I decided to stop writing, and I was going to reapproach it at some point in the future. After my week in the Maldives and feeling uncomfortable with my book, I decided I had too much to lose and that I needed to give work one more try. I then travelled back home feeling grateful in terms of what I had achieved with my business, and I was sure I could turn things around.

When I returned from my holiday, the same problems occurred straight away, and I fell into a stressful pattern again. I had gone above and beyond to accommodate everyone. I was very giving, and I rewarded my staff with bonuses—Nick was on a bonus for each engineer that completed a week's worth of work. It was not a huge amount, but it was an extra £150 to £300 a week for him. I took out a van policy in my name, then one of the guys smashed up the van, and I had to pay £2,000 out of my own pocket. I

253

completed various engineers' paperwork when they didn't do it correctly or just could not be bothered to do it, which was not my responsibility, and most nights, I would be sitting in my office well past 10 pm doing what I was paying other people to do. If you consider the fact that these were not direct staff, they were all subcontractors, and it was their responsibility to have everything in order, such as vans and insurance policies, you can now see how much I was bending over backwards to accommodate everyone.

I remember my accounts woman Sharron turned round to me one day and said, "Jamie, stop being so nice. They don't respect you, and they think you're weak." I indulged in them in the hope that I could buy their loyalty, just as my dad had done with me in my childhood. It was one of my ingrained beliefs, which I was living out daily. The more I gave, the more they took. I was always looking for constant approval in my work life because I never had guidance from my dad or in my childhood, so I was scared to trust or assert myself.

Early in 2021, I snapped one day physically and broke down on the floor of my office, crying in front of Shenade. I then rang my mum in desperation and said I could not carry on anymore—I was fully done. I remember the week it happened clearly: one of my roofers had a heart attack, I sacked someone for drinking alcohol again on the job (he was caught drinking gin on a roof), two other members of the team quit, Shenade's dog got run over, my dog ended up in hospital with food poisoning, Nick and I had an explosive argument, and it just became too much effort me. I was constantly fighting, and I had no fight left in me.

The only positive aspect of the job was my bank balance each month, but even that now was not enough for me to carry on. I realised I finally had enough financial security to step away, and it was time to focus on myself. In my mind, I thought I would be able to walk away into the sunset and that would be that, but Nick had other ideas.

When I told Nick that I was finished and closing the company, we agreed that we would complete any outstanding jobs we had pencilled in. This would have taken around three months in total because we had so much work; I also did not want to let my clients down as I had built a good relationship with most of them. Because I had committed to a date, I thought I could carry on with the end in sight, but I could not even get to the end of the week. Throughout this week, knowing that I was closing my business gave me the strength to release everything I had been burying, and whenever Nick threatened something, my response was, "Then do it. Quit now, go home. I don't care. I'm done. If you don't want to fulfil the remaining work, then don't." He no longer had a hold over me, and this caused massive arguments every day, but me arguing with a fool only confirmed one thing: that there were two fools.

By the end of the week, I could not carry on a day longer, so I then proceeded to cancel over a quarter of a million pounds worth of work. I explained to my clients that I could not carry on due to the state of my mental health. The response I got only added to my stress further: I was sworn at on the phone, I was asked how I could do this, and I was told that I had left everyone in the shit. I proceeded to apologise to each client and explained that I could not physically carry on anymore as the job was making me ill.

After I closed my business, I had an idea of setting up a flooring company which Shenade could run. I found that the flooring jobs were very simple, and I had a trustworthy company I could use to carry out the work that never caused me any stress, so I did not need to hire vans, pay for insurance policies or any of the general crap that came with trying to keep staff happy. I also did not need to get involved as much as Shenade could

255

manage the work. With Shenade focusing on the flooring business, I could then concentrate on finishing my book and trying to make sense of my life. Although I could not carry on working physically due to the stress, I wanted to try and be responsible and still have a source of income.

After I parted with Nick and closed the business, I began to feel less stressed, and the two weeks after my decision, I had never felt so good and light. Shenade was a trained Reiki healer, and she began performing this healing on me every day in the office. Feeling better was confirmation that I had made the right decision. However, after two weeks passed, I started to find out through various people that Nick had set up a company on Companies House in anticipation of stealing my business from the offset. With the company now shut, Paul, who had now left due to his age and wanting a less stressful job, was now my friend and someone who had always stuck by me. Paul had decided to ring me, and his wife Jill had come on the phone and said, "Jamie, I told Paul a year ago, within the first week of Nick starting, that I could tell by his voice that he was going to try and steal your business." This was common knowledge to everyone, but due to Nick being controlling and intimidating, people were afraid to tell me anything substantial until I closed my business.

In my last conversation with Nick, it was time to tell him that I knew he had been overcharging me for materials. I could not hold it in any longer, and I needed to face the truth. This happened when a few weeks passed, and my new flooring company received three Google reviews slandering my name in person. These were 1-star reviews, and I knew they had come from Nick. I had never received lower than a 4-star review in 18 months, let alone three 1-star reviews in ten minutes. Looking back, Nick was gone and out of my life, and I should have left him to it, but I decided to ring him. For my own safety I recorded the conversation because I knew he was going to start threatening me again.

After ringing Nick, I told him that I knew he had been stealing from me all along and that if he didn't remove the online slander by 5 pm, I would take him to court and sue him for breach of contract. Nick had signed a contract with my company, and Clause 2:1 stated that he could not take any of my clients for a 12-month period. I had also received several phone calls from my clients telling me about the business Nick had set up and that he was actively pursuing my old clients.

After I confronted him over the phone and recorded him, he laughed at me and said, "I know how much you love your animals. You know what I am capable of."

I said, "I am not scared of you, Nick. I will just take you to court."

His reply was, "Then you will see your animals hanging from the side of your balcony. You are a closet gay, no one likes you, and I have people watching you outside your place."

The conservation ended with me telling him that he had been recorded and I put the phone down, not really fearing his threats, but my painter, who knew Nick, was at my house and had heard the conversation, then packed his stuff up out of fear and left. I then contacted the police and sent the voice recording I had and awaited their response. Two weeks then passed, and I got a knock on my door on 22nd May at around 6.05 pm. There was a big man wearing a Covid mask and a high-vis jacket who said he was from building management. I had reported an issue with my balcony, so I assumed he was coming to fix it. As I opened the door and turned my head to invite him in, I was punched to the floor, then strangled and threatened to have my kneecaps blown off with a shotgun if I was to carry on with my

257

"keyboard tactics" as he put it, referring to me going to the police or taking Nick to court by producing the contract he had signed.

After the person left, I went to stay with my mum, fearing for my safety, but when I returned, pictures of my balcony were taken and then sent to me along with threatening emails and text messages to my account's woman, slandering me.

While this was all happening, Nick had started to build relationships with my clients and tarnished my name by fabricating lies and stories about me. This resulted in me not being able to get all the money I was owed, and as I write this book, I am still owed over £150,000, although today, the money is irrelevant because it no longer carries the significance and hold over me that it once did. Despite me having physical proof, such as the voice recording of Nick threatening me, emails he had sent me from fake accounts, and CCTV evidence from a bar across the road where I lived that showed the man who had attacked me as well as the car park where he had parked which showed the number plate of his van, Nick was not arrested for three months, and I was passed between 17 different police officers in total. The crimes, I believe, were listed incorrectly, and instead of blackmail or extortion, which carries up to 14 years in prison, he was arrested for low-level charges such as malicious communication and Section 39, which were later dropped. Despite me being attacked and a marker put on my address, the police had said that if anything further happened, they would aim to be at my property within ten minutes, but when a man came back with a gun the second time, I called the police at 6 pm, but they did not turn up until 1.30 am, six and a half hours later. With the police not helping me or ensuring I was kept safe, I contacted my local MP, Lucy Powell, and I made a complaint to the IOPC twice (the police governing body). Today I have still not received the outcome of this, but I no longer need to waste any of my energy on justice or even revenge. My justice has already come for me in the fact that I would go on to create a new life, and today I am grateful for what these experiences have taught me because they moulded me into a better person by altering the direction of my life.

To paraphrase an old chess saying, the only way I could eventually get smarter and learn was by playing a smarter opponent. When you take such a massive action in life, you need to expect to be criticised, and the second you start achieving great results, you will immediately be judged by people who cannot operate on the same level as you. Constantly getting caught up in these work skirmishes meant that my energy was always focused on areas that were not going to enable me to truly heal.

Finally ending this toxic relationship with Nick liberated me, although it was incredibly difficult. Once I was finally able to do this, and after some time had passed, I increased my vibrational state and created a positive life for myself. Having time and perspective then enabled my healing and growth finally as a person.

When the dust had finally settled, I began to see that I had no one to blame for my life, and the harsh reality was that my problems were due to my ingrained beliefs which were contributing towards my destruction. The hardest challenge you will ever face in life is your opponent, and that opponent is yourself.

I want to point out that your self-worth is not defined by the way people treat you. I had recognised I deserved a better life than the continuous toxic one I became trapped in, and although there were consequences, this was ultimately the best decision I ever made. The more I stayed in a threatening environment with such harmful conditions, the more I would sabotage my own life.

Looking back, when people took advantage of me, it was usually a result of my failure to enforce a boundary. People did what they wanted, and I allowed that to happen. Feeling angry was a clear sign that a boundary had been overstepped, but I had not communicated this properly or with purpose, and when I had, and it was not heeded, I backed down instead of enforcing it because I was scared of the consequences of doing so. Setting boundaries saves a person from a lot of unnecessary negative emotions and feelings that we will otherwise go on to experience. When you set boundaries, they allow you to stop people from being hurtful or resentful towards you. Since I had not learned to set boundaries because I was not taught any as a child, this would impact on me severely, but Nick was my final test. I was violated, used, and made to feel uncomfortable. I adjusted to accommodate this pain because I believed it was necessary to remain where I was. There was also the matter of safety, and because I was working in dangerous situations, trying to set boundaries resulted in me being threatened. Setting boundaries also brought up feelings of abandonment and being rejected, so once again, this was another deep-rooted component because I would rather be attached to destruction than left rejected and alone as I was when I was a child. Living without boundaries was like leaving my front door wide open for any person to enter anytime they wanted to do what the fuck they wanted.

I ended up becoming addicted to the emotional cycle, and although I had different relationships, the dynamics were always the same. This traumatic bonding was an addiction for me, just as real as my crack addiction. Being rejected and fearful in my childhood formed the earliest parts of my relationships, so I was compelled to seek adult relationships that mirrored exactly that conditioned cycle. Today I can see why children born into environments such as mine will then seek out familiar environments as they become adults. Because I existed in a state of fear, my body had adapted on a molecular, physiological, and neurochemical level. Being creatures of comfort, humans love to predict the future even when that future is dangerous, terrifying, or scary because it's safer than the unknown.

Being addicted to my past meant that I had made my past the future; each time I did this, I would feel ashamed for making the same mistake with no conscious knowledge of why I had done it. My shame came from knowing that I deserved better than what I was receiving, but the problem was that my subconscious mind did not allow me to take the more rational and safer path. Engaging in a trauma bond meant that I had no access to my rational mind and was constantly dragged into my past through my subconscious, and by doing this, I was living on autopilot mode, which was a pattern that became rooted in my familiarity. Trauma bonding is a process that has to be unlearned, and advising me to just walk away or say, "Well, this has happened before. You should know better, Jamie," is not helpful and does not come from a place of understanding how the dynamics connected with trauma work.

Having an addicted mind meant that my recovery was not over from early addictions through the absence of drugs or alcohol. The underlying cause was my psychological dysfunction which needed to be healed. I needed to turn my negative psychology into a positive one, and this would then help to build my self-esteem. To do this, though, I would need to create a healthy and positive environment which would enable me to excel, and just using my willpower was not going to be enough to see a fundamental change. I was trying to recover without truly healing, and the 12-step programme refers to this as "white knuckling". The addicted mind does not get cured; instead, it remains ever present, simmering under the surface, waiting for any excuse to establish its dominance again. The only way to break out of this cycle was to have a different type of therapy and maintain ongoing daily care and maintenance, which would contribute towards my eventual success.

I had lived an unhealthy life without boundaries, but that was not going to work for me anymore. It was time to change. Once a manipulative and selfish person begins operating within our boundaries, we become sucked into the chaos at the expense of our own life and sanity. By creating boundaries, I could ensure necessary self-care measures as well as develop healthy relationships with others. Each person should receive the basic respect they are entitled to. With this newly adopted attitude, I could no longer be manipulated by others into doing things I did not want to do.

I have compiled a list below regarding boundaries:

- Each person has the right to say no if they do not feel comfortable. As well as saying no, you do not need to feel guilty or even give an explanation.
- Your needs are what is important.
- You have the right to be treated with respect.
- You have the right to express your opinions freely without feeling like you will be belittled.
- You have the right to speak up in circumstances which threaten or violate you.
- No one has the right to treat you with disrespect.

Boundaries are necessary because if you do not have them, people will treat you in any way they like, and that then can compromise your well-being. We are the ones who are responsible for our happiness, and relying on others to determine that is a disaster waiting to happen as it takes the control away from us. Trying to keep quiet and people-pleasing is the basis of a dysfunctional relationship. Without setting boundaries, you're placing a target on your back for people to hit time and time again. Manipulators such as Nick are very hard to escape from, and when we start saying no to these types of characters, they will start with emotional blackmail. People like this are only happy when we give in to their demands and do things their way at our own expense. Each time you surrender to these individuals, they will want more and place more expectations on you, knowing that you will retreat and surrender again. Trying to hold onto relationships that depend upon a lack of boundaries attracts the wrong people into our life. When we finally draw a line for our own sanity, disaster can occur, such as in my case, but my disaster was the final turning point in my life.

By me being so concerned with financial safety and external goals, I saw that I had severely neglected my spiritual growth. I saw flaws in Nick, Jason, and in the world in general, and that was my problem. As long as I was concerned with other people's faults, I could never focus my energy on accepting myself and working through what I needed to do to move forward in my own life. Closing my business down and removing all forms of negativity would lead to the start of my new life, and finally, we are here.

"May your choices reflect your hopes, not your fears."
—Nelson Mandela

Chapter 14 – Energy

(Work done by the mind or body: energy used to do something)

Love for myself was the only way I was going to be able to finally create the life I yearned for. The threats and violence had pushed me to re-evaluate my life in its entirety, and the first step was to close my flooring business. I now had no job or form of income, but I had saved up enough money to feel safe about making this decision.

I had now started the process of creating some solitude in my life, just as I had done after my spiritual awakening. This enabled me to focus my energy on self-care and dissecting what I had been through in my life. I remember being left seriously confused by my intentions, which meant that this confusion had projected out into my existence.

The next couple of months were particularly hard, and the decision I had made to close my business was not an easy one as I had no idea what the future held in store for me.

With money no longer my main objective and with no business or further distractions, I was left to face the true nature of my reality. Everything was now finally coming to the surface to be released, and despite feeling extremely upset, I never once considered turning back to the alcohol or drugs to numb my pain.

As the months gradually passed, I decided to write again, and this became an emotional outlet for me. Writing was a purposeful tool to identify the patterns that had kept reoccurring, and I had found a place where I could start to make sense of my life with no pressure or time frame attached. I would quickly go on to discover that my drive to achieve financial success was a big contributor to the decline in my life. The problem was not so much the money I was chasing; instead, it was the perception I had of money and the lengths I was prepared to go to achieve that desire. Another factor which played an important part was the fear of ever being homeless again, and this really drove me on uncontrollably at times. It was finally time to understand that no amount of money was going to heal me, and it had taken a situation as severe as the one with Nick to finally realise this.

As I continued writing, I decided to set myself some goals for 2021. These were no longer financial; instead, they revolved around removing any toxicity from my life (which I had already started the process of doing) and understanding myself with clarity and healing. Having money in the bank allowed me to feel comfortable and not let time alter any of my decisions. I had suffered with so much pain throughout my existence, but the one positive I took was that I was still here, I was still fighting, and this proved to me that whatever had tried to destroy me had lost; I deserved a better life, and it was now time to focus all my energy on how I would finally achieve this.

The more space I created, the more the experience of my spiritual awakening came back into my conscious mind, and without it, I felt lost. I was finally ready to accept what had happened to me, and I can tell you that acceptance is one of the most important components on the road to recovery for any person.

Accepting where I was and no longer beating myself up enabled me to create a foundation point to work from. I then began to immerse myself in books again as I recognised that reading had previously contributed towards my growth. Living in Batley, I had learned through reading that failure was only temporary and because I was not prepared to give up, I would try different approaches; over a sustained period of time, this knowledge I had acquired meant that I was always going to find the right path despite my many repetitive failures. Although reading had contributed massively to my life, my actual life experiences were what solidified any permanent change I was able to make. By viewing my experiences and recognising the consistent patterns that had played out, I could finally start the process in transforming. I had now set an intention, and the universe responded by presenting me with a natural path to follow.

At first, I started with what I knew I could change, and that was my environment. I had removed any work distractions, I was now writing regularly and expressing my emotions, I was reading again, I was spending time with my animals as much as possible, I was going out into nature, I began meditating again, and I was eating as many natural foods as possible. With no work on the horizon or financial goals to achieve, I was no longer killing myself.

The process of change did not take long. I would say that after around four weeks of consistent habits, I started to raise my vibrational state once again. I had now recognised through experience that I had viewed my daily routine as a destination to reach, and once I had reached it, I no longer maintained it. To succeed in life, my routine needed to remain a constant theme throughout my future. Creating a positive environment was what I knew I could do, but I had no idea where to go from there, so I then surrendered myself to the universe by asking for help and a direction to follow. I had admitted that I needed guidance, and I would trust in the signs that I would be presented with.

Not too long then passed before my first clear apparent sign appeared. After receiving a phone call from Sharron, we began speaking, and she said that she was going to see a hypnotherapist. Sharron had said her friend had been to see this hypnotherapist to quit smoking, and it had worked. I then asked Sharron for his number as I thought that he might be able to help me. I was now about to find what I had always been searching for, but the journey was not going to be an easy one. It was time to go deeper than I had ever been before and explore the root of my issues.

Stage 12: Return with the Elixir. This is the final stage where I returned to the ordinary world as a changed man. I have grown as a person, learned many things, and faced many dangers, but I now look forward to starting a new life.

I had now taken a step forward, and this time there would be no more steps going back.

As I began to change the direction of my life, many people seemed to have a problem with me. I had decided to put myself first, and nothing was going to stop me doing that. I then changed my phone number and only gave it out to a select few people I trusted. I did not owe anybody any money, I did not owe anyone any of my time, and more importantly, I did not owe anyone an explanation. My thought process at the time was this: if you have a problem with me, then call me. If you don't have my phone number anymore, then that means you don't know me well enough to have a problem.

After finally calling the hypnotherapist, whose name was Chris, I booked some sessions with him, and I began travelling to his office to see him weekly. The first couple of times went well, and Chris made me feel safe and at ease. As I have explained previously, feeling safe is the most important aspect of any therapy one wishes to have. Chris did not rush me. Instead, it was a gradual process. During our sessions, I explained the hurricane I had been through since I was born, what I thought my problems were, and what I was trying to accomplish by going to see him.

As the sessions progressed naturally, I began to understand myself and make further sense of my life with a heightened sense of awareness and clarity, which I never had been afforded before. Hypnosis induced me into a state of calm so I could view the traumatic experiences from my childhood without becoming overwhelmed. Being able to observe critically and calmly enabled me to integrate my dissociated memories into my conscious mind so I could then work through them in the correct way. The main focus of the sessions consisted of what had happened to me as a child and how this was impacting on my everyday life. I found that my childhood experiences had influenced my brain's development, which had formed key destructive components in my brain. With no pressure in my life, I was able to attend hypnotherapy, go home and contemplate what I had unearthed each time.

Hypnotherapy afforded me the insight to take a step back from my emotional reactions and view each situation from where it was originating from; I was then able to start the process of questioning then changing my inherent beliefs by creating new neuron pathways in my brain, and this then enabled me to react differently to situations which would trigger me. Over a sustained period of time, these new pathways became more prominent than my old destructive ones.

I would go on to find out that because I did not love myself, I had created an environment that was no different from the one in my childhood. The mind has a fundamental need to feel good about itself, and my low self-esteem created a source of psychological discomfort for me. My mind had tried to compensate for this low self-esteem by projecting a false and exaggerated pride which I had achieved through external validation. Psychologists identify two types of pride: authentic (good) pride versus hubristic (bad) pride. Hubristic pride is the kind that's arrogant, boastful, self-absorbed, and conceited. Authentic pride is when we are proud of a legitimate accomplishment, but we aren't shoving it in everybody's faces. The dysfunctional pride that had ruled my life up until this point was hubristic, and it was an attempt to cover up my rock-bottom self-esteem. Each new car or material item I bought would be a form of external validation which I needed to mask my underlying pain.

The trauma I was exposed to in my childhood forced me to betray myself, and I felt rejected, worthless, and not good enough. My dad had denied me what I required; he unconsciously taught me to reject what I inherently felt. The more I learned to distrust myself, the more I distanced myself away from my feelings, and this then caused me to grow up with a lack of understanding of how I felt, so I always struggled to express myself; this then created a fundamental belief that I must betray who I am in order to survive in this world. I looked to other people to shape the nature of my reality. These people I looked to were familiar with what I was exposed to as a child, so I became attached to violence, danger, and pain. When you are not heard as a child, it is exhausting and upsetting, and to be abused becomes confusing and disturbing; I can tell you through experience that being acknowledged is one of the deepest human requirements each of us need.

Being conditioned to accept and then bury the abuse I suffered in my childhood, and the fact that my screaming and pleading never led to a change in my dad's behaviour, meant that in my adult life, many times, I just accepted how people treated me. I would refuse to stand up for myself because I thought I was not strong enough to change my circumstances, which was no different from how I behaved in my childhood. The consequence of this meant that I was vibrating at a low frequency which was dominated by my fear and trapped negative emotions, and I then attracted low-vibrational people into my life as I was vibrating at that same level as them.

As hypnotherapy continued, I finally got to the root cause of why I always felt like everything was my fault throughout my life. I had found that I was conditioned to think this way as a child because growing up, my dad had blamed me for Tracy leaving, Gizmo shitting on the bed and everything that went wrong in his life.

Another important aspect which came up was my perception of love. With my dad having sex with various females and being directly exposed to this as a child, my brain had formed a perception that to receive love, I had to repeat my dad's actions. This is why I looked for love in the wrong places in my adult life. The situation with Tracy and my mum had also contributed massively to the trust issues I had formed, and this is why I struggled to form a connection with any female. When someone did get close, I would always sabotage any potential positive relationship, so I did not have to risk the feelings of being rejected and abandoned again, as I was when I was a child. These were some of my first ingrained perceptions, and I had created a world based on every dysfunctional belief I had formed without understanding the importance of how my childhood had impacted on me.

One very important belief that came up was the attachment I had formed to accept abuse as long as it came with some form of a financial reward. When I was a child, I was subjected to varying degrees of abuse from

270

my dad, which was then always followed by a reward in fear that I might ever tell on him again. This ingrained perception was something I carried with me throughout my adult life, and as long as I received money in exchange for the abuse I would have to endure, it would be acceptable and also familiar to me. I had no conscious thought as to why I kept finding myself in similar patterns with destructive and abusive people, but hypnotherapy enabled me to understand and then finally break this cycle of devastation which had been destroying my life. I was then able to see that I was not a terrible person and when I came to this realisation, I remember I cried to myself because it was confirmation that my core beliefs were the contributing factor to the disasters so far in my life and not because I inherently thought I was a "bad child".

Now, money was a very important subject that came up several times. *If I had enough money,* I thought, *I would never have to worry about being homeless again when I was cold and could not afford to buy food to feed myself.* Every time I had a bad day at work, I would become triggered and sent straight back to that moment in time, and the fear which would come through to the surface only ever destroyed the present moment. Inherently I still did not trust myself or truly believe in what I was doing, and with outside influences affecting me, every negative comment or bad day would knock me completely off balance, and I would automatically think of the extreme worst-case scenarios.

Another component tied in with money was my belief that money would make me happy, just as I thought it made my dad happy. So, for me, money was a direct source to find happiness, but once achieved, I was unable to understand why it did not fulfil me, and I then tried to obtain more money in the hope of it making me happy at some point; I was searching for my happiness through external means, and again this was another inversion.

271

With money meaning so much to me, I was prepared to let people walk all over me by not enforcing any boundaries. Boundaries were hard for me as I was never taught any as a child, but it was now time to start putting them in place to protect me from other people and also myself. My perception of money and what I was prepared to do in order to obtain it had become just as destructive as the alcohol I drank, the cocaine I sniffed, or the crack cocaine I smoked. Like money, a lot of my problems were interlinked and fed off each other.

As time progressed, I began living in the present moment a lot more. I realised that taking a day at a time was important for me, and no more than that. I am only afforded today, and if I am lucky enough to wake up tomorrow, then I will work through tomorrow when it arrives. I was now taking my time by slowing everything down, and whenever I became unsure about something, I would ask myself the following:

- Is this a decision I truly want to make, and I am not making it due to some outside influence?
- When I think about making this decision, does it make me feel sad, happy, or even forced?
- If I take money out of the equation, would I still make this decision?
- Do I have to change as a person when making this decision, or can I feel comfortable in my own identity?
- Does my energy feel good about making this decision, or does it make me feel drained, low, and tired?
- Do I feel safe, understood, and respected?
- Does this situation feel like there is some ulterior motive? Do I feel anxious? Feeling anxious was a sign that the decision was most likely not the right one.

Hypnotherapy became a crucial tool in changing my life, and although it was extremely painful, it finally gave me the clarity I needed to understand my upbringing, myself, and the new path I would need to take to become the best version of myself. It takes a huge amount of courage to allow yourself to remember, and my heart goes out to anyone who is prepared to go through this painful process. Talking about distressing feelings definitely helps to resolve them, but unfortunately, the experience of trauma can get in the way of people reaching out. No matter how much insight I had developed in my life up until this point, I was unable to know who I truly was without understanding my inherent beliefs through hypnotherapy.

So, what is an inherent belief? It is a belief that is a practised thought derived from a lived experience. Beliefs are formed over many years through thought patterns, and they require interior and exterior validation. Beliefs we hold about ourselves are how we then go on to view the world. The more these thoughts are practised, the more the brain wires itself to these default thought patterns. This is especially true if our thoughts activate a stress response as this then creates internal turmoil, which over time becomes compulsive, and this is the definition of a conditioned trauma reaction we know as emotional addiction.

Without boundaries, I became emotionally attached to destructive individuals who would violate me, and this is what we call a trauma bond. What I can now see is the most prominent addiction I had in my life was not the drugs or alcohol I took. Instead, it was my emotional addiction which I was repeating time and time again. The more we think about something, the more we are likely to believe it and the more it is likely to manifest in our lives. These practised thoughts became my reality, and these

273

conditioned patterns of physiological dysregulation meant that I had to reconstruct myself to change my deep-rooted beliefs. When a belief is instilled and consistently validated, it becomes a core belief. Core beliefs are the deepest perceptions about our identity, and they are installed into the subconscious mind when we are children. Though our core beliefs may seem as if they are our own, they come from our parent figures and earliest experiences from our environment. Many of these core beliefs are shaped by different forms of trauma that a person has been exposed to. Once a core belief has been formed, a person will begin to attach to that belief through the evidence they acquire, which then validates that belief. The more you fall into this destructive cycle, the more prevalent negative bias becomes, which is a state when a person prioritises negative information over positive. This bias is evolutionarily hardwired from the earliest parts of our species, and this is because, as humans, we are much more likely to survive if we focus on things that could kill us rather than things that make us happy. This bias is built into our operating system at the physiological level and is largely removed from our conscious control. Now, just as each person is not every thought they have, they are also not their core beliefs, although it can feel like we are. I found this very hard to accept at first as this new information contradicted my ingrained beliefs. These beliefs shaped my daily life; they were not formed overnight, and this meant that they did not change overnight either. This took serious dedication and persistence to see transformation.

Everyone's real long-term goal is to find security inside of themselves without external means. We all need to feel good enough and not become reliant on others to determine our happiness. Through hypnotherapy and accessing my inner child, I could start the process of doing just that.

Each person's inner child represents their first original self that entered this world. Listening to my inner child's voice helped me remove the shame and disappointment I felt about myself. Connecting with my inner child reconnected me to the wounded part of myself that had become lost in my childhood. I had to grow up so fast that I had to repress my inner child, and although I grew into an adult physically, I never reached emotional or psychological maturity.

What I would find was that my ego had developed and formed through my beliefs, and my self-identity lived deep inside my subconscious mind. My ego had created a story based on my childhood experiences, and this kept me living in painful, familiar settings because they were my predictable, and predictability feels safer than uncertainty. My ego's main objective was to protect the identity I had formed at whatever cost. Our egos are defence and fear-based, and any criticism a person receives becomes a direct and forceful threat.

Going to see a hypnotherapist meant that I was given insight into myself and guidance about what I needed to do in order to change. When I had previously gone to see a doctor, I was asked about my family history of mental illness and offered anti-depressants to numb my pain and alter my reality. When we become diagnosed, it decreases the incentive to change or explore the root cause of an inherent issue. When we do not ask how we can contribute towards our own wellness, we become helpless and dependent. The reality is that each of us can potentially become sicker. As I started to question the status quo, I realised that people find themselves unable to change because they are not being told the truth about the human experience. When our body expects to get better, it sends out messages to start the healing process. Hormones, immune cells, and neurochemicals are all released. The placebo effect provides proof that when we believe we are

275

going to get better or feel better, we often do; it's a testament to the power of the mind to affect the body with a mere suggestion.

Professionals will tell you that you are suffering from major depression when you are down and upset, and you could then be recommended anti-depressants. If you are restless and lack attention, you could be categorised as having ADHD and treated with Ritalin or other stimulants; if the doctor looks at the history of your trauma and finds you are suffering from flashbacks, you might receive a diagnosis of PTSD. None of these diagnoses will be completely wide of the mark, but at the same time, none of them confirms who the patient is and what the root cause of their suffering is.

A psychiatric diagnosis has serious consequences: diagnosis implies that treatment is required, and getting the wrong treatment can have disastrous effects. Also, a diagnostic label is likely to attach to a person for the rest of their lives and profoundly influence how they define themselves. None of these diagnoses account for the unusual talents many develop or the creative energies they mustered to survive. All too often, diagnoses are mere tallies of symptoms, leaving patients to be viewed as if they need to be straightened out.

Let me make this clear: nobody can treat a war, abuse, rape, molestation or other violent events that sadly occur in some people's lives. What has happened cannot be erased and undone, but what we can deal with is the imprints of the trauma on the body, mind and soul, the crushing sensations in your chest that you may label as anxiety or depression, the fear of losing control and always being on alert for danger, the self-loathing, the nightmares and the flashbacks, the cloud that keeps you from staying on task and from engaging fully in what you are doing, so you are unable to fully open your heart to another human being. Trauma robs a person of the feeling that they are in charge, and the challenge of recovery is to re-establish ownership of your body and mind. This means feeling free to know what you know and feel what you feel without becoming overwhelmed, disgusted, or ashamed.

Mainstream trauma treatment has paid scant attention to helping terrified people safely experience their sensations and emotions. Medications such as serotonin reuptake blockers and Seroquel have increasingly taken the place of helping people to face their sensory world. The most natural way that we as humans calm down our distress is through simple interaction as we are designed to be social beings; being touched, hugged, heard, understood and able to express ourselves helps with excessive arousal and makes us feel warm, safe and protected.

As my knowledge grew, I began to see that I was not damaged, and I found that my habits and behaviours were learned responses that my body used to help me to survive. I then recognised that if my body had learned this way to keep me alive, it could also learn a new, healthier way to progress through life.

By beginning to connect with my internal state, I was able to listen to my intuition and further strip away everything that I was not aligned with. When the cost became too great for me to bear, I would set the ultimate boundary with people: complete separation. This type of boundary has completely re-directed my life positively. After removing everything which was unnecessary and destructive, I created enough space to allow in what was necessary and productive. These acts of self-care and valuing myself were not self-indulgent; they are a fundamental part of any true healing process. I was now finally learning to take care of my emotional and physical needs, which I was denied in my childhood.

277

Once I started to understand my inner child and the belief system which had formed, my addictions disappeared, my relationships improved with those closest to me, my health got better, I started to sleep more consistently without nightmares, I felt less anxious, my appetite increased, and I started to trust myself and the decisions I was making. Most importantly, the biggest change was I started the process in loving myself.

The more beliefs I brought back into my consciousness, the more energy I had at my disposal. I was no longer expending energy in areas that were not beneficial for me.

I have listed some key components which helped me through this process:

1. I created healthy daily rituals, which I consistently stuck to.

2. I created solitude in my life.

3. I expressed my emotions.

4. I removed myself from anything I did not feel aligned with.

5. I did everything in my power to increase my vibrational state.

6. I accessed and then worked through my subconscious mind and started to reconstruct my inherent beliefs by first making them conscious.

Although it felt like I had so many issues to work through, it turned out that they all stemmed from a couple of major problems in my childhood. I would come to realise that I spent my whole life trying to let go of my past by forgetting it, but how ironic it was that I had to get as close to it as possible to finally be freed.

The more I became present and acknowledged my feelings, the more I began to feel in control of my life and destiny. This is the opposite of dissociation and when I was not connected with my body. Trauma that is not worked through correctly creates further trauma, and the consequence is that hurt people will then proceed to hurt other people.

With my newly formed clarity, I started to look at each singular incident collectively by connecting the dots of my life through writing my book, and I could then see that The Talking Universe had been communicating to me all along by trying to push me in a direction towards healing and feeling comfortable in my own skin.

With hypnotherapy coming to an end, I began meditating frequently, but when I had meditated previously, I was spiritually bypassing, and although meditation is an effective tool, I had not been using it correctly because I had been denying inherent parts of my subconscious mind. I had now accessed my subconscious mind, so I was able to find mindfulness meditation helpful; I was no longer meditating to try and remove my problems, but instead, I was embracing them because they were a direct route for me to find further answers. Practising mindful meditation also decreased my chances of going into fight or flight mode because it helped to calm down my sympathetic nervous system. Meditation began to help me control my mind and stop it from jumping off in various directions. My mind was prone to making snap decisions without integrating my higher reasoning capabilities. Through meditation, I could discipline my mind, integrate my

279

higher functioning capabilities, rationalise situations better, and stop instinctual reactions which had previously been dominant. When I encounter stressful situations, which will always happen in life, I could give a measured response rather than lashing out and reacting in the heat of the moment.

An important aspect of meditation is breathing; the brain makes up two per cent of our body, but it uses 25 per cent of our entire oxygen intake, and our brain needs to breathe, especially during meditation because we want to direct fresh oxygen to the brain. I had never understood the importance of breathing before, but I began to learn that this was an essential part of my healing process.

The more I meditated, the more disciplined my mind became. When my mind tried to travel off in another direction, I was able to pull it back, and after a while, this ability began to show itself in my everyday life and not just through meditation. Psychologists refer to this as "trait mindfulness", and there is evidence that links mindfulness to self-control as well as numerous other measures of health and happiness. Various brain imaging studies suggest that mindfulness practices are associated with the amygdala part of the brain. The amygdala reacts to threats by generating emotion. Mindfulness practices appear to calm down that specific area, so they can assist in reducing fear, panic and anxiety. Rather than having anger carry me down an unwanted path, I began to stay centred in times of stress. A disciplined mind is an imperative asset which can be learned through meditation.

At this point, the stressors in my life did not impact me like they once did. I had put such a huge amount of pressure and stress on myself that it was inevitable that any person would crack under the circumstances I had created. What I noticed was that when I responded in a calmer state, people tended to react to me in a much better and more appropriate way. This then helped me to turn any difficult situations that would arise into more manageable ones.

Six months had now flown by, and I had begun to change, although there were some up and down moments, which is natural as this process is not linear. Through understanding myself, I saw that I was the creator of my life, and I could not blame anyone for what had transpired. I then began to forgive all the people who contributed towards my grief because I knew that holding on to any form of pain would only affect me in the future. However, that forgiveness did not open the door for these people to come back into my life, and just because I had forgiven them, it did not mean I had to reach out and entertain any of these people again. I can't change other people's actions, and Jason and Nick, for example, have their own paths and destinies. One thing I do know is how the universe works, and when you behave in such a negative way, then life will always catch up with you at some point, and that's what we have the word karma for.

With me working through my past and connecting all the dots, I went on to have another moment of enlightenment in how the process of manifestation really works. Previously, I had been using the conscious mind to manifest, and I had no idea how significant the subconscious mind was. My subconscious mind had 37 years of embedded experience and evidence from past events, which consisted of pain, suffering and survival. And this is why I had manifested monetary wealth alongside all of my inherent beliefs.

My conscious mind had shown me that I could indeed manifest. In order to manifest what I wanted, I needed to focus on healing, and the part that was holding me back was my inherent belief system, which I had now accessed through hypnotherapy. Positive thoughts have a profound effect on our lives, but only when they are in connection with our

281

subconscious programming. Once recognised and you decide to act, transformational results occur.

The power of the subconscious mind is so huge that it has more than a million times more power than the conscious mind. That should put into perspective how important this part of the mind is in the manifestation process. No matter how strong the will of the conscious mind is, it will not overpower the subconscious mind. I can tell you if you think you're running your life, then you're not; your subconscious mind is the one who is really in control. The programmes acquired by the subconscious mind shape 95 per cent or more of our life experiences (Szegedy-Maszak, 2005). This means that our lives are mostly a projection of our subconscious programming, which we acquire when we are children.

Once I knew what my subconscious mind was doing, I could draw energy back that I was expending in non-constructive areas and put that towards strengthening my conscious intent. By changing my subconscious mind, I could align with my goals, aspirations, and needs. If we go even deeper, I can say the following statement: both unconscious and conscious intention is the creative force of the universe, and this is why there is so much suffering in life because a lot of people are just unconscious. If everyone was conscious, we would not have created the world we are all currently living in. All the problems in the world we see today are due to a lack of consciousness.

When the mind changes, it also begins to affect a person's biology. If you believe you can or you can't, guess what? You're right either way. While we cannot change our genetic blueprint, we can change our minds, and in that process, we can switch the blueprints used to express our genetic potential. You can live a life of fear or a life of joy, the choice is yours.

Where attention is directed is where you will see the most prominent results in your life, and that is what started to happen for me. With my healing process well underway, I began to see myself improve, and I had not taken any medication recommended by a doctor or the online therapist I had spoken to. My cure was always found in changing my life around and understanding the basic laws of energy and how I interacted with my environment. The reality is this: harnessing the power of your full mind can be more effective than any medication that is prescribed.

Now I was on the right path, and I began having moments of enlightenment each day. I had been looking outwardly to fill a void inside of myself, and I did this through various addictions and careers which I thought would give me the monetary wealth I so desperately craved. I now realised my gold all along was found right in front of me by going deep inside of myself and healing then changing my life around through internal and not external means. Not only could I now change my life, but by writing a book, I could communicate the message to help change other people's lives too.

Everything I had read about increasing my vibrational state and healing through natural means proved to be true, so I began to read further into natural medicine and energy, and this then took me back to acupuncture again. Acupuncture stimulates the release of endorphins, which are the body's natural pain-relieving neurohormones, through the insertion of needles into specific points throughout the body. This then allows the energy to flow correctly without blockages, encouraging the body to heal itself naturally.

I then decided to book some sessions with a local acupuncturist called Renata, just as I had done with Chris, my hypnotherapist. Traditional Chinese medicine really fitted in with what I had learned regarding energy, and after attending my first session, I sat with Renata and explained to her what I was looking to achieve, which was to live a more healthy and balanced life. I had no physical symptoms, but I knew my energy had been severely affected due to the years of suppressed trauma I had accumulated. Renata then gave me further insight into acupuncture, and she explained the following:

Traditional Chinese medicine has roots in Taoism, a philosophy that originated in China nearly 3,000 years ago. Back in those days, the philosophical approach was rather simple: accept what is in front of you without trying to change it, and instead adjust and adapt to it and harmonise your inner environment with whatever situation arises. This adaptation process assures survival and longevity. A person who can't adapt, whatever the reason, can run into all sorts of problems, including ill health. Adaptation doesn't necessarily mean you join in with whatever everyone else is doing; instead, you connect with the wisdom within and respond appropriately, always accepting where you are at the time, maintaining balance, and staying calm within. We are all connected to the earth and use its natural resources to keep us alive and healthy. Wherever there is a separation, we will find that disease and disharmony will set in. Acupuncture can calm the mind and soothe excessive emotions, resolve stagnated energy, and promote blood and energy flow, which brings that feeling of openness and calm.

The scientifically proven physiological effects of acupuncture on the body are pain relief and an anti-inflammatory effect, but traditional Chinese medicine takes this further, creating a bigger picture, bringing together, and connecting the pieces (body, mind, spirit) that modern science separates into individual subjects or dismisses completely. Unlike modern science, which has tools to show us how things work on a minuscule level and in isolation from everything else, the philosophy behind traditional Chinese medicine is teaching us how to "be", how to maintain life and restore balance through interconnectedness. I believe it offers wisdom and a balanced viewpoint. Energy cannot be destroyed; instead, it can only be transformed into something else.

As well as acupuncture, Renata also explained the importance of massages, which she also did for me. We all carry a lot of tension in our bodies, especially in our shoulders and back, and this creates stress for us in our lives. By having regular massages and looking after my body, I could relieve myself of any stress that I had been carrying. I then began to feel less stressed; it improved my flexibility, I started sleeping better, I felt more relaxed, it improved my circulation, and it reduced my stress responses as they were no longer accumulating and causing devastating effects in my life.

As I built momentum, I looked further into what could help me. Next on my list was crystals, as I had begun to read about their benefits. Crystal healing boosts low energy, prevents bad energy, releases blocked energy, and transforms the body's aura. The crystal that related most to my needs was rose quartz. Each crystal has a different effect on the energetic field of the human body, so if you are looking into crystals, take your time in choosing one that you think would be best suited to you, as each one has different properties which will be aligned to your specific needs.

After my research on crystals, I then created a visualisation board on which I put all my targets, such as healing and future ideas, one of which was to write and finish my book. I would then read and view this every morning. This then created purpose in my life as I was working towards set specific targets, and integrating all my daily actions towards my goals, brought significance to my existence. Achieving inner harmony for me meant that my feelings, thoughts, and actions started to align with one another.

The more I progressed, the more I refined my routine and went in search of other information. I then found through reading that sex is the most powerful creative force in the universe, as it is what creates life when two human beings connect together. This sacred connection has been downplayed throughout society to fulfil a bodily pleasure. We owe a large proportion of this to pornography. What I found was that when a male climaxes during sexual activity, he will deplete his core and give up his life force energy. This occurs through sex and masturbation. As a result, the mind is not sharp, your balance and stability decrease, your core strength is weakened drastically, your energy level is lowered, and it increases the desire for bodily pleasures. To continue reaching my potential, I needed to use this creative energy in another way. I then began abstaining, and although this was extremely hard at first, over a sustained period, it became easier. Eventually, it became a routine for me, just like everything else had. The benefits of doing this have been incredible on both a physical and a creative aspect.

To elaborate on this topic further, our sexual desire can be converted into a weapon once we understand this. We all become creative when sexual desire is at its peak. Your imagination becomes vivid, awareness increases, and you are motivated to pursue a source of sexual satisfaction diligently. That same energy can be transformed and channelled into a creative outlet. We would be better able to conceptualise and innovate ideas that we want to birth into existence. Sexual desire is natural, and it is the force that is responsible for all life on Earth. The key is not to deny that the desire exists but rather to refrain from overindulgence and understand the creative power attached to our sex drive. When we are aware of our sexual energy and accept its presence, we can better use it to "birth" other ideas into existence, and this helped me to transform my book from a good one to a great one.

Preserving this life force has powerful benefits for males, both physically and mentally. There are many examples throughout history of men who have abstained from sex intentionally or, as a result of isolation and because of it, have exercised superpowers in their thinking and physical lives. Russel Wilson, Malcolm X, Nikola Tesla, Isaac Newton, Beethoven, Leonardo Da Vinci, and Muhammad Ali are all examples of how abstinence empowers you to exercise the creative superpower within yourself.

The more I began to heal, the more I trusted the new environment I had created, which in turn enabled me to grow further. What I began receiving back were loving experiences instead of my past familiar destructive ones.

I now began to see that my purpose in life was to show others through my story that you can transform and change despite what may have happened to you. My book was no longer going to be about money and having a successful business; instead, it was going to be about the healing process and sharing the wisdom I have gained to try and make a difference in other people's lives, just like I have in my own. Although my book was the hardest, scariest, and most painful thing I have ever done, it has also been the most rewarding, beneficial, and important thing in my life.

The more I wrote, the more I realised that some of the books I have read about being successful, manifestation and pushing yourself are detrimental to the world. I took some of the advice in these books literally and pushed myself to the point of extinction. Some of the books I read portrayed a message of working oneself into the ground, and when everyone is sleeping, make sure you are working. A lot of books portray the wrong message of manifestation; think happy thoughts, and that's what becomes your reality. What they do not explain is the importance of the subconscious mind. Please be careful with what you choose to read because what is written in books is not always factual. In many cases, it is a complete inversion.

I now felt happier than I had ever done in my life; however, my story is no magic recipe for happiness. Life is about feeling a range of emotions, and there are still days when I feel down. I am not ashamed to admit that, and life is about understanding duality. Today I am happy more often than I am sad, and when I do feel down, I have healthy coping strategies in place to fall back on that make my down days more manageable. This is part and parcel of being a human being, and the Instagram world that portrays eternal happiness is not the real world. We all get down, we all have flaws, and that's okay because we are all human beings, and we are not made to be perfect. My story can't offer you guaranteed happiness, but it can offer you a realistic expectation of what life is and what you can do to give yourself the best opportunity each day. I can't offer you anything apart from that, which is the truth.

Once I surrendered and allowed the path of my life to take its natural course, I could reconnect with my soul, which would bring me closer to truly healing myself. Forgiveness and acceptance of who you are deep down are imperative, and this includes the beautiful and the horrible aspects of yourself. When I began to start loving myself, I saw that I had a tolerance for the weaker aspects of myself; I then began to see that everything in life was not personal and the journey I had been on had no blame attached to anyone anymore.

How has the world changed for me as a result of my new insights? I have finally woken up and seen the world as a place that provided me with a path for everything I needed once I became clear with my intentions. When each coincidence happened, and I acted on the signs of the universe, I grew, and each time I grew, I existed at a higher vibration. Yes, there were still mistakes, and I did not always perceive the signs correctly, but guess what? Life is about making mistakes, then getting back up and trying again. Everything you require in this world will be found through other people, good and bad. Experiences that I felt were negative at that moment were true gifts and blessings in disguise now when I look back.

The fundamental reality is this: the negative aspects of life are just as important as the positive, and it is part of the human experience we are all having. I will always carry a certain amount of pain with me, but that's okay because my pain now has meaning, and I understand it.

Life for me was about taking full responsibility for my thoughts and actions to find the right answer to all the problems I encountered along the way. Whenever I got side-tracked, life always seemed to have a funny way of throwing me back on track, and yes, it was often in the most distressing ways imaginable, but without my suffering, the growth that I was able to achieve would not have been possible for me. Today I am no longer the chess piece. I am the chess player.

No one was ever going to knock on my door and make all my wishes come true. Due to my dysfunctional upbringing, there was no other way; I had to go out there and make mistakes to get where I finally am. I can tell you it never got easier, I just ended up getting better, and lots of small changes eventually added up to huge results for me.

It's crucial that if you are looking to improve and self-develop, you need to maximise the opportunities you get whilst in solitude. What you will find is that people who struggle to control their attention in solitude will inevitably resort to external solutions to try and solve their problems. My path has not so much been a trip, but instead, it has been a search for my identity. Every person on this planet has something to discover within themselves. It is an amazing feeling to finally know oneself.

No matter how great the teacher is, if the student is unable to understand the message, then it means nothing. My teacher was The Talking Universe, and only when I was able to understand how it communicated by becoming consciously aware could I then begin to transform. My sensitivity, which was once a curse, has been a true gift all along.

The reality is that not everything in life is light. It's about surrendering to the destruction of every limiting belief you've ever thought and felt about yourself, other people, and the world. Spirituality is not always pretty. Trust me on that. In fact, often, it is the most shattering, shitty, and testing experience we can go through in life. Only once we emerge from the embers of our destruction can we be reborn into new lives with clarity.

A big problem I had was that I was asking people who had never been where I had been for directions, and when nothing went right, it was time to follow my intuition and turn left. When you become mature, every insult you receive just becomes constructive feedback. Life can only be understood backwards, I have found that out through writing my book, but the paradox is that life can only be lived by moving forwards. Understanding we are born to be real and not perfect is crucial. Change what you believe, and you will start to change what you experience.

Humanity has evolved at such a rate through technology, but the negative aspect of this is the disturbing problems that coincide with this technology, such as soul loss. The divide in society shows that something is clearly wrong. While the population increases year on year, our ecological systems are suffering, resources are becoming scarcer, the food that we eat is being contaminated and genetically modified, the rich get richer, and the poor get poorer. We are at a crossroads with humanity, and if we carry on down this same road, then annihilation is the course this path will take. We as a society are so concerned with progressing externally that we have each forgotten to explore ourselves internally, and this neglect is prevalent in the world today as it has been projected and then manifested out for all to see. We look for others to solve the problems that we have today in the world, but this strategy does not work. Instead, we all need to focus on what each and every one of us can do, and that starts with the self and going deep inside to heal. I believe that one of the major issues we see today in the world is that we are not taught that self-love is the most important aspect of life.

The most powerful force on earth is love, and to become your true self and reconnect with your soul, you must develop a relationship with your heart. When love is given and received, it is dependent on the ability to be present, attuned and responsive to another human being. When you are connected to the heart, it does not matter if you are Christian, Muslim, or a Hindu because you are able to see that all religion does is create further separation. When you are connected to the heart, it does not matter what someone's beliefs are because what you can see is that we are all made from the same ingredients. We are all interconnected, and any form of separation in any context only leads to something that is coming from a place that is not love.

As nobody had ever explained to me the importance of connecting to my heart, I am sure many of you have also not understood the importance of this, so I will share some basic knowledge with you. Connecting with yourself and the heart is a simple process of just becoming present and appreciating what you have. Practise gratitude, notice and seek out true beauty rather than the manufactured kind, listen to music you enjoy, write about or express your feelings, show kindness whenever you can, practise self-compassion, open up to others and learn to trust them, kiss, laugh, hug, show affection, and just celebrate life.

All my pain stemmed from what had happened to me and not due to what was wrong with me. Simply being alive and present to tell you my story makes me worthy and shows there is hope for everyone. If you don't believe in yourself, how can you expect others to? If you don't love yourself, how can you expect others to? It all starts inwardly and not outwardly, as society portrays it.

The more I looked into the consequences of trauma, the more I saw that our schools, doctors, hospitals, the police, the courts, and many other government establishments that are supposed to help us citizens are, in fact, doing the opposite. Unfortunately, a lot of life is an inversion, and changes cannot be made until humanity awakens from this unconsciousness. As I have explained, everything is interconnected, and for us as a society to move forward from these dark times we are currently living in, everything will need to be integrated and connected together to see a fundamental change instead of each establishment being treated discretely with its own rules, own language and own methods and structures, which have no correlation with the next establishment. It just does not make sense how the world has formed because it is a recipe for disaster, and if an ex-homeless person who never attended school, a former criminal and a crack addict can work that out, why can't the people in charge of us? Trauma penetrates all aspects of life, so let's stop looking at the symptoms of trauma and start dealing with the root causes.

We are profoundly affected by social media. It's part of society now, but the influence we receive from these media images affects how we perceive the world, and the human brain is not designed for the modern world we have created. The rate at which we produce new inventions has far exceeded the rate at which we can problem-solve. One of the most damning facets of human life today is that science has gathered knowledge faster than

292

we as a society have gathered wisdom. The result is increased suicide rates, depression, anxiety, and a whole host of other negative consequences. Society is fast approaching a point where empathy will no longer exist if we carry on. With more online interaction and fewer relational interactions, children will become more self-centred, less mature, less socially aware, and more self-absorbed and narcissistic. Real conversations have been replaced by more liking, posting, tweeting, and messaging. This new quality of life breeds a new type of human being which is one that is going to cause serious complications for humanity, not only in the future but today as it's happening already. So many people I have met in my life feel empty and are seeking some form of connection, and that connection is often found in very unhealthy ways, as I can surely testify. The more we disconnect from the true self, the more vulnerable we will become as a species.

If we want a healthy society, I recommend that schools start teaching children how to raise their vibrational state. This is free, by the way, and it does not cost anything because everything we need is already here, apart from the communication of this knowledge. With a clear understanding of the human energy system and how it functions, it is possible for people to heal themselves just as I did. The earliest parts of our lives are so significant, and it is also paramount that parents and the educational system understand the impact of this as well.

Today I do not suffer from a loss of imagination or mental flexibility. My imagination is vivid, and I have shown that I can adapt to my new environment and change in accordance with my new conditions.

My healing began to happen when I started to understand I deserved better. This enabled me to open up and trust the correct people in my life who would help me along my journey. The more I used my brain to support my growth, the more its ability grew to function correctly. Our cells are like programmable chips whose behaviour and genetic activity are primarily controlled by environmental signals. This means that once I could change my environment, I could start experiencing a different reality. Today, I am not affected as much by outside influences or what people think of me as I am more grounded, confident, and stronger, with a lot more balance in my life.

Today my fuel comes from a positive place which is deep inside of me. Now I am safe and secure, I can focus my energy on trying to help others by sharing the knowledge and wisdom I have gained. Success did not bring me happiness; happiness brought me success, and the external locus I once had has been replaced with an internal locus, and I now understand that my behaviour can affect the outcome of my environment.

Finishing my book is only the start of my journey; my destiny and the reason I have been put on this planet is to help others by sharing my story, but before I could do that, I first needed to help myself.

I hope you have all enjoyed reading my book, it has been difficult and uncomfortable for me to share my experiences, wisdom, and knowledge with you, but the end result is very satisfying. The foundation for recovering from trauma is self-awareness, and now that I have achieved this, my life is no longer a pointless existence as I have finally found a certain degree of peace. The most significant message of my book is about the importance of truly loving yourself.

"Life's a test, mistakes are lessons, but the gift of life is knowing that you have made a difference."
—Tupac Shakur

Acknowledgements

I want to thank my friends, Nana, Mum, Dad, stepdad Ian and all the people with whom I have crossed paths. Each and every experience, positive and negative, has shaped my present-day life. Having come through such a complicated journey has now given me the tools to succeed in whatever I choose to do in my future. When I look back at some of the most negative situations in my life, I realise that they have been the most important components to enable me to look in the mirror and make the necessary changes to become a better person.

Special acknowledgement:

Chris, my hypnotherapist, you gave me a level of clarity which I was never afforded before. Only after our sessions could I begin to progress in my life and stop the repeating patterns of devastation which I had no conscious knowledge of. I will be eternally grateful for your support, guidance and wisdom, which has enabled me to start moving forward in my life.

Printed in Great Britain
by Amazon